NEWCOMER'S HANDBOOK ™

for New York City

First Books, Inc.
P.O. Box 578147
Chicago, IL 60657
(312) 276-5911

14th Edition.

Publisher: Jeremy Solomon
Cover Design: Miles DeCoster
Interior Design and Production: Miles and Gale DeCoster
Maps: Ann Crews

Contributors: Jennifer Cecil, Belden Merims, David Ravel, Martha Hanson, Patty Moosbrugger, Robert Mitchell.

ISBN O-912301-24-4

Manufactured in the United States of America by Versa Press, East Peoria, Illinois.

Published by First Books, Inc., P.O. Box 578147, Chicago, IL 60657, 312-276-5911.

Contents

Introduction

This book is dedicated to the proposition that it is as rewarding to live in New York City as it is to work here. However, the transition from new-comer to New Yorker isn't necessarily achieved without some discomfort. To minimize the difficulties involved in moving to New York, we have written the *Newcomer's Handbook for New York City.*

The *Newcomer's Handbook for New York City* has been continually updated since its 1980 inception in order to chronicle accurately the constant changes taking place in this fastest-paced of cities.

Whether you are looking for the right neighborhood or the right health club—the right synagogue or merely the right radio station—these chapters will guide you, the newcomer, in your search.

Some feel the city's rough edges have gotten even rougher in the 1990's. Troubled times have meant a softer real estate market which is good news for newcomers. Now more than ever it is important to know your neighborhood: establishing a sense of community where you live will make your life in New York happier and more rewarding.

In addition to the regular updating, this 14th edition includes a new section on New York's bountiful greenmarkets and a section on how to treat building staff. Also, at the suggestion of our readers, we have added an index. As usual, we welcome readers' suggestions and comments on the tear-out page at the back of the book.

We hope that the information presented on the following pages help you establish a New York City residence smoothly and speedily. We also hope that once you select your neighborhood and settle in, the book will help you get on with the pleasure part: enjoyment of the city's myriad and unrivaled resources.

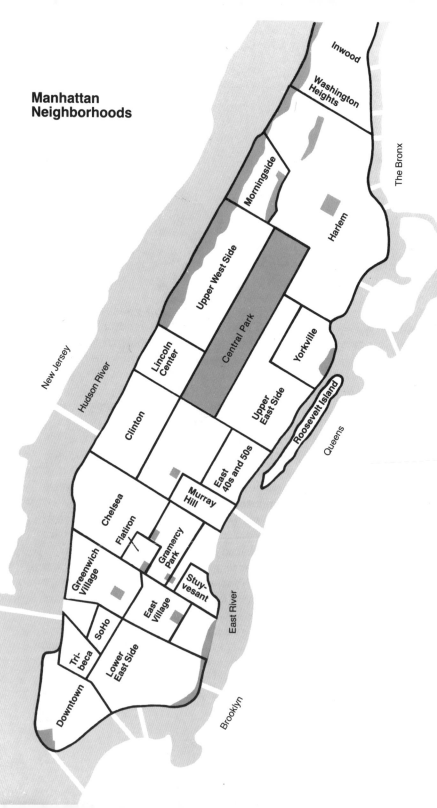

Manhattan Neighborhoods

Inwood

Washington Heights

The Bronx

Morningside

Harlem

New Jersey

Hudson River

Upper West Side

Central Park

Yorkville

Lincoln Center

Upper East Side

Roosevelt Island

Queens

Clinton

East 40s and 50s

Chelsea

Murray Hill

Flatiron

Gramercy Park

Stuy-vesant

Greenwich Village

East River

SoHo

East Village

Tri-beca

Lower East Side

Downtown

Brooklyn

Neighborhoods

From the wind-whipped corner of East End Avenue and 86th Street on an icy January evening, Greenwich Village seems as accessible as Alaska. So you cancel plans to meet a Village acquaintance downtown, call a friend on East 85th and get together at an uptown locale instead. There is no question but that the neighborhood in which you live affects what you do and who you see in New York City. Like attracts like and most newcomers tend to pay more attention to where they live than how they live there. The protestations of I-want-to-be-aloners fade when faced with the choice between a nicely renovated one-bedroom apartment in Brooklyn's Park Slope for $800 a month (45 minutes from Manhattan by D train) and a two-person share in a one-bedroom apartment in Yorkville for $900, or more. The cachet of the Upper East Side (or another of Manhattan's established communities) usually has more allure for the neophyte than privacy in the boroughs or a newly gentrified enclave. It takes time, familiarity with the city and a certain street-honed sophistication to be totally at ease in distant or just-emerging districts. Nevertheless, unless money is no object, Manhattan's rental market often requires compromises, not only in the way you live but also in the neighborhood you choose. But no matter where you land, once established you'll probably become a booster of your own very special area.

Not for nothing are New Yorkers neighborhood proud. More than just an address or a source of necessary services, neighborhoods provide residents with identification and a sense of belonging, which in turn gives the individual sufficient sustenance and heart for daily confrontations with the city's size and pace. Most people feel profoundly chauvinistic about their area and take great delight in extolling its virtues and, being New Yorkers, its faults as well. There are few streets or blocks in the city that don't fall into one of any number of recognizable enclaves—

the list is as long as Manhattan itself.

Manhattan neighborhoods are listed clockwise (picture an exceedingly elongated clock) starting with Yorkville, continuing south along the East River downtown around the tip of the island and then uptown along the Hudson ending with Washington Heights Inwood. Descriptions of communities in The Bronx, Brooklyn, Queens and Staten Island as well as two in New Jersey follow Manhattan. No description, however, can substitute for your own experience. You are strongly encouraged to visit the neighborhoods that interest you and talk to residents before signing a lease. (Among other things, it is an excellent way to get leads on apartments that might otherwise escape your attention.) Resources and city services within each neighborhood are included in order to facilitate orientation once you're settled.

Suggestions on how to go about finding an apartment and how to best enjoy the city come after **Neighborhoods** in **Apartment Hunting** and in other sections.

MANHATTAN

Yorkville

Boundaries and Contiguous Areas: North: East 96th Street and **East Harlem;** East: East River; South: East 79th Street and **Upper East Side;** West: Lexington Avenue and **Upper East Side.**

What distinguished Yorkville from its Upper East Side surroundings until recently was the character imbued by immigrants from Germany and Eastern Europe. Now, however, you'll find more co-op signs and health clubs than residents of Hungarian and Czechoslovakian ancestry. In the 1980s, a co-op, condo and rental apartment boom finished off what World War II started: the erosion of Yorkville's ethnicity. Old walkups were first leveled in the late 1940s to make way for new apartment buildings attractive to professionals—white-collar types who, once drawn to the neighborhood, began replacing the immigrants in the remaining railroad flats. Only traces of Yorkville's European heritage remain, and while Yorkville is still the most accessible part of the Upper East Side, what began as a scattering of stolid brick apartment buildings in mid-century is now an area that overflows with living space unlike any other part of the city. From the East 90s south is a forest of ever-more-fanciful towers and fortresses.

86th Street from Lexington to First Avenues has been attempting to redefine itself into a pricier shopping strip. However, the hoped for stability has not entirely materialized. Large residential projects like the 17-story Park Avenue Court (really on Lexington) and the Colorado luxury apartment building are offering prime retail space (and lots of it) that has been attracting upscale, international stores.

Yorkville was a pleasant rural community when the first wave of German and Irish immigrants arrived on these shores in the 1850s. Tranquil pastures surrounded river estates owned by wealthy merchants, many of whom—John Jacob Astor, the Rhinelanders and the Schermerhorns—were of German origin. In the 1880s the completion of the Second and Third Avenue elevated lines opened the area to settlement, and German immigrants, many attracted by jobs in the developing breweries, moved north from the Lower East Side. Irish immigrants followed and then, as they grew more prosperous, Hungarians, Czechs and Slovaks. Today, the second and third generations are more likely to be found in Queens and Westchester than in Yorkville, and it is a dwindling, elderly Middle European population that patronizes the few remaining ethnic bakeries, butcher shops and restaurants. Not that these stores are empty; customer ranks have been swelled by appreciative young professionals lately come to dominate the area.

The inviting mix of buildings, old and new, that characterizes Yorkville, as well as the community's relatively low crime rate and good public schools, makes it an attractive destination for the determined apartment seeker. Housing construction, co-ops and rentals, spurred by development of the former Ruppert Brewery site between 90th and 93rd Streets, still booms south of 96th Street. Those bulky red brick blocks and columns east of Second Avenue are part of the Ruppert project, a complex that contains subsidized low income housing and middle income rentals, for which New York State residency is one of the qualifications. The Sunday *Times* Real Estate Section is thick with ads drumming those amenity-laden new Yorkville buildings as well as shareable one-bedroom apartments in newly renovated brownstones and tenements.

For a refreshing pause, explore Carl Schurz Park bordering the East River at 86th Street, where you can also spy the mayor's residence, graceful Gracie Mansion built in 1799. Jutting over F.D.R. Drive, this semi-sylvan oasis recalls Yorkville of yore and affords a spectacular view of the East River, its islands, boats and barges.

Area Code: 212

Post Offices: Yorkville Station, 1619 Third Avenue, NYC 10028, at 90th Street, 369-2230; Gracie Station, 229 East 85th Street, NYC 10028, 988-6682.

Zip Codes: 10128, 10028, 10021

Police Precinct: Nineteenth, 153 East 67th Street, NYC 10021, 452-0600.

Emergency Hospitals: Mt. Sinai Hospital, Fifth Avenue at 100th Street, NYC 10029, 241-6500; Metropolitan Hospital, 1901 First

Avenue, NYC 10029, 230-6262; Doctors Hospital, 170 East End Avenue, NYC 10128, 870-9000.

Library: Yorkville, 222 East 79th Street, NYC 10021, 744-5824.

Public School Education: School District #2 (see **Chelsea**).

Cultural Resources: 92nd Street Y, Young Men's and Young Women's Hebrew Association, 1395 Lexington Avenue, NYC 10128, 427-6000.

Transportation—Subway: *Lexington Avenue IRT* (#4, #5, #6) 96th Street, 86th Street (Exp), 77th Street, 68th Street, 59th Street (Exp).

Transportation—Bus: Crosstown *96th Street* (#19); Crosstown *86th Street* (#86); Crosstown *79th Street* (#79); Crosstown *72nd Street* (#72); Crosstown *66th/67th Street* (#66); Crosstown *57th Street* (#57, #58); Uptown *First Avenue*-Downtown *Second Avenue* (#15); Uptown *Third Avenue*-Downtown *Lexington Avenue* (#98, #101, #102).

The Upper East Side

Boundaries and Contiguous Areas: North: East 96th Street to Lexington Avenue and **Yorkville, East Harlem**: East: Lexington Avenue to 79th Street and the East River; South: 59th Street and the **East Forties and Fifties**; West: Fifth Avenue.

The affluent heart of the Upper East Side—that quadrant caught between Fifth, 79th, Lexington and 60th Street and the panhandle stretching from 79th along Fifth to 86th Street—has landmark status and as a result may remain ever thus. But this does not mean that Manhattan's most popular neighborhood for the wealthy and the upwardly mobile is completely homogeneous. Each avenue that traverses the area, from Fifth east to York, has a distinctive character all its own.

Fifth Avenue, flanking Central Park, glitters with some of the city's most magnificent museums, most exclusive cooperatives and some of its most glamorous relics, those wonderfully ornate mansions which so clearly reflect the tastes and fortunes of our turn-of-the-century million-aires. Fricks, Dukes, Carnegies, Whitneys—their copies of palaces, chateaux and Gothic castles established the avenue as highly fashion-able. Dominating Fifth in the East 80s, the Metropolitan Museum, not content with being the major physical and artistic presence on the Upper East Side, is also the site of one of the liveliest street scenes in town. Its sprawling stone steps, while providing access to the museum, offer seats and a meeting place from which to watch the mimes, musicians and street vendors who use the sidewalk around the entrance as per-forming space.

Madison Avenue between 60th and 86th Streets is a veritable Maginot Line of classy international boutiques and fine arts galleries. This solid wall of chic has been pepped up some with the addition of The Limited, Ralph Lauren, Timberland and the latest arrival: a Barneys. Around 81st Street and P.S. 6, the premier elementary school on the Upper East Side, a number of trendy designers have set up shop. Above 86th Street, where Andrew Carnegie built the elaborate mansion that now houses the Cooper-Hewitt Museum, most of the other palatial Beaux Arts residences constructed in the early 1900s have been acquired by schools, consulates and cultural institutions. Today these grand buildings, interspersed with bow-fronted, brick Georgian homes and solid pre-World War II apartment buildings, form an exceedingly har-monious neighborhood.

On Park, the handsome center strip of year-round greenery and seasonal plantings make the stately square cooperative buildings that proceed shoulder to elegant shoulder up the avenue more gracious still.

Lexington Avenue has largely taken over from Madison as purveyor of quality produce to Upper East Siders. Immaculate, and imaginative, shops harboring fishmongers and florists, greengrocers and bakers are crowded into the ruddy, rustic brick buildings that line the street.

The area from Third Avenue east to the river, once the province of the "el" and tenements, has been Trumped up. Today, sleek glass and granite shafts intersperse postwar brick apartment blocks that loom over the once characteristic, and now fast disappearing, five-story walkups. And turnover is a constant among the clubs, bars and restaurants cater-ing to east-of-Third singles.

The softer real estate market of the 1990s has meant more afford-able rents along the Upper East Side and in Yorkville. While rents used to range from high to astronomical, today's newcomers have a previously unheard-of power to negotiate with landlords, brokers and sellers.

Area Code: 212

Post Office: Lenox Hill Station, 217 East 70th Street, NYC 10021, 879-4402. Nearby: Gracie Station, 229 East 85th Street, NYC 10028, 988-6682.

Zip Codes: 10128, 10028, 10021, 10022

Police Precinct: Nineteenth, 153 East 67th Street, NYC 10021, 452-0600.

Emergency Hospitals: Lenox Hill Hospital, 100 East 77th Street, NYC 10021, 434-2000; New York Hospital-Cornell Medical Center, 525 East 68th Street, NYC 10021, 746-5454; Manhattan Eye, Ear and Throat Hospital, 210 East 64th Street, NYC 10021, 838-9200. Nearby: Mt. Sinai Hospital, Fifth Avenue at 100th Street, NYC 10029, 241-6500.

Libraries: 96th Street Branch, 112 East 96th Street, NYC 10128, 289-0908; Webster, 1465 York Avenue between 77th and 78th Streets, NYC 10021, 288-5049. The New York Society Library, 288-6900, a private institution with membership dues and 250,000 volumes, is an outstanding resource located at 53 East 79th Street, NYC 10021.

Public School Education: School District #2 (see **Chelsea**).

Adult Education: Marymount Manhattan College, 221 East 71st Street, NYC 10021, 517-0400; Hunter College, 695 Park Avenue at 68th Street, NYC 10021, 772-4000.

Cultural Resources: 92nd Street Y, Young Men's and Young Women's Hebrew Association, 1395 Lexington Avenue, NYC 10128, 427-6000; Central Park; "Museum Mile," an association of the ten museums (from Goethe House to the Guggenheim) located on or near Fifth Avenue between 82nd Street and 105th; not to mention the Frick Collection, 1 East 70th Street, The Asia Society,

725 Park Avenue (at 70th Street) 288-6400, the Center for Inter-American Relations, Park Avenue and 68th Street, the China Institute, 125 East 65th Street, Society of Illustrators, 128 East 63rd Street, and numerous other societies, museums, galleries and auction houses.

Transportation—Subway: *Lexington Avenue IRT* (#4, #5, #6) 96th Street, 86th Street (Exp), 77th Street, 68th Street, 59th Street (Exp).

Transportation—Bus: Crosstown *96th Street* (#19); Crosstown *86th Street* (#86); Crosstown *79th Street* (#79); Crosstown *72nd Street* (#72); Crosstown *66th/67th Street* (#66); Crosstown *57th Street* (#28); Uptown *Madison Avenue* (#1,#;2, #3, #4); Downtown *Fifth Avenue* (#1, #2,#3, #4).

Roosevelt Island

Located off 59th Street in the East River.

Roosevelt Islanders have always had an unusual commute: a silent aerial float to and from 59th Street—Second Avenue in Manhattan (every 5 to 15 minutes for $1.45) up and over the East River with the city's skyline first at eye level and then, incredibly, beneath your feet. Small wonder that the trams find favor with tourists and day-trippers. Residents used to be reduced to taking cabs or a roundabout bus ride through Queens to Manhattan when the funicular occasionally faltered. Now, however, the city's Transit Authority has a subway line (the Q train) connecting the island with Queens (at 21st Street and 41st Avenue) and Manhattan (at 63rd and Lex).

An appealing small-town quality pervades this island community of modern apartment buildings. It's quiet. Automobile access is limited, and a minibus (10¢) provides regular service between the tram terminal and high rises lining relatively spotless streets where strolls with baby carriages and street corner chats are ritual—a sort of time zip to the '40s. Sunbathers crowd the greensward on a warm afternoon, joggers pad silently along the Promenade, and the contemplative sit observing sailboats and barges parading Manhattan's skyline. Roosevelt Island has extensive recreational facilities and stores supplying the basic needs, if not the exotic or ethnic ones. Built by early farmers in 1796, the Manor House is preserved at the top of Main Street. The Octagon Lighthouse has recently been restored. Superior schools go up to the eighth grade and are part of District #2 (information in the **Chelsea** section).

Inauguration of the long-awaited subway line came not a moment too soon: the red brick five-building Manhattan Park development recently opened on an eight-acre site just north of the original concrete buildings added 1,100 units to the housing stock and some 2,500 inhabitants to the island's existing population of 5,200. Manhattan Park, unlike Roosevelt Island's rent-subsidized housing, is attracting upper middle class families (no studios) with stunning views and concierges at prices about 20% below comparable Manhattan rents. Residents hope these changes and the future development of the island's south point will do nothing to disturb the peaceful, low-crime character of the island.

Manhattan Park buildings are managed by Grenadier Realty Corp., 308-4040, with a rental office in Building 2 at 30 River Road. The Roosevelt Island Housing Management Corp., 838-4747, at 552 Main Street manages the rental units and subsidized apartments (for which there are specified income limits) in the original buildings; co-ops are managed by Dwelling Managers Inc., 308-7271. NB: If you own a dog, Roosevelt Island isn't for you; dogs aren't allowed on the narrow 2 1/2-mile-long island.

Area Code: 212

Post Office: Island Post Office, 752-5564.

Zip Code: 10044

Police Precinct: One Hundred and Fourteenth, 34-16 Astoria Boulevard, Astoria, New York 11103, (718) 626-9311.

Emergency Hospital: Goldwater Memorial Hospital, Roosevelt Island, 750-6800.

Transportation: *Tramway* (59th Street and Second Avenue). *Bus:* Queens (Q32). *Subway:* 63rd Street (B, Q).

East Forties and Fifties

Boundaries and Contiguous Areas: North: 59th Street and the **Upper East Side**; East: East River; South: 42nd Street and **Murray Hill**; West: Lexington Avenue.

In the 18th century, this urbane neighborhood was known as Turtle Bay Farm, a charming name that still applies to the tree-shaded community lying in the shadow of the United Nations. The mid-19th century brought industrialization and the "el" rumbling over tenements built along the East River. A construction boom in the 1920s left the heart of Turtle Bay much as you see it today; handsome blocks of carefully maintained brownstones interspersed with relatively small apartment buildings. But not until the 1940s, when the squalid slaughterhouses that had replaced the riverside slums were razed to make room for the United Nations, and the 1950s, when the "el" came tumbling down, did Turtle Bay become eminently respectable from Lexington Avenue clear to the East River. Now the area is one of the most prestigious—and one of the safest—in town, a self-assured place with toney restaurants and charming cul de sacs like Amster Yard on 49th Street, Greenacre Park on 51st and the private, somewhat secret, garden enclosed by twenty Italianate townhouses in which Katharine Hepburn and E.B. White once lived.

Apartment prices, as befits a neighborhood embracing exclusive Sutton Place, Beekman Place and the two glass towers at United Nations Plaza, are among the highest around. For the least rarefied rates look along First and Second Avenues and the side streets in between.

Tudor City lies southwest of Sutton Place and somewhat downscale. Bounded by 40th and 43rd Streets, this huge complex of Tudor-style buildings between First and Second Avenues includes a hotel, church and private parking area. Unfortunately for would-be tenants, eleven of the twelve buildings completed in 1930 have been converted to cooperatives.

Area Code: 212

Post Office: Tudor City Station, 5 Tudor City Place, NYC 10017, 697-8656.

Zip Codes: 10022, 10017, 10016

Police Precinct: Seventeenth, 167 East 51st Street, NYC 10022, 826-3211.

Emergency Hospital (nearest): New York Hospital-Cornell Medical Center, 525 East 68th Street, NYC 10021, 746-5454; New York University Hospital and Medical Center, 560 First Avenue, NYC 10016, 263-7300.

Libraries (nearest): 58th Street Branch, 127 East 58th Street, NYC 10022, 759-7358; Mid-Manhattan, 455 Fifth Avenue, NYC 10016, 340-0849.

Public School Education: School District #2 (see **Chelsea**).

Cultural Resources: Young Men's Christian Association of Greater New York, Vanderbilt Branch, 224 East 47th Street, NYC 10017, 755-2410; YWCA of the City of New York, 610 Lexington Avenue, NYC 10022, 755-2700; Japan Society, 333 East 47th Street, NYC 10017, 832-1155.

Transportation—Subway: Crosstown *42nd Street Shuttle* Crosstown *Flushing Line #7*; *Lexington Avenue IRT* (#4, #5, #6) 59th Street (Exp), 51st Street, 42nd Street (Exp).

Transportation—Bus: Crosstown *49th/50th Streets* (#27, #50); Crosstown 42nd Street (#42); Uptown *Madison Avenue* (#1, #2, #3, #4); Uptown *Third Avenue*—Downtown *Lexington Avenue* (#98, #101,#102); Uptown *First Avenue*—Downtown *Second Avenue* (#15).

Murray Hill

Boundaries and Contiguous Areas: North: 42nd Street and the **East Forties and Fifties**; East: East River; South: 34th Street and the **Gramercy Park Area**; West: Fifth Avenue.

Murray Hill is the kind of neighborhood where you can walk into a compact ground floor apartment, open a back door and have access to a garden larger than the flat. Time was when the great mansions of Fifth and Madison Avenues lastingly elegant buildings like J.P. Morgan's magnificent McKim, Mead and White-designed library — conferred social status on the houses highest on the hill. Below these were the stables and carriage houses serving them, and in the shadow of the old Third Avenue "el," tenements. The tenements are gone now and as Fifth Avenue became more commercial, residential Murray Hill shifted east and the carriage houses proved to be fashionable — indeed, charming homes. The streets are a mix of tranquil landmarks like Sniffen Court, a private mews at 150-158 East 36th Street, nondescript brick apartment buildings and postmodern fantasies like the undulating, 57-story Corinthian. And brownstones: these solid and unpretentious turn-of-the-century buildings are nonetheless elegant and lend a particularly substantial quality to the crest of Murray Hill.

This popular area is made more attractive still by the vitality of its early evening street life. The doctors, nurses and other young professionals employed by University and Bellevue Hospitals and related New York University medical facilities are a major presence on the scene, and the casual, inviting shops and restaurants crowding Second and Third Avenues play to a youthful audience. Housing possibilities include proliferating high rises on the flatlands east of Third as well as brownstones and carriage houses on Murray Hill itself.

Area Code: 212

Post Office: Murray Hill Station, 115 East 34th Street, NYC 10016, 679-9127.

Zip Code: 10016

Police Precinct: Seventeenth, 167 East 51st Street, NYC 10022, 826-3211.

Emergency Hospitals (nearest): New York University Medical Center, 560 First Avenue (and 33rd Street), NYC 10016, 263-7300; Bellevue Hospital Center, 462 First Avenue (and 27th Street), NYC 10016, 561-4141.

Library: Kips Bay, 446 Third Avenue, NYC 10016, 683-2520.

Public School Education: School District #2 (see **Chelsea**).

Adult Education: American Academy of Dramatic Arts, 120 Madison Avenue, NYC 10016, 686-9244.

Cultural Resources: J. Pierpont Morgan Library, 29 East 36th Street, NYC 10016, 685-0008.

Transportation—Subway: Crosstown *42nd Street Shuttle* (S) Lexington Avenue; Crosstown *Flushing Line* (7) Lexington/Third Avenues; *Lexington Avenue IRT* (#4, #5, #6) 42nd Street (Exp), 33rd Street.

Transportation—Bus: Crosstown *34th Street* (#16,#34); Uptown *Madison Avenue* (#1, #2,#3,#4); Uptown *Third Avenue*—Downtown *Lexington Avenue* (#101, #102); Downtown *Second Avenue* (#15).

Gramercy Park Area

Boundaries and Contiguous Areas: North: 34th Street and **Murray Hill**; East: Second Avenue and **Stuyvesant Area**; South: East 14th Street; West: Park Avenue South/**Chelsea** and the **Flatiron District**.

The Gramercy Park is a verdant, block-square, fenced and locked enclave to which only residents of the surrounding buildings hold keys. With its lovely old trees, squirrels, flowering spring plantings and the occasional nanny, the park is reminiscent of a quiet London square. But it wasn't the work of a homesick Brit; a real estate developer, to increase the value of 66 lots he owned nearby, laid out the private park in 1831. That this strategy was successful is evidenced by the quality of the ornate later-19th century buildings that still surround the square—elaborate structures like The Players Club (Edwin Booth's former home) and the National Arts Club (designed by Calvert Vaux in a Gothic Revival style).

The air of dignified elegance which permeates Gramercy Park and sets such a pleasant tone for the neighborhood as a whole is reinforced by historic Stuyvesant Square (located four blocks to the southeast at 15th Street) with its lovely white clapboard Friends Meeting House and brownstone St. George's Church, where J.P. Morgan once worshipped. In general, this is an enclave of small townhouses and rows of trim brick-fronts dappled with upgraded tenements, modest apartment houses and an occasional highrise.

And, propelled by emergence of the East 20s and of the Union Square area as a major publishing and public relations neighborhood, more are on their way. On Park Avenue and on Second Avenue, and in the 20s and low 30s, new condos have sprouted like field mushrooms after a warm fall rain. Pricey rentals are available at the Rutherford Place apartments overlooking Stuyvesant Square and in the older and highly desirable Waterside complex between 23rd and 28th Streets overlooking the East River.

Gramercy Park is a desirable place to live, but you probably have a better chance of finding an apartment in one of these newer high rises that ring the neighborhood than in one of the townhouses adjacent to the park itself. In any event, the Gramercy area is relaxed and neighborly, and it pays to walk through the community talking with doormen and building superintendents when searching for an apartment here.

Area Code: 212

Post Offices: Murray Hill Station, 115 East 34th Street, NYC 10016, 679-9127; Madison Square, 149 East 23rd Street, NYC 10010, 673-3771.

Zip Codes: 10016, 10010, 10003

Police Precincts: Seventeenth (above 30th Street), 167 East 51st Street, NYC 10022, 826-3211; Thirteenth, 230 East 21st Street, NYC 10010, 477-7411.

Emergency Hospitals (nearest): New York University Hospital Medical Center, 560 First Avenue at 33rd Street, NYC 10016, 263-7300; Bellevue Hospital Center, First Avenue and 27th Street, NYC 10016, 561-4141; Cabrini Medical Center, 227 East 19th Street, NYC 10003, 995-6000; Beth Israel Medical Center, 16th Street at First Avenue, NYC 10003, 420-2000; New York Eye and

Ear Infirmary, 310 East 14th Street, NYC 10003, 979-4000.

Library: Kips Bay, 446 Third Avenue, NYC 10016, 683-2520.

Public School Education: School District #2 (see **Chelsea**).

Adult Education: School of Visual Arts, 209 East 23rd Street, NYC 10010, 679-7350; Baruch College of Adult and Continuing Education, 48 East 26th Street, NYC 10010, 447-3020.

Cultural Resources: The Players, 16 Gramercy Park South between Irving Place and Park Avenue South, NYC 10003, 228-7610, contains important collections of letters, playbills, prompt books, plays and materials relating to 19th century British and American theater which can be seen by appointment. Theodore Roosevelt House, 28 East 20th Street, NYC 10003, between Broadway and Park Avenue South, 260-1616; Roosevelt's exuberantly Victorian birthplace contains letters, books and objects collected from his many trips.

Transportation—Subway: Crosstown *14th Street* (L) Union Square, Third Avenue; *Lexington Avenue* IRT (#4, #5, #6) 33rd Street, 28th Street, 23rd Street, 14th Street/Union Square (Exp).

Transportation—Bus: Crosstown *34th Street* (#16, #34); Crosstown *23rd Street* (#23); Crosstown *14th Street* (#14); Uptown *Madison Avenue* (#1, #2, #3, #4); Uptown *Third Avenue*—Downtown *Lexington Avenue* (#101, #102); Downtown *Second Avenue* (#15).

Stuyvesant Town and Peter Cooper Village

Boundaries and Contiguous Areas: North: 23rd Street; East: FDR Drive; South: 14th Street and the **East Village;** West: First Avenue and **Gramercy Park Area.**

Two of the oldest and best known housing developments in New York City, Stuyvesant Town, 14th Street to 20th Street, and its upscale (larger apartments and rents) big brother, Peter Cooper Village, 20th Street to 23rd Street, are difficult to penetrate. In addition to income requirements, there is a long waiting list where time is meted out in years, not weeks or months. What makes these developments so desirable, besides the relatively reasonable rents, is their resolutely middle-class family-oriented population, relative safety and—after twenty years' growth of trees, flowers, ivy and climbing hydrangea against the otherwise unrelieved brick walls—unpretentious attractiveness. So, if you care to pursue the matter, apply at the renting office for both developments, which are owned by Metropolitan Life Insurance Co., at 629 East 14th Street, NYC 10009, SP 7-1600, and get in line, or "on line," as we say in New York.

The community surrounding Peter Cooper and Stuyvesant includes luxury buildings as well as owner-occupied brownstones and upgraded tenements. When scouting the area (First Avenue west to Lexington), try the side streets. The neighborhood is a comparison shopper's dream, with all the major supermarkets and many ethnic food stores (especially south on First Avenue), clothing shops and decorating showrooms along First and Second Avenues vying for your dollars. There are large, quiet tree-shaded parks for breaks between apartment visits, and in warm weather the renovated public swimming pool at 23rd Street and Asser Levy Place is available for a cooling few laps. (In fact, look for this turn-of-the-century stone Roman bath even if you can't swim; it's a beauty.) And if you're beset by hypochondria, this location with five top hospitals within walking distance merits serious consideration.

Area Code: 212

Post Office: Peter Stuyvesant Station, 432 East 14th Street, NYC 10009, 677-2112.

Zip Codes: 10010, 10009

Police Precinct: Thirteenth, 230 East 21st Street, NYC 10010, 477-7411.

Emergency Hospitals: New York University Hospital Medical Center, 560 First Avenue at 33rd Street, NYC 10016, 263-7300; Bellevue Hospital Center, First Avenue and 27th Street, NYC 10016, 561-4141; Cabrini Medical Center, 227 East 19th Street,

NYC 10003, 995-6000; Beth Israel Hospital Medical Center, 16th Street and First Avenue, NYC 10009, 420-2000; New York Eye and Ear Infirmary, 310 East 14th Street, NYC 10003, 979-4000.

Libraries: Epiphany, 228 East 23rd Street, NYC 10010, 679-2645; Kips Bay, 446 Third Avenue, NYC 10016, 683-2520.

Public School Education: School District #2 (see **Chelsea**).

Adult Education: School of Visual Arts, 209 East 23rd Street, NYC 10010, 679-7350; Baruch College of Adult and Continuing Education, 48 East 26th Street, NYC 10010, 725-7172.

Transportation—Subway: Crosstown *14th Street* (L) Lexington Avenue, Third Avenue, First Avenue; *Lexington Avenue IRT* (#4,#5, #6) 23rd Street, 14th Street/Union Square (Exp).

Transportation—Bus: Crosstown *34th Street* (#16) goes across 34th Street and down Second Avenue, then east across 23rd Street and uptown to 34th Street along F.D.R. Drive; Crosstown *23rd Street* (#26); Crosstown *14th Street* (#14); Uptown *First Avenue*— Downtown *Second Avenue* (#15).

East Village

Boundaries and Contiguous Areas: North: 14th Street and the **Stuyvesant Area;** East: Avenue B; South: Houston Street and the **Lower East Side;** West: Broadway and **Greenwich Village.**

"I've lived in my rent-controlled apartment for years and pay $115 a month," says a Manhattan resident quoted in *New York* magazine. "I live on the Lower East Side. The young kids who just moved in upstairs and pay $700 a month for the same amount of space—they live in the East Village." Indeed, long-time residents do call this colorful (in the singular life-style sense of the word) neighborhood the Lower East Side, but sometime in the 1960s, perhaps in an attempt to bestow a bit of cachet, the then-emerging avant-garde colony was dubbed the East Village. The name stuck, and while the East lacks the charm of Greenwich to the west, this Village no longer has the depressing poverty and crime of much of the Lower East Side to the south.

What this up-beat but slightly off-center community of homesteaded tenements does have is a combination of ingredients that makes it one of the most desirable alternative neighborhoods in town: an abundant and often eye-popping street life, art galleries, boutiques on the cutting edge of fashion, inexpensive hangouts, and beauticians expert in the latest asymmetrical hairstyle. The East Village also boasts an influential ethnic population. Italians, Poles, Ukrainians, Lithuanians and Hispanics, and the bakeries, butcher shops, restaurants and various cultural institutions they have nurtured for decades, add not only diversity but depth and interest to the neighborhood.

The retaking of Alphabet City, the A, B, C and D Avenues east of First Avenue, from the control of drug dealers and junkies has been a major factor in the redevelopment of the East Village. Since 1984, Operation Pressure Point, a joint effort of the Police Department, city agencies and community groups against dealers and addicts, has been largely successful. Now Avenue B boasts co-ops and the renovation of Tompkins Square has saved the park from the Calcutta-like squalor of the 1980s and brought back the East Village's leafy back yard. Consequently rents, while still more affordable than other areas, have been rising here.

To the west, the Astor Place area bubbles with student life centered around Cooper Union and nearby NYU, the ever-lively Public Theater, and good buys in books, booze and latest-look clothing along a revivified Broadway. Connecting Astor Place with the Second Avenue heart of the East Village is St. Mark's Place, actually part of 8th Street, where hippies and flower children frolicked, the Electric Circus drew limousines from uptown and W. H. Auden lived. That's gone now and St. Mark's is a little quieter, visually and audibly, but little changed.

Throughout the East Village, pocket-sized boutiques selling wild and exotic clothing coexist nonchalantly with The Boys Club of New York, Hell's Angels headquarters and the "Indian Block" on Sixth Street lined with curry parlors. In these surroundings, briefcase-toting law associates and young bank trainees look somewhat out of place but they, no less than faddishly dressed art dealers and be-jeaned students, are attracted by the neighborhood's decidedly lively pace and comparatively reasonable rents. Although condo renovations, beginning with the Cristadora on

Tompkins Square Park, are a trend, be prepared for walk-ups; most of the housing stock consists of improved tenements. Start your apartment search by studying ads in *The Village Voice*, then check Cooper Union and NYU bulletin boards, walk the streets and talk to people who live here.

Area Code: 212

Post Offices: Cooper Station, 93 Fourth Avenue, NYC 10003, 254-1389; Peter Stuyvesant Station, 432 East 14th Street, NYC 10009, 677-2112; Tompkins Square Station, 244 East Third Street, NYC 10009, 673-6415.

Zip Codes: 10003, 10009

Police Precinct: Ninth, 321 East Fifth Street, NYC 10003, 477-7811.

Emergency Hospitals: Beth Israel Hospital Medical Center, 16th Street and First Avenue, NYC 10009, 420-2000; New York Eye and Ear Infirmary, 310 East 14th Street, NYC 10003, 979-4000.

Libraries: Ottendorfer, 135 Second Avenue, NYC 10003, 674-0947; Tompkins Square, 331 East 10th Street, NYC 10009, 228-4747.

Public School Education: School District #1: Community School Board, 80 Montgomery Street, NYC 10002, 602-9700.

Adult Education: Third Street Music School Settlement, 235 East 11th Street, NYC 10003, 777-3240; Stuyvesant Adult Center, 345 East 15th Street, NYC 10003, 254-2890, offers a wide variety of inexpensive evening adult education courses, from languages to sewing.

Cultural Resources: La Mama Experimental Theater Club, 74A East Fourth Street, 475-7710, on the cutting edge of avant-garde theater for over two decades, and PS (Performing Space) 122, 150 First Avenue, 477-5288, a reclaimed public school, to say nothing of the Public Theater just over the East Village line on Lafayette

Street, indicate the lively state of this neighborhood's arts. Second Avenue was the Yiddish rialto until 1940. Now the Theater for the New City performs new plays in a converted city market building at 155 First Avenue, 254-1109, and CSC Repertory Theater has been successfully producing classics at 136 East 13th Street, 677-4210, for nearly 20 years. The Third Street Music School (see above) also offers concerts and recitals, and Cooper Union at Third Avenue and 7th Street, 353-4195, has frequent exhibits, concerts and lectures. Theater and opera thrive even on the Bowery: classics at the Jean Cocteau Repertory, at 330 Bowery, 677-0060, and Italian opera at The Amato Opera Theater at 319 Bowery, 228-8200.

Transportation—Subway: Crosstown *BMT* (L) Third Avenue, First Avenue; *Lexington Avenue IRT* (#4,#6) Astor Place, Bleecker Street; *Sixth Avenue IND* (F) Houston Street/Second Avenue.

Transportation—Bus: Crosstown *14th Street* (#14); Going East: Crosstown *West 10th Street/West Eighth Street* (#13); Going West: Crosstown *West Ninth Street/Christopher Street* (#13); Uptown *Third Avenue/Lexington*—Downtown *Lexington/Third Avenue* (#101, #102); Uptown *First Avenue*—Downtown *Second Avenue* (#15).

Lower East Side, Little Italy and Chinatown

Boundaries and Contiguous Areas: North: Houston Street and the **East Village**; East: East River; South: **Downtown**; West: Broadway and **SoHo**.

"Give me your tired, your poor . . ." wrote Emma Lazarus, and when they arrived, many of them, it was to the Lower East Side. Between 1870 and 1920, wave on wave of immigrants from Italy, Bohemia, China and the ghettos of eastern Europe poured into the warren of fetid tenements on Mulberry, Elizabeth, Hester and Division Streets, where they lived and worked until able to move up and out to the suburbs, or at least The Bronx, leaving room for the next wave.

Although public housing, especially along the easternmost strip of the Lower East Side, has alleviated crowding and let in some light and air, much of the area remains unchanged from the turn of the century. Whole chunks of the neighborhood are rat-, roach-and drug-infested— and dangerous. Along the fringes, however, there are enclaves where the young and impecunious—artists, students and the like—have established beachheads. Even grungy Ludlow Street is showing unmistakable signs of gentrification: among the grim tenements, a thriving cafe in the basement of a newly renovated building with an incredible *trompe l'oeil* facade.

Actually, at least three Lower East Sides exist, with imprecise and constantly changing borders: (1) the old Jewish Lower East Side, now largely Puerto Rican, to the east; (2) Chinatown in the southwest portion, which is expanding rapidly northward into (3) Little Italy. Colorful Orchard Street is still chockablock with little stores and Yiddish-speaking shopkeepers, many of them bearded, black-hat-wearing Hasidim. On Sunday in particular, crowds flock in from New Jersey, Long Island and uptown in search of bargains and Jewish food specialties. But shop owners live elsewhere, most of them, and at night all that remains of a once vibrant Jewish community are forlorn old synagogues, deserted or converted to pentecostal churches.

Thousands upon thousands of recent arrivals have burst Chinatown's traditional seams past East Broadway into the old Jewish enclave and north over Canal Street into Little Italy, which is now two-thirds Asian. Continuing immigration via Hong Kong has also severely split the once stable social and political fabric of the Chinese community. Housing is impossibly crowded, and sweatshops are said to be increasing. But walking the almost impassable sidewalks of Chinatown on a Saturday, one would think this area existed solely to satisfy the city's insatiable appetite for Chinese food. Like bounty hunters, mavens stalk the crowded streets, pouncing on new restaurants with cries of delight. On Saturdays, there are numerous street vendors.

Little Italy, between Canal and Houston Streets, has a declining Italian population and an expanding selection of Italian restaurants and cafes. Along Mulberry Street on a warm spring evening the combined hisses of uncountable cappuccino machines sound like a locomotive gathering steam. The neighborhood seems destined to become a restaurant district operated increasingly from Long Island, Staten Island and New Jersey. And although beansprouts have replaced fagioli and frozen dim sum take the place of frozen ravioli in innumerable small stores, a bit of the old Southern Italian character still remains, as does the community's reputation as a don't-mess-with-us, low-crime neighborhood with strong ethnic ties around the old, original St. Patrick's. Infiltration of the Lower East Side by the middle class has begun. In fact, it's old news. In 1984 intrepid souls brave enough to sign leases on The Bowery, Rivington or Pitt Streets were featured in *The New York Times*. Now bright banners advertising slick co-ops flutter in Little Italy and Chinatown. Most notably the recently refurbished Police Building at 240 Centre Street, a granite Renaissance Revival palazzo built in 1909, reopened with crystal chandeliers and 54 luxury condos behind a statuary-cluttered facade in the heart of Little Italy. Rents in the neighborhood move ever upward, and the unmonied and creative have moved to Queens. Still, apartment listings are sparse. Best to talk to someone who lives in the neighborhood, and do walk around, exercising caution and looking (carefully) block by block.

Area Code: 212

Post Offices: Knickerbocker Station, 128 East Broadway, NYC 10002, 227-0089; Chinatown Station, 6 Doyers Street, NYC 10013, 267-3510.

Zip Codes: 10012, 10013, 10002

Police Precincts: Fifth, 19 Elizabeth Street, NYC 10013, 334-0711; Seventh, 19 1/2 Pitt Street, NYC 10002, 477-7311.

Emergency Hospital (nearest): New York Downtown Hospital, 170 William Street, NYC 10038, 312-5000.

Libraries: Hamilton Fish Park, 415 East Houston Street, NYC 10002, 673-2290; Seward Park, 192 East Broadway, NYC 10002, 477-6770.

Public School Education: School District #1: Community School Board, 80 Montgomery Street, NYC 10002, 602-9700; School District #2 (see **Chelsea**).

Cultural Resources: The Henry Street Settlement is actually a variety of resources, with its Arts for Living Center, Settlement Playhouse and New Federal Theater at 466 Grand Street, NYC 10002, 598-0400. The Lower East Side Tenement Museum, 97 orchard Street, NYC 10002, 431-0233, includes exhibits in three buildings (one of which has been "unrestored" to illustrate life as it was) as well as neighborhood walking tours.

Transportation—Subway: *Lexington Avenue IRT* (#4, #5, #6) Spring Street, Canal Street (Exp); *Sixth Avenue IND* (F) Houston/Second Avenue, Delancey Street, (B, D) Grand Street (Exp); *BMT* (N, R) Canal (Exp); *Nassau Street Local* (J, M) Canal, Bowery and Essex Street.

Transportation—Bus: Crosstown *West-East Houston* (#21); Uptown *First Avenue*—Downtown *Second Avenue* (#15); Uptown *Bowery/Third Avenue*—Downtown *Third Avenue/Bowery* (#101, #102).

Downtown

Boundaries and Contiguous Areas: North: Chambers Street and **Tribeca;** East: East River; South: Upper New York Bay; West: Hudson River.

The streets of downtown New York are so convoluted and irrational in design that even natives sensibly carry maps. It is an area which encourages the visitor to look up—to the top of the World Trade Center, where television airwave receptors hover like rocket launchers; up at the four limestone sculptures (of Asia, America, Europe and Africa) emerging from the granite palace which was once the US Customs House at Bowling Green and Bridge Street; up at the delicate spire of Trinity Church (Broadway and the beginning of Wall Street), where lunchtime crowds gather for concerts at noon and munch sandwiches while walking among the historic tombstones; up at the masts of ships docked at the South Street Seaport Museum alongside the Fulton Fish Market and the Rouse Development Corporation's South Street Seaport renewal.

Consisting of renovated Schermerhorn Row, museum shops, a new

Fulton Market and a shopping mecca on Pier 17, the Seaport edges the East River at Fulton Street and, just like sister developments in Boston and Baltimore, is a pleaser. Crowds browse craft stands and upscale boutiques, stroll and nosh their way through a tantalizing assortment of ethnic snack bars, queue for the multimedia show at the Trans-Lux Theater, and dine in the glamorous glass-enclosed pavilion shimmering over East River waters.

Visitors downtown also look up at old wholesale houses, offices and bank buildings in the process of conversion to residential use and new structures going up expressly for that purpose. Downtown is slowly adjusting to the fact that people live (as opposed to work) there, 24 hours a day, seven days a week. The 1970 census showed only 7,000 residents in the oldest part of Manhattan; you could take tea in the middle of Wall Street on a Sunday afternoon—if you could find some tea to take. An estimated 25,000 people live here now, serviced by dry cleaners where there were none, day care centers, supermarkets, and food specialty shops (stocked with tea). Indeed, the community is on its way to becoming a full-fledged neighborhood, with its own handsome, new Public School 234, several hotels, and plans for a Downtown branch library.

Battery Park City, built between West Street and the Hudson River on landfill excavated from the World Trade Center site, is the largest development ever constructed in Manhattan. The recently developed 92 acres is made up of a collection of architecturally diverse residential and financial complexes managed by the Battery Park City Authority. The World Financial Center—four stunning, copper-topped buildings fastidiously designed by Cesar Pelli—faces the World Trade Center and forms Battery Park City's hub.

At its center like an imperial gateway to the city, the soaring, glass and polished-steel Winter Garden with sixteen California palms set in gleaming marble provides an elegant site for free concerts edging the North Cove Yacht Harbor. The beautifully landscaped Esplanade—connecting the Winter Garden with South Gardens and North Park—constitutes the spine of the development as it stretches over a mile along the Hudson River.

With two residential complexes occupied and more to come, along with a huge fifth office building, public parks and gardens, a floating skating rink, and a museum of the Holocaust, Battery Park City is a work in progress. Gateway Plaza consists of 1,712 apartments in six (three tall, three short) buildings, which are fully rented. All ten of the mostly-Deco, brick and limestone mid-rises that form Rector Place are now in place, with a total of 2,200 rental apartments and condominiums. Three new upscale condo buildings have opened in Battery Place to the south with 630 units.

Battery Park City residents tend to be young professionals who work in Lower Manhattan. Some 25,000 people will live, another 35,000 will work, within sight of the Statue of Liberty when the mammoth project is completed. The whole is even now surrounded by parks and sculpture-filled plazas and connected by ferry service to New Jersey and by climate-controlled walkways to the World Trade Center, public transportation and the Financial District. Bravura new world.

The size and splendor of this mega-project should not, however, obscure the presence in Lower Manhattan of other residential possibilities. For example, small, architecturally distinguished condominiums like Greenwich Court have sprung up on the West Side below Chambers Street, and conversions are rife throughout lower Manhattan.. Today, a many of the older office towers near Wall Street contain nary a brokerage firm but, rather, cooperative residences instead.

Area Code: 212

Post Offices: Church Street Station, 90 Church Street, NYC 10007, 330-5247; Peck Slip Station, 1-19 Peck Slip, NYC 10038, 964-1055; Bowling Green Station, 25 Broadway, NYC 10004, 363-9490.

Zip Codes: 10007, 10038, 10047/48 (World Trade Center), 10006, 10004, 10005, 10041, 10280, 10281, 10282

Police Precinct: First, 16 Ericsson Place, NYC 10013, 334-0611.

Emergency Hospital: New York Downtown Hospital, 170 William Street, NYC 10038, 312-5000.

Library (nearest): Chatham Square (Chinatown), 33 East Broadway, NYC 10002, 964-6598.

Public School Education: School District #2 (see **Chelsea**).

Adult Education: Pace University, 1 Pace Plaza, NYC 10038, 346-1200; New York Institute of Finance, 2 Broadway, 5th Floor, NYC 10004 344-2900.

Cultural Resources: South Street Seaport Museum, Fulton and Water Streets, NYC 10038, 669-9424; The Whitney Museum of American Art's Downtown Branch, 33 Maiden Lane, NYC 10013, 943-5655 (offices); also see **Tribeca.**

Transportation—Subway: Seventh Avenue IRT (#1, #2, #3) Chambers (Exp), Cortlandt, Rector, South Ferry/Battery Park, Park Place/Broadway, Fulton (Exp), Wall; Eighth Avenue IND (A, C, E) World Trade Center, Broadway/Nassau; BMT (N, R) City Hall, Cortlandt, Rector, Whitehall; Lexington Avenue IRT (#4, #5, #6) Brooklyn Bridge, Fulton, Wall, Bowling Green; Nassau Street Local (J, M) Fulton; PATH (to New Jersey) World Trade Center.

Transportation—Bus: Crosstown *Chambers/West/Vesey/Park Row to Madison Street* (#22); Uptown *Church/Hudson/Eighth Avenue*—Downtown *Seventh Avenue/Varick/West Broadway* (#10); Uptown *Church/Sixth Avenue*—Downtown *Broadway* (#6); Uptown and Downtown *Grand Central Terminal—Wall Street Express* (#X25) weekdays only.

Tribeca

Boundaries and Contiguous Areas: North: Canal Street and **SoHo;** East: Broadway; South: Chambers Street and **Downtown;** West: Hudson River.

South of Canal Street, where the island of Manhattan narrows toward its tip, Greenwich Street angles to intersect West Broadway, leaving in its wake not only the loft district dubbed Tribeca (triangle below Canal) but triangular blocks and crossroad parks unique in the city. Felicitous little Duane Park, the most charming of the lot, breathes into an area composed of 19th century brick and cast iron structures, sprawling warehouses and commercial space, an air of peace and tranquility rare in the Big Apple.

Before becoming Tribeca-ized, the area consisted of a warren of scruffy walkups that housed the city's wholesale fruit, vegetable and flower district, the Washington Market, as well as the butter and egg district. Most of the market was razed and sent packing to The Bronx in the late 1960s, to be replaced in part by the ponderous brick Independence Plaza project at 40 Harrison Street, but a few vestiges of the produce district remain. A row of Federal houses has been tucked under Independence Plaza's angular wing, and the satisfying scents of roasting coffee beans and nuts, ground spices, chocolate and an occasional wheel of aging cheese perfume air already salted by breezes blowing off the Hudson.

Tribeca is also home to a number of elegantly sculptural cast iron buildings—the first built not far from Duane Park by James Bogardus in 1849. The noticeably cleaner of the arched and colonnaded facades front residential lofts and cooperatives skillfully adapted from commercial space, as well as the galleries and offices of the avant-garde establishment (the pioneering fringe has moved to the Lower East Side and across the East River into Queens and Brooklyn). Loft living is now an accepted urban lifestyle, and Tribeca has changed radically from the quiet backwater it remained throughout the 1970s. It is a prime destination for those who like their buildings wide and their spaces open.

The vaunted, often vaulted warehouses just south of the Holland Tunnel sheltered the clubs responsible for Tribeca's dominant position on the late-night-life scene during the 1980s. Long after midnight, limos, cabs and private cars from New Jersey jostled for curb space, much as their passengers, confined behind red velvet ropes, angled for positions at the head of the waiting line. The restaurants that the disco devotees haunted remain, catering these days to a more staid clientele. Tribeca hosts a kaleidoscopic range of restaurants—Ethiopian, streamlined hangouts, trattorias and French cafes—for the young, the chic and the up-and-coming; middays they nourish neatly pressed Wall Streeters and rumpled denizens of City Hall.

Competing pressures—southbound from booming SoHo, from 10,000 students at Manhattan Community College in its midst, and most insistently from affluent, ever-expanding Battery Park City to the South—are transforming Tribeca into a thriving, cohesive mixed-use community. Conversion of commercial buildings to handsome residential lofts proceeds; service businesses spring up among the faded signs of the vanished butter, egg and cheese trade. But the real estate activity has yet to

seriously disturb the fine community feeling which, along with unimped-
ed bike-riding on weekends, the architecture and night life, is one of the
great attractions of living in Tribeca.

Area Code: 212

Post Office: Canal Street Station, 350 Canal Street, NYC 10013,
925-3378.

Zip Code: 10013

Police Precinct: First, 16 Ericsson Place, NYC 10013, 334-0611.

Emergency Hospital (nearest): New York Downtown Hospital, 170
William Street, NYC 10038, 312-5000; St. Vincent's Hospital and
Medical Center, 153 West 11th Street (at Seventh Avenue), NYC
10011, 790-7000.

Library (nearest): Hudson Park, 66 Leroy Street, NYC 10014,
243-6876, has an excellent film program for children.

Public School Education: School District #2 (see **Chelsea**).

Adult Education: Borough of Manhattan Community College,
Office of Continuing Education, Room S763, 199 Chambers Street,
NYC 10007, 346-8000, offers a variety of inexpensive evening and
weekend courses ranging from computer to business to
self-improvement. Concerts and theater are also presented regularly in the College's Triplex Theater.

Cultural Resources: Tribeca quarters alternative spaces displaying
works for and by the avant-garde much as Madison Avenue in the
70s houses deluxe galleries catering to the establishment. These
include Artists Space, 38 Greene Street, 3rd Floor, NYC 10013,
226-3970; Franklin Furnace, 112 Franklin Street at West Broadway,
NYC 10013, 925-4671; and The Clocktower (Institute for Art and
Urban Resources), 108 Leonard Street, 13th floor, NYC 10013,
233-1096. Also, Borough of Manhattan Community College, 199
Chambers Street, NYC 10007, 346-8000..

Transportation—Subway: *Eighth Avenue IND* (A, C, E) Canal Street (Exp), Chambers Street (Exp); *Seventh Avenue IRT* (#1, #2, #3) Canal Street, Franklin Street, Chambers Street (Exp).

Transportation—Bus: Crosstown *Madison & Chambers Street/West Street & Grand Street* (#22); Uptown *Hudson Street/Eighth Avenue*—Downtown *Seventh Avenue/Varick Street* (#10); Uptown *Sixth Avenue* (#6); Uptown and Downtown *Grand Central Terminal—Wall Street Express* (X25) weekdays only.

SoHo

Boundaries and Contiguous Areas: North: West Houston Street and **Greenwich Village;** East: Broadway and **Lower East Side;** South: Canal Street and **Tribeca;** West: Sixth Avenue.

SoHo's cast iron buildings are justifiably famous and a visual delight. Look up to appreciate the beauty of the patterns—columnar shapes, Greek Revival capitals and other architectural embellishments—pressed into the cast iron facades. Windowsill houseplants, paintings and some of the city's most colorful walls reveal the loft residences which now occupy most of what was manufacturing space. Behind these slightly grimy fronts live some of New York's trendiest setters, often in 4,000-square-foot spreads.

The structures are based on a technique perfected by James Bogardus around 1850. Forerunners of today's "curtain wall" skyscrapers, these cast iron buildings are supported by interior columns, obviating the need for thick walls and allowing the use of much more glass than was previously possible. As a result, the graceful windows, many of them arched, nicely complement the strong, solid buildings, and the whole is extremely harmonious. The buildings are also exceedingly attractive to the city's artists, ever on the lookout for good light and space. In the early 1960s they began to move into the area, just as industry had moved into what had been the city's raunchy Tenderloin a century before; loft living became legal in 1971. With the subsequent discovery of SoHo by the affluent, high prices have driven many of the original artists to less costly neighborhoods. But art galleries and audacious boutiques remain to prosper and proliferate.

The popularity of SoHo has in no way diminished. On the contrary, monied *arrivistes* commingle with painters and sculptors on the upper floors of the converted cast iron structures while at street level, hard-edged, minimalist (whatever the fashion-of-the-moment) show-rooms spread their plate glass windows far and wide. What Madison Avenue, with its French designer boutiques and galleries, is to the Upper East Side, West Broadway is to Lower Manhattan, and at similar prices. You can buy the latest in wearable art, Japanese designer clothes, French *pret-a-porter*, exquisite antique blouses and accessories, Art Deco furniture of the 1930s. Bring money.

What has changed in recent years is the eastern edge of SoHo. Galleries, clothing shops, and even offices, have spread east from West Broadway past Wooster, Greene and Mercer to Broadway and beyond. Once drab and lifeless, Broadway is undergoing a personality change as faux marble and hand-grained surfaces replace the tatty showrooms of fabric wholesalers. The relocation of Dean and DeLuca's extraordinary food emporium to a vast, white space resembling an edible art gallery is a sure sign of the Broadway revival. As SoHo crawls ever eastward, the boundary between SoHo and Little Italy is blurring.

While loft living is legal in many buildings, and you need not necessarily qualify as an artist to rent or sublet SoHo space, caution is advised in taking over a lease or paying key money for a loft or apartment. Checking with a local tenants' association is a good idea; Lower Manhattan Loft Tenants, Inc., 280 Broadway, Room 412, 212-344-8866, can inform about legal rents and living situations (see Lofts). Many artists teach and sublet when they go on sabbatical or receive grants which take them to other parts of the country. If you're not in the market for a condo, the best line on housing availability down here is by word-of-mouth (and conversation is lively at the local art galleries and show openings, which anyone can attend) and bulletin boards. Try the one at the Broome Street Bar.

Area Code: 212

Post Office: Prince Street Station, 103 Prince Street, NYC 10012, 226-7868.

Zip Codes: 10012, 10013

Police Precinct: First, 16 Ericsson Place, NYC 10013, 334-0611.

Emergency Hospitals (nearest): St. Vincent's Hospital and Medical Center, Seventh Avenue and 11th Street, NYC 10011, 790-7000; New York Downtown Hospital, 170 William Street, NYC 10038, 312-5110.

Libraries (nearest): Jefferson Market, 425 Avenue of the Americas, NYC 10011, 243-4334; Hudson Park, 66 Leroy Street, NYC 10014, 243-6876.

Public School Education: School District #2 (see **Chelsea**).

Adult Education: The French Culinary Institute, 462 Broadway, NYC 10013, 219-8890, offers a variety of professional and non-professional cooking courses (lunch and dinner too at their restaurant, L'Ecole, 219-3300 for reservations); Pratt Manhattan, the local branch of Brooklyn's Pratt Institute, 295 Lafayette Street, NYC 10012, 925-8481, has extensive evening and weekend course offerings in the arts and professional areas.

Cultural Resources: New Museum of Contemporary Art, 583 Broadway, NYC 10012, 219-1355; Guggenheim SoHo, 575 Broadway, NYC 10012, 423-3500; Museum for African Art, 593 Broadway, NYC 10012, 966-1313. The district is crammed with great and small gallery spaces—investigate them at leisure. Most are closed Sunday and Monday. A scan of Art Now's *Gallery Guide*, available in galleries throughout the city, gives a total picture of the area's resources and current shows. The best weekly guides to arts events in SoHo are *The Village Voice* and the Weekend section on Friday and the Arts and Leisure section on Sunday in *The New York Times*. Nearby Tribeca also offers opportunities to explore the more avant-garde side of the arts, as does the East Village, from which, amoeba-like, galleries have begun to spread throughout the Lower East Side.

Transportation—Subway: *Eighth Avenue IND* (A, C, E) Spring Street, Canal Street (Exp); *Sixth Avenue IND* (B, D, F, Q) Broadway/Lafayette; *BMT* (N, R) Prince Street, Canal Street (Q stops here, too); *Lexington Avenue IRT* (#4, #6) Bleecker Street,

Spring Street, Canal Street.

Transportation—Bus: Crosstown *West-East Houston* (#21); Uptown *Sixth Avenue*—Downtown *Fifth Avenue* (#5); Downtown *Seventh Avenue/Broadway* (#10); Uptown *Sixth Avenue*— Downtown *Broadway* (#6).

Greenwich Village

Boundaries and Contiguous Areas: North: 14th Street, **Chelsea** and **Flatiron District;** East: Broadway and the **East Village;** South: West Houston Street and SoHo; West: Hudson River.

Greenwich Village is the kind of community where neighbors look after each other's plants and pets and where people *do* call the police or fire department if they notice something amiss. Residents still tend to be arts-oriented and more liberal and politically active than most, particularly when it comes to incursions, real or threatened, on the free-wheeling life style adopted by some or on the hallowed six-story maximum building limit. It was the Village's great good fortune to have its streets laid out along the original 18th century farm lanes and property lines before city planners superimposed the grid pattern on most of Manhattan. The crooked streets that intersect major arteries at ungainly angles prevent the standardization, through traffic, and large buildings (not to mention urban boredom) that mar other neighborhoods.

Since the 19th century, the brick, Federal-style structures along these crooked streets have housed more than their share of the city's talented and creative. Writers came first: Edgar Allan Poe in 1837, later Mark Twain, Henry James and Walt Whitman. Artists and intellectuals followed. A handful of people and institutions played key roles in the evolution of the Village as a magnet for those in the vanguard of the arts and letters. Gertrude Vanderbilt Whitney opened her first studio here, exhibiting and encouraging the artists who subsequently became the nucleus of the "Ashcan School" of social realist painters. Mabel Dodge's famed literary salon was on Washington Square, and the Provincetown Players established an early experimental theater on MacDougal Street in 1916. New York University was founded on Washington Square in the

1830s, the New School on West 12th Street in the 1920s. By then the local populace included John Dos Passos, e.e. cummings, Willa Cather, Henry Miller and Edna St. Vincent Millay, and the Village was the avant-garde capital of the nation.

After World War II, abstract expressionists, method actors, controversial novelists and muckraking journalists all coexisted, bringing creative vitality to the area. The early 1960s may have changed the surface look of things, with its beaded and feathered hippies garlanding the streets, but the foment and ferment of past decades continued unchecked. Only as recently as the early 1970s and the advent of spiraling rents has the Village's appeal lessened as a haven for artists and writers. These days there are probably more appreciators around than doers, but the charm of the Village, with its pleasing proportions and special kind of peacefulness, remains.

Greenwich Village contains a balanced mix of high rise elevator buildings, older rent stabilized apartments, lofts, renovated tenements and brownstones (a harmonious ensemble threatened, in the West Village at least, by the emergence of several buildings above the prescribed height limit to obtain remunerative Hudson River views). New, pricey rental apartments and condos in now-fashionable converted warehouses lining West and Washington Streets and in the handsome conversions found in the wholesale antiques district bordering University Place are widely advertised.

A recent addition to Village housing stock is The Archive, a handsome, landmarked Romanesque Revival monolith which was originally a waterfront customs warehouse and most recently a post office. It has been cleaned and refitted into 479 upscale duplex rentals by Rockrose (212-691-9800), the largest rental outfit in the Village.

Because the area is essentially an assembly of small communities—the predominantly Italian South Village, the central Washington Square neighborhood, and the West Village bounded by Seventh Avenue and the Hudson River—searching for rentals is best done on foot and through reliable real estate agents.

Area Code: 212

Post Offices: Patchin Station, 70 West 10th Street, NYC 10011, 475-2534; West Village Station, 527 Hudson Street, NYC 10014, 989-5084; Cooper Station, 93 Fourth Avenue, NYC 10003,

254-1389; Village Station, 201 Varick Street, NYC 10014, 989-9741.

Zip Codes: 10014, 10011, 10012, 10003

Police Precinct: Sixth, 233 West 10th Street, NYC 10014, 741-4811.

Emergency Hospital: St. Vincent's Hospital and Medical Center, Seventh Avenue and 11th Street, NYC 10011, 790-7000.

Libraries: Jefferson Market, 425 Avenue of the Americas, NYC 10011, 243-4334; Hudson Park, 66 Leroy Street, NYC 10014, 243-6876.

Public School Education: School District #2 (see **Chelsea**). Greenwich Village has two elementary schools. P.S. 41 offers "traditional" public school education, while P.S. 3 with an "open corridor" program is more experimental.

Adult Education: Parsons School of Design, 66 Fifth Avenue, NYC 10011, 229-5600; The New School for Social Research, 66 West 12th Street, NYC 10011, 229-5600; The Cooper Union for the Advancement of Science and Art, Third Avenue and 7th Street, NYC 10003, 254-6300; Greenwich House Music School, 46 Barrow Street, NYC 10014, 242-4770; Greenwich House Pottery, 16 Jones Street, 242-4106; New York University, 50 West 4th Street, NYC 10003, 998-1212.

Cultural Resources: The District Office of Community Planning Board No. 2 has a resource directory of all Greenwich Village associations, service organizations and cultural agencies. The directory is up-to-date and free (3 Washington Square Village, Suite 1A, NY 10012, 979-2272).

Transportation—Subway: Crosstown *BMT* (L) Eighth Avenue, Sixth Avenue, Broadway/Union Square; *Eighth Avenue IND* (A, C, E) 14th Street (Exp), West 4th/8th Street (Exp); *Seventh Avenue IRT* (#1, #2, #3) 14th Street (Exp), Christopher Street/Sheridan Square, Houston Street; *Sixth Avenue IND* (F, D, B) 14th Street,

West 4th/8th Street (Exp); *Lexington Avenue IRT* (#4, #5, #6) 14th Street/Union Square (Exp), Astor Place, Bleecker Street at Lafayette; *BMT* (N, R) 14th Street / Union Square, 8th Street / NYU; PATH (between New Jersey and 33rd Street) Christopher at Hudson, 9th and 14th Streets at Sixth Avenue.

Transportation—Bus: Crosstown *14th Street* (#14); Going east: Crosstown *West 10th Street/West 8th Street* (#13); Going west: Crosstown *West 9th Street/Christopher Street* (#13); Uptown *Greenwich Street/Tenth Avenue*—Downtown *Ninth Avenue/Hudson Street* (#11); Uptown *Hudson Street/Eighth Avenue*—Downtown *Seventh Avenue* (#10); Uptown *Sixth Avenue* (#5, #6, #7); Uptown *University Place*—Downtown *Fifth Avenue* (#2, #3).

Flatiron District

Boundaries and Contiguous Areas: North: 23rd Street and Madison Square; East: Park Avenue South and **Gramercy Park Area**; South: 14th Street and **Greenwich Village**; West: Sixth Avenue and **Chelsea**.

Thanks to the famous wintry photograph by Edward Steichen, the thrusting nose of the Flatiron Building is familiar, even to out-of-towners. The triangular structure at the convergence of Broadway and Fifth Avenue at 23rd Street was a wonder, a skyscraper, when completed in 1902. The 21-story steel-frame structure was also at the apex of the Ladies' Mile, New York's elegant shopping district. Macy's, Altman's, Lord & Taylor, W&J Sloane and other luxurious emporiums now forgotten cut a fashionable swath down Broadway, Fifth and Sixth Avenues in the late 19th century.

But just as the rumbling Sixth Avenue elevated had stimulated the development of the Ladies' Mile, so the city's booming economy caused the great stores to move uptown. The elegant buildings with rhythmic cast iron fronts, elaborate mansard roofs, Byzantine columns and Gothic finials were abandoned to a dim and sooty half-life as manufacturing lofts and warehouses.

Today, there's a reawakening south of 23rd Street, and the wedge-shaped Flatiron Building has lent its name to New York's newest neighborhood. Andy Warhol was, perhaps, the first to set up in the Flatiron District when he established his notorious Factory on Union Square. Professional photographers began moving bed-and-tripod into the neighborhood's vast manufacturing lofts in the 1970s. Photo supply houses and model agencies came next, followed by publishing houses and advertising agencies. And now Lower Fifth Avenue is experiencing a retail renaissance, becoming a veritable outpost of midtown shops. Cavernous spaces and relatively low rents have already attracted fashion heavyweights like Armani, Paul Smith and Matsuda. So you can lunch among the literati and leggy lovelies in sprawling theme restaurants, furnish your kitchen at Williams-Sonoma and outfit yourself in the latest Italian threads at Barneys (both on Seventh Avenue), shoot billiards till dawn and boogie the night away, all in the Flatiron District.

There are some rentals available in the handsome Zeckendorf Towers set back from Union Square with airy, teal pyramid points atop the brick towers and a 24-hour super-A&P downstairs. Madison Green, overlooking restful Madison Square Park, is among the notable modern condominiums. More typical of the Flatiron District, however, are the elegant, converted living lofts hidden away in the stolid manufacturing buildings which darken the side streets. Consult a real estate broker for the occasional sublet that comes on the market when the owner's away shooting photos in Crete. Besides a prime location with good public transportation, you'll have the graceful, green breathing space that is now Union Square for a front yard. The four day a week greenmarket (see **Greenmarkets**) is the Square's *piece de resistance*. Manhattanites trek year round to the northwest corner at East 16th and Broadway for fresh produce, fish, sausages, cheese, pretzels, breads, honey . . . oh, endless edibles.

Area Code: 212

Post Offices (nearest): Cooper Station, 93 Fourth Avenue, NYC 10003, 254-1389; Madison Square Station, 149 East 23rd Street, NYC 10010, 673-3771.

Zip Codes: 10003, 10010, 10011

Police Precinct: Thirteenth, 230 East 21st Street, NYC 10010, 477-7411.

Emergency Hospitals (nearest): Cabrini Medical Center, 227 East 19th Street, NYC 10003, 995-6000; St. Vincent's Hospital and Medical Center, Seventh Avenue and 11th Street, NYC 10011, 790-7000.

Libraries (nearest): Muhlenberg Library, 209 West 23rd Street, NYC 10011, 924-1585; Epiphany, 228 East 23rd Street, NYC 10010, 679-2645.

Public School Education: School District #2 (see **Chelsea**).

Adult Education: School of Visual Arts, 209 East 23rd Street, NYC 10010, 679-7350; Baruch College of Adult and Continuing Education, 48 East 26th Street, NYC 10010, 447-3020.

Transportation—Subway: Crosstown *14th Street BMT* (L) Sixth Avenue, Union Square; *Lexington Avenue IRT* (#4, #5, #6) 23rd Street, 14th Street/Union Square (Exp); *BMT* (N, Q, R) 14th Street/Union Square (Exp).

Transportation—Bus: Crosstown *23rd Street* (#23); Crosstown 14th Street (#14); Uptown *Park Avenue South/Madison Avenue* (#1, #2, #3); Uptown *Sixth Avenue* (#5, #6, #7); Downtown *Park Avenue South* (#1); Downtown *Fifth Avenue* (#2, #3, #5); Downtown *Broadway* (#6, #7).

Chelsea

Boundaries and Contiguous Areas: North: 34th Street and **Clinton**; East: Sixth Avenue and **Flatiron District**; South: 14th Street and **Greenwich Village**; West: Hudson River.

Residential Chelsea is a sunny community renowned for peace, quiet and four and five-story brownstone row houses, but its origins date back to 1750, when Capt. Thomas Clarke's farm encompassed the area. Over the years Chelsea has had its ups and downs, largely visible in the housing stock; using this yardstick, the last thirty years have been one long, steady up.

Clarke's grandson, Clement Clarke Moore, began selling off farm lots in the 1830s, developing Chelsea as a highly desirable suburb and donating land for the block-square General Theological Seminary between 20th and 21st Streets and Ninth and Tenth Avenues. The tree-shaded Seminary Close is still a neighborhood oasis, and the adjacent seminary library is available to the public for scholarly research. The complex is just across the street from the Gothic Revival style St. Peter's Episcopal Church, where Moore read his A Visit from Saint Nicholas to family and parishioners.

To the west, the Hudson River Railroad attracted slaughterhouses, breweries and shanties, and in 1871 Chelsea was darkened by the city's first elevated railroad on Ninth Avenue. Successive decades saw the brief emergence of 23rd Street as the city's theater district; the raising of vast cast iron structures on Sixth Avenue to house fashionable emporiums such as the original B. Altman's, and in the 1920s and 1930s a thriving vice district; the beginning of the nation's movie industry; and the opening of one of the city's first cooperative apartment houses, now the Chelsea Hotel, home over the years to artists and writers and still a fascinating building. Urban renewal in the 1950s and 1960s removed chunks of slums from the district, spurring the restoration of many fine townhouses and making way for two low-income housing projects and the middle-income International Ladies Garment Workers cooperative extending from 23rd to 27th Streets between Eighth and Ninth Avenues.

Sharing the side streets with restored one-and two-family houses are the occasional apartment house and tenement, not to mention formidable London Terrace, 405 West 23rd Street, with 14 buildings, four of which are co-op. The lofts in the photography, flower, fur and fashion districts (roughly 15th to 30th Streets between Fifth and Eighth Avenues, which includes the Flatiron District) were discovered by artists in the 1950s and now attract young families and professionals.

In 1982 the down-at-the-heels Elgin, a 1930s movie house on Eighth Avenue, was transformed into the exuberantly Deco Joyce, the first theater in the dance capital of the world to be specifically designed for small and medium-sized dance troupes. Since then, Chelsea has become something of a dance and performance district. The Dance Theater Workshop is a block east of the Joyce on 19th Street. The relatively avant-garde Kitchen recently relocated on 19th near the Hudson River. Way west—any further and your feet would get wet—several nightclubs have nestled in between auto-repair shops and factories, usurping Tribeca's reign over the night club scene. Eighth Avenue, between 15th and 23rd Streets, has become Main Street, Chelsea, and bears witness to the latest residential trends. The bodegas, Cuban-Chinese restaurants, Irish bars and kosher butchers catering to resident Hispanics, longshoremen and garment workers are being crowded out by mauve-walled cafes, bistros, croissanterias and punk, preppy and Victorian clothing stores. With a lively restaurant scene and trendy boutiques punctuating the relatively unobtrusive condos and co-ops, Eighth Avenue has taken on the youthful character of Columbus Avenue in the West 70s and 80s.

Area Code: 212

Post Offices: General Post Office, Eighth Avenue at 33rd Street, NYC 10001, 967-8585, open 24 hours; London Terrace Station, 234 Tenth Avenue, near 24th Street, NYC 10011, 242-8248; Old Chelsea Station, 217 West 18th Street, NYC 10011, 675-2415; Port Authority Station, 76 Ninth Avenue, NYC 10011, 929-9296.

Zip Codes: 10001, 10011

Police Precincts: Midtown South, 357 West 35th Street, NYC 10001, 239-9811; Tenth, 230 West 20th Street, NYC 10011, 741-8211.

Emergency Hospitals (nearest): St. Clare's Hospital and Health Center, 415 West 51st Street, NYC 10019, 586-1500; St. Vincent's Hospital and Medical Center, Seventh Avenue and 11th Street, NYC 10011, 790-7000.

Library: Muhlenberg Library, 209 West 23rd Street, NYC 10011, 924-1585; Library for the Blind and Physically Handicapped, 40 West 20th Street, NYC 10011, 206-5400.

Public School Education: Chelsea is in the NYC Board of Education's School District #2, one of the best in Manhattan. School Superintendent, 330 West 18th Street, NYC 10011, 337-8700; Committee on the Handicapped, District Manager, P.S. 33, 281

Ninth Avenue, NYC 10011, 244-6426. Bayard Rustin High School for the Humanities, 351 West 18th Street, 675-5350, is the city's newest college preparatory high school.

Adult Education: Fashion Institute of Technology, 227 West 27th Street, NYC 10001, 760-7650, classes plus art gallery open to the public.

Cultural Resources: McBurney YMCA, 215 West 23rd Street, NYC 10011, 741-9210; the Joyce Theater, 175 Eighth Avenue at 19th Street, 212-242-0800; Dance Theatre Workshop, 219 West 19th Street, NYC 924-0077; Dia Center for the Arts, 548 West 22nd Street, NYC 431-9232..

Transportation—Subway: Crosstown *BMT* (L) Eighth Avenue and 14th Street (crosses 14th Street and continues into Brooklyn); *Seventh Avenue IRT* (#1, #2, #3) 34th Street/Penn Station (Exp), 28th Street, 23rd Street, 18th Street, 14th Street (Exp); Eighth Avenue IND (A, C, E) 34th Street (Exp), 23rd Street, 14th Street (Exp); PATH (between New Jersey and 33rd Street) 14th, 23rd and 33rd Streets at Sixth Avenue.

Transportation—Bus: Crosstown *34th Street/Ninth Avenue* (#16); Crosstown *23rd Street* (#23); Crosstown *14th Street* (#14) also down Avenue A and Avenue D; Uptown *Tenth Avenue*—Downtown *Ninth Avenue* (#11); Uptown *Eighth Avenue*—Downtown *Seventh Avenue* (#10)

Clinton

Boundaries and Contiguous Areas: North: 59th Street and **Lincoln Center;** East: Eighth Avenue and the Theater District; South: 34th Street and **Chelsea;** West: Hudson River.

Not so long ago Clinton was "Hell's Kitchen," the neighborhood—and it *is* a real neighborhood—that produced gangster Owney Madden and inspired *West Side Story*. Traditionally a poor workingman's district with often squalid tenements and rooming houses, Clinton still has a few Irish and Puerto Rican gangs and raunchy blocks catering to transients. Reason enough to explain why this area, so close to midtown that developers are calling it "Midtown West," has remained something of a backwater until the incursion of desirable living space brought semi-respectability.

Upgrading began in the 1970s when Manhattan Plaza, 400 West 43rd Street, with its two towers, pool and tennis courts, was built. People with enough money to pay the high rents originally charged for the apartments were disinclined to live in the neighborhood, so the buildings were converted to subsidized housing for long-time residents displaced by the complex and for people in the performing arts. This new population helped found and now supports the thriving off-Broadway Theater Row on the south side of 42nd Street, a bonanza for New York's theater-going public, not to mention the theater world. The new respectability is firmly anchored on West 42nd Street (albeit with entrances on quieter 43rd Street) by The Strand condo tower and the Riverbank West rental complex near Eleventh Avenue. Now, in an area noted for sleaze and depression, there are good restaurants catering to the theater trade, a few blocks of spiffed-up townhouses, and handsome co-op renovations like the Piano Factory. The gentrification of Clinton is in full swing, and the gentry are mostly young, mostly gutsy.

Two mammoth projects that have had a profound effect on Clinton are the 1,800-room Marriott Marquis Hotel on West 46th Street and the Jacob K. Javits Convention Center, 655 West 34th Street.

One Worldwide Plaza, a 49-story tower capped by an ever-so-fashionable nouveau mansard roof, is the latest symbol and powerful instrument of change in Clinton. Prestigious law firms and ad agencies now serve a classy clientele at Eighth Avenue and 50th Street, where the shabby, old Madison Square Garden once squatted and winos, hookers and pushers roamed. A plaza separates the office spire in the mixed-use Zeckendorf development from the residential area, which is located to the west in the block-square complex. There a 39-story high rise and a series of attractive brick low rises contain some 650 condo units. Eighth and Ninth Avenues and the adjoining side streets are moving up.

Because the neighborhood is in the midst of a radical transformation, any apartment hunting here should be done block by block on foot. Besides the possibility of lucking into a reasonable rental on a decent block, Ninth Avenue in the 30s and 40s offers foods of every ethnic variety and outdoor stands heaped with tantalizing fresh fruits and vegetables. Consult the weekly *Chelsea Clinton News* as an informative neighborhood reference, 989-5761.

Area Code: 212

Post Offices: Midtown Station, 223 West 38th Street, NYC 10018, 944-6598; Times Square Station, 340 West 42nd Street, NYC 10036, 244-0111.

Zip Codes: 10019, 10036, 10018

Police Precincts: Midtown North, 306 West 54th Street, NYC 10019, 760-8300; Midtown South, 357 West 35th Street, NYC 10001, 239-9811.

Emergency Hospitals: St. Luke's-Roosevelt Hospital Center: The Roosevelt Hospital at 428 West 59th Street, NYC 10019, 523-4000; St. Clare's Hospital and Health Care Center, 415 West 51st Street, NYC 10019, 586-1500.

Libraries: Mid-Manhattan Library (research, patents and newspapers), 455 Fifth Avenue at 40th Street, NYC 10016, 340-0833; Donnell Library Center, 20 West 53rd Street, NYC 10019, 621-0618, includes Record Lending Service and foreign language sections.

Public School Education: Clinton falls within Community School District #2 (see **Chelsea**).

Adult Education: John Jay College of Criminal Justice, 445 West 59th Street, NYC 10019, 237-8000.

Cultural Resources: St. Clement's Episcopal Church, 423 West 46th Street, NYC 10036, 246-7277, has a special mission to the arts community, and its services are as likely to consist of theatrical performances as liturgy. The Intrepid Sea-Air-Space Museum, Pier 86 at West 46th Street and 12th Avenue, 245-0072, is housed in and around the aircraft carrier Intrepid and contains, among other permanent and changing exhibits, the Museum of the Medal of Honor.

Transportation—Subway: Seventh Avenue IRT (#1, #2, #3) 59th Street, 50th Street, 42nd Street (Exp), 34th Street (Exp); *Eighth Avenue IND* (A, C, E) 59th Street (Exp), 50th Street, 42nd Street (Exp), 34th Street (Exp).

Transportation—Bus: Crosstown *57th Street* (#57, #58); Crosstown *49th/50th Streets* (#27, #50); Crosstown *42nd Street* (#42); Crosstown *34th Street* (#16, #34); Uptown *Tenth Avenue*—Downtown *Ninth Avenue* (#11); Uptown *Eighth Avenue*—Downtown *Seventh Avenue* (#10); Downtown Broadway (#104) to 42nd Street and then crossing to the East Side along 42nd Street.

Lincoln Center Area

Boundaries and Contiguous Areas: North: 72nd Street and the **Upper West Side;** East: Central Park West; South: 59th Street and **Clinton;** West: Hudson River.

This neighborhood, dubbed Lincoln Square, is a prime example of the change a major new facility can effect in a marginal New York location. Just as Cinderella's slipper transformed the hapless char girl, so the construction in 1960 of the glass and travertine Lincoln Center complex with theaters, opera and ballet houses, concert halls, library and the Juilliard School transformed a dreary stretch of rundown tenements and warehouses. Now it seems every other pedestrian carries a musical instrument or moves with the marked grace of a ballet dancer, and limousines queue up where once trucks double-parked.

Columnar apartment and office buildings rise above the cafes, restaurants and boutiques lining Broadway, Columbus and Amsterdam Avenues. Fordham University's West Side Campus and ABC/Capital Cities are also firmly planted in the neighborhood. The whole adds a boost to the renaissance of Columbus and Amsterdam Avenues, which cater to the food, drink and clothing needs of the West Side's relatively affluent young residents. Tall white brick luxury buildings compose most of Lincoln's Square's housing: typical is the huge Lincoln Towers co-op—3,897 apartments contained in eight high rises fronting West End Avenue between 66th and 70th Streets. Recently condo spires and columns have shot up south and west of the culture complex, even on barren Tenth Avenue, which may be the new frontier of Lincoln Square.

There are probably more rental apartments on the Upper West Side than around Lincoln Center. However, this will change if Trump City, the much-heralded riverfront project, ever gets off the drawing board. When Donald Trump purchased the site of the now-defunct railroad yards fronting the Hudson River between 59th and 72nd Streets, plans for the development of an enormous housing (condos, most likely), shopping and business complex to the west of Lincoln Center received a boost. Alexander Cooper, lauded for his humane master plan for Battery Park City, is designing what amounts to a new city from scratch. But resistance to the Trumping of Lincoln Square has solidified among residents and community planners, NBC has backed out, and future development, now at a crawl, is likely to be less dense, less grandiose than the original Trump model.

Area Code: 212

Post Office: Columbus Circle Station, 27 West 60th Street, NYC 10023, 265-7858.

Zip Codes: 10023, 10019

Police Precinct: Midtown North, 306 West 54th Street, NYC 10019, 767-8400.

Emergency Hospital (nearest): St. Luke's-Roosevelt Hospital Center: The Roosevelt Hospital at 428 West 59th Street, NYC 10019, 523-4000.

Library: Library of the Performing Arts at Lincoln Center, 111 Amsterdam Avenue, NYC 10023, 870-1630.

Public School Education: School District #3, 300 West 96th Street, NYC 10025, 678-2800; Committee on Special Education, 234 West 109th Street, NYC 10025, 865-2002.

Adult Education: Fordham University, 113 West 60th Street, NYC

10023, 636-6000; The Juilliard School, Lincoln Center Plaza, NYC 10023, 799-5000; Art Students League of New York, 215 West 57th Street, NYC 10019, 247-4510; The Elaine Kaufman Cultural Arts Center, 129 West 67th Street, 362-8060, offers courses in music, dance, art and the theater.

Cultural Resources: For the plethora of cultural events, theaters, library, shops, restaurants, exhibits and tours at Lincoln Center, consult the telephone directory; Merkin Hall, 129 West 67th Street, 362-8060, presents a variety of concerts, primarily ethnic and chamber music. Museum of American Folk Art, 2 Lincoln Square, NYC 10023, 595-9533.

Transportation—Subway: *Seventh Avenue IRT* (#1, #9) 66th Street, 59th Street; *Eighth Avenue IND* (A, B, C, D) 59th Street (Exp).

Transportation—Bus: Crosstown *72nd Street* (#72); Crosstown *66th/67th Streets* (#66); Crosstown *57th Street* (#57, #58); Uptown *Tenth Avenue*—Downtown *Columbus Avenue* (#11); Uptown *Eighth Avenue*—Downtown *Central Park West/Seventh Avenue* (#10).

The Upper West Side

Boundaries and Contiguous Areas: North: 110th Street and **Morningside Heights;** East: Central Park West; South: 72nd Street and **Lincoln Center;** West: Hudson River.

Large sprawling apartments and an active community life have been luring writers, musicians, intellectuals, psychiatrists — in general, those seeking an alternative to the Upper East Side's more constrained life-style — to the West Side for decades. Indeed, the city's first large apartment buildings, with lofty ceilings, thick walls and space to waste, were built here around the turn of the century. Grand structures rose first along Central Park West (note the famed Dakota at 72nd Street), claimed by some aficionados to be the most architecturally elegant avenue in New York; next on Broadway (the neoclassical Ansonia between 73rd and 74th Streets and the block-square Apthorp between

78th and 79th are particularly grand), which was to be Park Avenue West but isn't; and then on West End Avenue and Riverside Drive.

Most buildings along the apartment-lined avenues — with the notable exception of Columbus and Amsterdam, which have only recently emerged from the Dickensian 19th to enter the trendiest century — managed to remain sufficiently attractive to hold the middle class. But the rows of brick, limestone, and brownstone townhouses built for the newly affluent on the cross streets during the early 1900s declined into squalid tenements and SRO (Single Room Occupancy) rooming houses. Not until the 1960s, when an ambitious urban renewal plan spurred building and renovation, did this veritable architectural museum again become an address for affluent achievers. Today, the typical brownstone houses the owner's family on the garden or parlor floors and tenants on the original bedroom floors above.

A golden ghetto has never been the goal of West Side planners. They have fought long and hard to keep the neighborhood diverse and representative of the city as a whole. However, the vogue-ish and often short-lived gourmet emporiums, bijou boutiques, clothing shops featuring somber Japanese designs, and fashionable hangouts decorating Columbus and Amsterdam Avenues attest to the fickle needs of the upwardly mobile.

Lately, ranks of condo towers have shot up along Columbus and, more recently, Amsterdam between 87th and 97th Streets — just outside the boundaries of the Central Park West historic district. These svelte and pricey (though cheaper than Lincoln Square) condominiums provide residents with plenty of play space: health clubs, pools, rooftop gardens, party rooms and in-house parking are standard. Meanwhile, Upper Broadway is being transformed as high rises are slotted, sleek cheek by shabby jowl, among the wearier old-timers between 97th Street and Columbia University. A short-term rental in one of these buildings offers the undecided newcomer an opportunity to try out the neighborhood before making a long-term commitment.

Most of the handsome stone buildings fronting Central Park are cooperatives now, as are the vast apartment houses lining West End Avenue and curving along Riverside Drive. Pioneers are staking their claims in the area known as Manhattan Valley east of Broadway in the upper 90s and 100s. For the less adventurous and thicker of purse, existing rental apartments are well worth pursuing, if only to live between Manhattan's greenest playgrounds, Central and Riverside Parks, and near one of its cultural stalwarts, the massive Museum of Natural History, which devotes almost 25 acres of floor space to some of the finest scientific collections in the world.

Area Code: 212

Post Offices: Cathedral Station, 215 West 104th Street, NYC 10025, 6629191; Planetarium Station, 127 West 83rd Street, NYC 10024, 873-3701; Ansonia Station, 138 Columbus Avenue, NYC 10023, 362-7486.

Zip Codes: 10025, 10024, 10023

Police Precincts: Twenty-fourth, 151 West 100th Street, NYC 10025, 678-1811; Twentieth, 120 West 82nd Street, NYC 10024, 580-6411.

Emergency Hospital (nearest): Both branches of the St. Luke's-Roosevelt Hospital Center: The Roosevelt Hospital at 428 West 59th Street, NYC 10019, and St. Luke's Hospital, 114th Street and Amsterdam Avenue, NYC 10025, both 523-4000.

Libraries: Bloomingdale, 150 West 100th Street, NYC 10025, 222-8030; St. Agnes, 444 Amsterdam Avenue, NYC 10024, 877-4380; Riverside, 127 Amsterdam Avenue, NYC 10023, 870-1810.

Public School Education: School District #3 (see **Lincoln Center Area**).

Adult Education: Bank Street College of Education, 610 West 112th Street, NYC 10025, 222-6700.

Cultural Resources: Central Park, stretching from 59th Street over 840 acres up to 110th Street. For literary events, Gilbert and Sullivan, live jazz, Afro-Cuban rhythms and the new modern directions: Symphony Space, 2537 Broadway at 95th Street, 864-5400. For a multiplicity of musical styles, played live: the Beacon Theater, Broadway and 74th Street, 496-7070. American Museum of Natural History and the Hayden Planetarium, Central Park West from 79th

Street to 81st Street, museum information: 769-5000, Planetarium information: 769-5920. The New York Historical Society, 140 Central Park West (at 77th Street) NYC 10024, 873-3400, at this writing the Society's galleries were closed, but the library and print shop were open to the public. Nicholas Roerich Museum, 319, West 107th Street, NYC 10025, 864-7752. Children's Museum of Manhattan, 212 West 83rd Street, NYC 10024, 721-1234.

Transportation—Subway: *Seventh Avenue IRT* (#1, #2, #3) 110th Street, 103rd Street, 96th Street (Exp), 86th Street, 79th Street, 72nd Street (Exp); Eighth Avenue IND (A) 110th Street, 103rd Street, 96th Street, 86th Street, 81st Street, 72nd Street.

Transportation—Bus: Crosstown *96th Street* (#19); Crosstown *86th Street* (#86); Crosstown *79th Street* (#79); Crosstown *72nd Street* (#72); Crosstown *66th/67th Streets* (#66) ending at Central Park West and 72nd Street; Uptown *Riverside Drive* — Downtown *Riverside Drive* (#4, #5); Uptown *Amsterdam Avenue* — Downtown *Columbus Avenue* (#7, #11); Uptown *Broadway* — Downtown *Broadway* (#104).

Morningside Heights

Boundaries and Contiguous Areas: North: 125th Street and **Harlem;** East: Morningside Drive; South: 110th Street and **Upper West Side;** West: Hudson River.

Academia amidst a gritty urban-scape, this lively community occupying the formerly rocky slopes of northern Manhattan is dominated — physically, economically and socially — by Columbia University, one of the nation's oldest, richest and largest educational institutions. In addition, Barnard College as well as two important religious seminaries, the Manhattan School of Music, a large teaching hospital, and two major churches share the Heights with a mixture of students, professors, professionals and urban poor. Up here next to the granite bulk of Ulysses S. Grant's pompous tomb, upper west side grey is relieved by Riverside Park, used extensively by residents as a front yard, and by Morningside Park, seldom used because it is safe only to contemplate from a distance.

When finally completed decades hence, the Episcopal Cathedral Church of St. John the Divine will literally tower over the community; now spireless, the world's largest Gothic cathedral just looms. (The tall Gothic church tower you do see rising northwest of Columbia belongs to Riverside Church, the Rockefellers' non-denominational gift to the city.) St. John's caters to cultural as well as spiritual needs, sponsoring a particularly rich and wide-ranging series of concerts from chamber music through liturgical works to jazz and other events including poetry readings, craft fairs and dance programs. The church dedicates a side altar to victims of AIDS.

Broadway, Morningside Heights' Main Street, showcases bookstores, all night fruit stands, student bars cum jazz joints, boutiques and restaurants ranging from fast food to ethnic and elegant. The lively street life that continues late makes the neighborhood relatively safe and certainly interesting.

As owners of one-third the community's housing stock, over half of which is occupied by tenants affiliated with the university, Columbia is the Heights' biggest landlord. Rent control is pervasive here and tenants unrelated to the university often came with their buildings; when these folk leave, their apartments are usually taken by university people. However, an occasional rental does hit the open market, and sometimes space becomes available when Columbia-connected roommates separate (graduate, marry or move) leaving behind an empty room and half the monthly rent bill.

Area Code: 212

Post Office: Morningside Station, 232 West 116th Street, NYC 10026, 864-6968.

Zip Codes: 10027, 10026, 10025

Police Precinct: Twenty-sixth, 520 West 126th Street, NYC 10027, 678-1311.

Emergency Hospital: St. Luke's-Roosevelt Hospital Center: St. Luke's Hospital, 114th Street and Amsterdam Avenue, NYC 10025, 523-4000.

Library: 115th Street Branch, 203 West 115th Street, NYC 10026, 666-9393.

Public School Education: School District #3 (see **Lincoln Center Area**).

Adult Education: Barnard College, 3009 Broadway, NYC 10027, 854-5262; Columbia University, Broadway and 114th Street to 120th Street, NYC 10027, 854-2752; Union Theological Seminary, Broadway and 120th Street, NYC 10027, 662-7100; Bank Street College of Education, 610 West 112th Street, NYC 10025, 875-4400; Jewish Theological Seminary, 3080 Broadway, NYC 10027, 678-8000; Manhattan School of Music, 120 Claremont Avenue, NYC 10027, 749-2802.

Cultural Resources: Cathedral Church of St. John the Divine, West 112th Street and Amsterdam Avenue, NYC 10025, 316-7540, also has on its large grounds a Biblical Garden with plantings inspired by the Old Testament; north of St. John the Divine, Riverside Church, 400 Riverside Drive (at West 122nd Street), NYC 10027, 222-5900, offers educational and cultural programs in addition to religious services.

Transportation—Subway: *Seventh Avenue IRT* (#1, #2, #3) 125th Street (Exp), 116th Street, 110th Street; *Eighth Avenue IND* (A, B, C) 125th Street (Exp), 116th Street, 110th Street.

Transportation—Bus: Crosstown *116th Street* (#20); Uptown *Riverside Drive* — Downtown *Columbus Avenue* (#11); Uptown *Broadway* — Downtown *Broadway* (#104).

The Harlems

Boundaries and Contiguous Areas: East Harlem: North and East: Harlem River; South: 96th Street, **Upper East Side and Yorkville;** West: Central Park. **Harlem:** North: 155th Street and **Washington Heights;** East: Harlem River; West: Hudson River; South: 125th Street and **Morningside Heights.**

This neighborhood, rich in culture, remains the spiritual focus of Black America. Although Harlem pockets some of the worst crime and poverty in New York City, many of its high-stooped, row-house-lined streets are perfectly safe.

Originally settled by Dutch farmers, Harlem thrived as a prosperous suburb in the 1800s. Black New Yorkers began settling into an abundance of apartment buildings left empty when real estate brokers' plans for a white middle class neighborhood never materialized.

Harlem in the 1920s is synonymous with the Harlem Renaissance. Musicians, playwrights and novelists flocked to the neighborhood bursting with jazz clubs and casinos.

Since the 1930s prominent African-American Harlemites have lived on Striver's Row, on 138th and 139th Streets between Seventh and Eighth Avenues. Dominated by brownstones now part of the St. Nicholas Historic District, this block is where Spike Lee filmed some of *Jungle Fever*. Abyssinian Baptist Church, New York's oldest Black church is located at 132 West 138th Street. Professionals also settle in the 140s near St. Nicholas and Convent Avenue, an area called Hamilton Heights.

Harlem's East side is known as Spanish Harlem or El Barrio. Here you'll find mostly tenements and housing projects. Above 100th Street, newcomers should take care and know where they're going. La Marqueta, a Latino produce, meat and houseware market keeps things bustling along El Barrio's busiest street, 116th to Park Avenue. The Canaan Baptist Church of Christ, 132 West 116th Street, welcomes visitors on Sundays for gospel music, American spirituals and rhythm and blues. New York City tour-guide books continue to mention Sylvia's ("Queen of Soul Food") off Lenox Avenue for a true taste of the neighborhood's traditional cuisine.

In the heart of Harlem at Lenox Avenue and West 135th Street is the Schomburg Center for Research In Black Culture, housing the world's largest collection of Black history. On West 135th Street is the facility's outdoor sculpture garden; the outdoor amphitheater is on West 136th.

Harlem celebrates its past and present history each August by hosting a one-week African-American and Hispanic festival. Call the Uptown Chamber of Commerce, 427-3315, for details.

Social and cultural tensions have kept Harlem somewhat isolated from the rest of Manhattan, but many say it is bringing itself to a second

Renaissance. Indeed, with new families restoring many of Harlem's brownstone buildings and a thriving cultural scene (see **Cultural Resources** below), this neighborhood is pumping with life.

Area Code: 212

Post Office: Hamilton Grange, 521 West 146th Street, NYC 10031, 281-8401; Manhattanville, 365 West 125th Street, NYC 10027, 662-1901; Hell Gate, 153 East 110 Street, NYC 10029, 860-3557; Triborough, 167 East 124th Street, NYC 10035, 534-0865.

Zip Codes: 100275,0 10029, 10031, 10035

Police Precinct: Twenty-third, 164 East 102nd Street, NYC 10029, 860-6411; Twenty-fourth, 151 West 100th Street, NYC 10025, 678-1811; Twenty-fifth, 120 East 119th Street, NYC 10035, 860-6511; Thirty-second, 250 West 135th Street, NYC 10030, 690-6311.

Emergency Hospital: Harlem Hospital, 506 Lenox Avenue at 135th Street, NYC 10037, 939-1000, includes a crisis intervention center for battered wives, children and rape victims; Mount Sinai Hospital, 101st Street and Madison Avenue, NYC 10029, 241-7171.

Library: A regional branch of the New York City Public Library, Countee Cullen, is located at 136th Street and Lenox Avenue, NYC 10037, 491-2070. The Schomberg Center for Research In Black Culture, 515 Malcolm X Boulevard (135th Street at Lenox Avenue), NYC 10037, 491-2200, houses the city's African archives and presents local artists' works.

Public School Education: East Harlem: District #4, 319 East 117th Street, NYC 10035, 860-5910; further West: District #5, 433 West 123rd Street, NYC 10027, 769-7600. High schools include the Manhattan Center for Science and Mathematics, FDR Drive and 116th Street, NYC 10029, 876-4639; and A. Phillip Randolph Campus, Convent Avenue and 135th Street, NYC 10031, 926-0113.

Adult Education: City College, City University of New York (CUNY) 138th Street and Convent Avenue, NYC 10031, 650-5310; Boricua College, a private Hispanic liberal arts college, 3755 Broadway at 155th Street, NYC 10032, 694-1000.

Cultural Resources: Apollo Theater, 253 West 125th Street, NYC 10027, 749-5838; Harlem Third World Trade Center on 163 West 125th; Studio Museum in Harlem, 144 West 125th Street, NYC 10027, 864-4500; Hamilton Grange, 287 Convent Avenue, NYC 10031, 283-5154; Black Fashion Museum, 157 West 126th Street, NYC 10027, 666-1320; The Museum of the City of New York, Fifth Avenue at 103rd Street, NYC 10029, 534-1672; El Museo del Barrio at Fifth Avenue and 104th Street, NYC 10029, 831-7272, (art, culture, heritage of Puerto Rico and Latin America); Dance Theater of Harlem, 466 West 152nd Street, NYC 10031, 690-2800 (see Dance section); Harlem School of the Arts, 645 St. Nicholas Avenue between 141st and 145th Streets, NYC 10030, 926-4100.

Transportation—Subway: *Lexington Avenue IRT* (#4, #5, #6), *Seventh Avenue IRT* (#1, #2, #3), Eighth Avenue IND (A, B, C).

Transportation—Bus: Crosstown *96th Street* (#19); Crosstown *116th Street* (#20); Uptown *Riverside Drive*—Downtown *Columbus Avenue* (#11); Uptown/Downtown *Broadway* (#7,#100,#104); Uptown/Downtown *St. Nicholas Avenue* (#3); Uptown/Downtown *Amsterdam Avenue* (#101).

Washington Heights-Inwood

Boundaries and Contiguous Areas: North: Harlem River and **Riverdale;** East: Harlem River; South: 155th Street and **Harlem;** West: Hudson River.

Up here, where outcroppings from the Hudson riverbed rise to form Manhattan's highest ground, the tawny stone arches rhythmically lining the central courtyard at The Cloisters are echoed by the exceptionally graceful curve of the steel suspension cables looping the twin towers of the silvery George Washington Bridge. Long before John D. Rockefeller gave the city the magnificent medieval Cloisters Museum as well as Fort Tryon Park, the land on which it stands, and long before the bridge was built in 1931, George Washington headquartered Revolutionary forces on the strategic terrain now called Washington Heights.

Six hundred acres of parkland, much of it boulder-strewn and covered with healthy trees and brush, refresh and beautify one of the most densely populated, and narrowest, sections of New York. On the map, the neighborhood looks like a knobby finger pointing across the Harlem River at The Bronx from the elongated fist of Manhattan. Washington Heights and Inwood are *all* "West Side"; the Harlem River lops off the "East Side" at 138th Street.

Commercial Broadway cuts through the area on a north-south bias, dividing the almost solidly Hispanic, Harlem River (eastern) half from the middle-income, Hudson River (western) half of the neighborhood. The western section contains the most coveted housing — solidly constructed one-and two-bedroom apartments, many with pleasing river and park views — situated in square, five- and ten-story buildings. The clusters of yellow, buff and occasionally red brick Art Deco buildings clumped along the riverbank have special appeal: Chittenden Avenue between 187th and 189th Streets contains some beauties and there's a beguiling section bordering forested Inwood Hill Park. Hudson View Gardens between 183rd and 185th Streets and Castle Village nearby, two of the most desirable complexes, are cooperatives.

Community feeling is particularly strong in Washington Heights and Inwood, largely as a result of a ten-year program that renovated an estimated 18% of the housing stock. Buildings have been going co-op on Riverside Drive and along the 181st Street corridor in Washington Heights. Another tangible sign of change in this working-class neighborhood are the several condos reconstructed from the shells of abandoned buildings in Inwood.

To get a sense of this other Manhattan — to feel fresh breezes blowing off the Hudson, to experience its slower pace and to realize that there are few pubby hangouts or one-of-a-kind boutiques in these latitudes — amble the Heights' main thoroughfare, 181st Street, and pick up a copy of "Northern Manhattan's Community Newspaper" at the office of the *Uptown Dispatch*, 833 West 181st Street. The paper is filled with local lore. For another dimension, travel up to Inwood and stroll the grassy banks of Inwood Hill Park. If you find the friendly unassuming neighborhood attractive, plan to search, and search hard, on foot, questioning supers and building managers. Certainly, you can check with a reputable real estate agent. However, few apartments ever reach a broker's office here; word of mouth is still the best way to find a rental in Manhattan's northernmost neighborhood.

Area Code: 212

Post Offices: Audubon, 511 West 165th Street, NYC 10032, 568-3311; Washington Bridge, 555 West 180th Street, NYC 10033, 568-7601; Fort George, 4558 Broadway, NYC 10040, 942-0052; Inwood, 90 Vermilyea Avenue, NYC 10034, 567-3032.

Zip Codes: 10034, 10040, 10033, 10032

Police Precinct: Thirty-fourth, 4295 Broadway, NYC 10033, 927-9711.

Emergency Hospital: Columbia-Presbyterian Medical Center, 622 West 168th Street, NYC 10032, 305-2500.

Libraries: Fort Washington Branch, 535 West 179th Street, NYC 10033, 927-3533; Washington Heights Branch, 1000 St. Nicholas Avenue, NYC 10040, 923-6054; Inwood Branch, 4790 Broadway, NYC 10034, 942-2445.

Public School Education: School District #6: Community School Board, 4360 Broadway, NYC 10033, 927-7777.

Adult Education: Yeshiva University, 500 West 185th Street, NYC 10033, 960-5400; Inwood Community Services, 651 Academy Street (just north of Dyckman Street), NYC 10034, 942-0043.

Cultural Resources: The Cloisters, division of the Metropolitan Museum of Art, Fort Tryon Park (193rd Street and Fort Washington Avenue), NYC 10034, 923-3700; Audubon Terrace Museum complex, Broadway between West 155th and 156th Streets, NYC 10032, including the National Museum of the American Indian Smithsonian

Institution, 283-2420, the American Academy and National Institute of Arts and Letters, 368-5900, and American Numismatic Society (public display on the history of money), 234-3130; Morris-Jumel Mansion and Museum, 1765 Jumel Terrace, NYC 10032, 923-8008, a colonial home in garden surroundings used by Washington during the Revolution and later redecorated by Eliza Jumel; Dyckman House, 4881 Broadway at 204th Street, NYC 10034, 304-9422, is a restored 18th century Dutch farmhouse-museum belonging to the city and well worth a visit.

Transportation — Subway: *Eighth Avenue IND* (A) 207th, Dyckman, 190th, 181st, 175th, 168th (Exp) Streets: stops along Fort Washington Avenue and Broadway; *Sixth Avenue IND* (B) 168th, 163rd, 155th Streets. *Seventh Avenue IRT* (#1) 215th, 207th, Dyckman, 191st, 181st, 168th and 157th Streets: all stops along St. Nicholas Avenue.

Transportation — Bus: Crosstown *181st Street* (#3, #11, #13, #35, #36, #38); Uptown/Downtown *Fort Washington Avenue* to Broadway (#4); Uptown/Downtown *Broadway* (#7, #100); Uptown/Downtown *St. Nicholas Avenue* (#3); Uptown/Downtown *Amsterdam Avenue* (#101).

**Neighborhoods in
Brooklyn, Queens,
The Bronx, Staten Island
and New Jersey**

Riverdale

THE BRONX

MANHATTAN

Astoria

Bayside

Hoboken

Sunnyside

Rego Park

Forest Hills

Kew
Gardens

Jersey City

QUEENS

NEW JERSEY

Brooklyn
Heights

Cobble
Hill

Boerum
Hill

Carroll
Gardens

Fort Greene/Clinton Hill

Park
Slope

Prospect
Park

St. George

Stapleton

Grymes Hill

BROOKLYN

STATEN
ISLAND

The Bronx

Poor The Bronx, a borough that's seldom mentioned without its article. The northernmost and smallest, though not by much, of New York City's five parts is more often celebrated for a rude cheer and for Fort Apache, the south central section that has begun to struggle back from dilapidation and worse, than for large verdant parks, colleges and top-flight high schools or for some singularly attractive neighborhoods. To set the record straight, then, you should know that The Bronx boasts all of these.

Just south of Westchester County, New England-esque City Island floats rather quaintly in placid Long Island Sound. And over on the Hudson shore, Riverdale shelters estates and sylvan lanes worthy of suburban Scarsdale. In between these two neighborhoods, apartment buildings embellished with Art Deco motifs line the once-elegant Grand Concourse.

Four of the city's finest high schools are situated in The Bronx: the prestigious Bronx High School of Science, from which so many Westinghouse Science Award winners graduate, as well as private Fieldston, Horace Mann and Riverdale Country Day School. Eight universities and colleges enhance the borough's scholastic character.

A wealth of public land is probably The Bronx's greatest asset; parkland accounts for almost a quarter of the 43-square-mile borough. Partially forested Van Cortlandt Park, a mecca for cross-country skiers in the winter, is the spot for soccer, rugby and football in the summer. Even larger Pelham Bay Park, from which little City Island dangles, harbors Orchard Beach along its sandy shore. But the star is Bronx Park with 500 acres about equally divided between two of the city's most illustrious scientific institutions: the Bronx Zoo (now officially renamed the New York Zoological Society's International Wildlife Conservancy) and the New York Botanical Garden. The Haupt Conservatory, a sparkling crystal greenhouse complex, displays thousands of plant varieties in natural micro-climates and must be seen. Kids of all ages, naturalists and explorers, too, frequent the Zoo, using the tram-like Skyfari for an overview of the African exhibit as well as to commute between pavilions that include the World of Darkness and World of Birds.

While chunks of The Bronx do flourish, the loft buildings and brownstones so dear to middle-income colonizers in search of inexpensive digs are in short supply. Cooperatives and condominiums continue to replace rental apartments, but The Bronx has few neighborhoods that attract the younger singles in the fashion of Brooklyn and Hoboken.

Riverdale

Boundaries and Contiguous Areas: North: 263rd Street and Yonkers; East: Broadway and Van Cortlandt Park; South: Harlem River and **Washington Heights-Inwood;** West: Hudson River.

Our boundaries outline a rather generous Riverdale, incorporating as they do the communities of Kingsbridge, Fieldston, Spuyten Duyvil as well as Riverdale. Each enclave has its own personality, but the first-time renter will probably head to Spuyten Duyvil or Riverdale in search of a post-war apartment that has yet to go co-op.

Spuyten Duyvil, a colony of apartment buildings edged by the Harlem River and the Hudson, faces Manhattan. Tall red-brick apartment towers cluster in clumps along Riverdale's narrow potholed lanes. There are plenty of mini-mansions in Riverdale, too, although perhaps the single largest concentration of elegant single-family residences is located in adjoining Fieldston, a somewhat exclusive community with private streets. All three communities share the same rocky outcropping beside the Hudson. The urban grid and bustle so typical of New York is found on the flats below in Kingsbridge.

The Riverdale that for most of its well-to-do length ridges the river seems more Westchester than New York. Posh private schools attract kids who drive in from New Jersey and the suburbs as well as those who arrive by subway and bus from New York. Shops are discretely curtailed to a few zones of Mom and Pop businesses. Supermarket complexes are built elsewhere. Riverdale's low, tree-shaded profile appeals not only to affluent New York professionals but to resident foreigners. The Russians built their white high-rise complex here, and many of the local estates house UN personnel and foreign executives.

For a great day in this country visit Wave Hill (call 718-549-2055 for directions; express buses run by Liberty Lines, 718-652-8400, provide direct service to West 252nd Street). You'll pass the white frame house at 252nd Street and Independence Avenue where JFK lived in the late 1920s before reaching Wave Hill's entrance gate at 249th Street and

Independence Avenue. The Hudson-side complex consists of two stone manor houses offering occasional chamber music, a greenhouse and 28 acres of perfectly gorgeous gardens, where in summer outdoor sculpture exhibits compete for your attention with lovely river views.

Area Code: 718

Post Offices: Riverdale, 5951 Riverdale Avenue, Bronx 10471, 549-7519; Kingsbridge, 5517 Broadway, Bronx 10463, 549-5500.

Zip Codes: 10463, 10471

Police Precinct: Fiftieth, 3450 Kingsbridge Avenue, Bronx 10463, 543-5700.

Emergency Hospital (nearest): Montefiore, 210th Street and Bainbridge Avenue, Bronx 10467, 920-4321.

Library: Riverdale Public Library, 5540 Mosholu Avenue, Bronx 10471, 549-1212.

Public School Education: School District # 10: Community School Board, 1 Fordham Plaza, Bronx 10458, 584-7070.

Adult Education: Manhattan College, Manhattan College Parkway and West 242nd Street, Bronx 10471, 920-0100; College of Mt. St. Vincent, Riverdale Avenue and West 263rd Street, Bronx 10471, 549-8000.

Cultural Resources: Wave Hill, West 249th Street and Independence Avenue, Bronx 10471, 549-2055; Riverdale YM-YWHA, 5625 Arlington Avenue, Bronx 10471, 548-8200.

Transportation—Subway: Seventh Avenue IRT (#1) 242nd Street, 238th Street, 231st Street and 225th Street (all in Kingsbridge).

Transportation—Bus: Commuters in Spuyten Duyvil, Fieldston and Riverdale tend to use Liberty Line, 652-8400, express buses to mid-Manhattan. Get a Bronx bus map for local MTA routes.

BROOKLYN

"For safety and real rental value, Brooklyn beats Manhattan hands down." The chauvinistic local real estate broker quoted might have added a qualifying "certain neighborhoods" in Brooklyn. But it is true that by crossing the East River to Long Island's westernmost purchase you can pay less for housing than you might in Manhattan. Even rents in staid, lovely old Brooklyn Heights are a bit cheaper than equally prestigious Manhattan locations. It follows that relative bargains can be found in the four and five-story row houses, more often than not lovingly restored by a Brooklyn brownstoner, that line the streets in less securely established communities such as Boerum Hill or Fort Greene/Clinton Hill. Among the salient features of these neighborhoods are the brick, board and, yes, brownstone row houses representing a virtual catalog of architectural styles from 1820s Federal through 1910s late Victorian.

Other pluses? Brooklyn boosters boast about excellent subway transportation, the quality of the public schools in District 15, and the lively cultural climate engendered by the culture scene's Big Three: the Brooklyn Museum, Brooklyn Botanic Garden and Brooklyn Academy of Music (BAM).

In 1985 Brooklyn, Queens and Staten Island were switched from the all-New-York-City 212 area code to 718. Far more than the area code has changed since then. 1987 marked the beginning of the long-overdue revitalization of downtown Brooklyn. First, 1 Pierrepont Plaza opened with 800 computer and back-office workers from Morgan Stanley. Now several mixed-use developments are in various stages of progress in the area. Metrotech, the largest, with 11 buildings when it is completed in 1996, already headquarters Brooklyn Union Gas and some 6,000 Chase Manhattan Bank workers, among others. Plans for Renaissance Plaza across Jay Street call for offices and a hotel. The Atlantic Center, a mixed office and residential complex on Flatbush Avenue, has begun to rise. These developments represent the most important change in Brooklyn since the completion of the Brooklyn Bridge. They are estimated to bring more than 37,000 new workers to the area. Over time, the ripple effect should be immense.

Names of Brooklyn realtors can be found under **Apartment Hunting**.

Brooklyn Heights

Boundaries and Contiguous Areas: North: Fulton Ferry Landing and Cadman Plaza West; East: Cadman Plaza and Court Street; South: Atlantic Avenue and **Cobble Hill;** West: The Esplanade overlooking the East River and Brooklyn-Queens Expressway (BQE).

A *New York Times* article described two young lawyers walking home along Henry Street in the Heights one summer evening discussing cooperative apartments they had just bought. Not only did they estimate the purchase prices to be about 20% lower than comparable real estate in Manhattan, but they believed the location couldn't be topped professionally. And as generalities go, that is a fair one. A large percentage of Heights residents have arrived, are established and will continue to lead the good life in carefully restored 19th and early 20th century townhouses built by earlier generations of successful Manhattan professionals.

Robert Fulton's steamboat ferry service, inaugurated in 1814, spurred the development of the rural Brooklyn settlement. Newly accessible to lower Manhattan, and cooled by East River breezes, the Heights attracted merchants and lawyers, who built the substantial homes and noteworthy churches which characterize the community today. Brooklyn Heights boasts 684 pre-Civil War houses alone, and more than a dozen mostly-Gothic Revival churches.

The opening of the Brooklyn Bridge in 1883 brought the Heights that much closer to Wall Street and provided its most spectacular landmark, the gossamer span Flung from Gothic tower to Gothic tower over the busy East River. Wealth crossed the bridge to Brooklyn Heights and created one of the richest communities in the nation by the turn of the century. But the Depression wiped out many residents, the bankers and businessmen who worked on Wall Street, and blight came to the Heights.

In the 1950s and early 1960s, Brooklyn's first "brownstoners", attracted by the innate quality of the rundown housing stock, discovered Brooklyn Heights. These pioneers began a wave of renovation that, in the ensuing decades, has swept over row upon row of dilapidated Brooklyn townhouses. Today, the Heights' relatively cohesive population resides in stolid prewar apartment buildings and lovingly restored brownstones, as well as in striking warehouse conversions down at Fulton Ferry Landing. Besides the obvious, a five-minute subway zip to

Manhattan, other commuting modes include the feet. Hearty residents stride briskly along the soaring raised center walkway of the Brooklyn Bridge to their jobs in Lower Manhattan.

From the start, accessibility to Wall Street attracted residents to the Heights, and the exceptional view of Manhattan and the harbor kept them there. The magnificent panorama brings a steady stream of day-trippers, who come to absorb the view while strolling the wide and gracious Esplanade and to enjoy the quiet, landmarked district with its informal restaurants and pleasant shops.

Area Code: 718

Post Offices: General Post Office, 271 Cadman Plaza East, Brooklyn 11201, 834-3000; Municipal Building Station, Municipal Building, 210 Joralemon Street, Brooklyn 11201, 875-1332.

Zip Code: 11201

Police Precinct: Eighty-fourth, 301 Gold Street between Tillary and Johnson Streets, Brooklyn 11201, 875-6811.

Emergency Hospital (nearest): Long Island College Hospital, 340 Henry Street at Amity Street, Brooklyn 11201, 780-1000.

Libraries: The Business Library, 722-3333, and Brooklyn Heights Branch, 722-3350, share the same address: 280 Cadman Plaza West, Brooklyn 11201. The Brooklyn Historical Society's private library, 128 Pierrepont Street, Brooklyn 11201, 624-0890, houses excellent historical and genealogical collections.

Public School Education: School District # 13: Community School Board, 355 Park Place, Brooklyn 11238, 636-3204; and School District # 15: Community School Board, 360 Smith Street, Brooklyn 11231, 330-9300.

Adult Education: Long Island University, University Plaza, Brooklyn 11201, 488-1000; New York City Technical College, 300 Jay Street, Brooklyn 11201, 260-5000.

Cultural Resources: St. Ann's and the Holy Trinity Episcopal Church, 157 Montague Street, 834-8794. This church and day school complex sponsors numerous concerts and other cultural events as well. Bargemusic, Ltd., Fulton Ferry Landing, Brooklyn 11201, 624-4061: chamber music concerts accompanied by gentle lapping from the East River. St. Francis College, 180 Remsen Street, Brooklyn 11201, 522-2300. The Brooklyn Arts & Culture Association, Inc. (BACA), 195 Cadman Plaza West, Brooklyn, 11201, 718-625-0080, coordinates and supports the efforts of a wide range of cultural programs within the borough; call to receive BACA's monthly Calendar of Cultural Events.

Transportation—Subway: *Seventh Avenue IRT* (# 2, # 3) Clark Street, Borough Hall; *Lexington Avenue IRT* (# 4, # 5) Borough Hall; *Eighth Avenue IND* (A, C) High Street/Brooklyn Bridge; *BMT* (R) Court Street; *Nassau Street Local* (M), Court Street.

Transportation—Bus: Stop by Brooklyn Transit Headquarters Information Center, 370 Jay Street, for a bus map of Brooklyn.

Cobble Hill

Boundaries and Contiguous Areas: North: Atlantic Avenue and **Brooklyn Heights;** East: Court Street and **Boerum Hill;** South: DeGraw Street and **Carroll Gardens;** West: Hicks Street.

If it were possible to walk across the Mediterranean, a stroll starting at Atlantic Avenue down Court, Cobble Hill's main shopping street, to Carroll Gardens could be compared to a walk from Lebanon and the Middle East to Italy. Atlantic's famed Near and Middle Eastern spice and grocery stores and restaurants filter along Court south for a couple of blocks before meeting up with the pizzerias, Neapolitan bakeries and shops selling Italian housewares that take over the street as it approaches heavily Italian Carroll Gardens on Cobble Hill's southern boundary. This intriguing ethnic mix results in topnotch food sources which attract shoppers from all over Brooklyn.

The row upon row of brownstones — cheaper and not quite as

grand as those in Brooklyn Heights — shaded by large, leafy trees (note particularly the plane trees that completely cover Clinton Street as it crosses Baltic, Veranda and Congress Streets on the way to the Heights) attract a young professional crowd. Cobble Hill is probably the most homogeneous of all the Brooklyn brownstone neighborhoods. Apartment buildings and converted industrial properties are beginning to spring up in Cobble Hill, notably The Henry Street Mews condos and One Tiffany Place, just west of the Brooklyn Queens Expressway. Other recent conversions include Cobble Hill Towers, the city's first low income housing project when it was built in 1878, and the P.S. 78 condominiums, lodged in a late-19th century public school on Pacific Street.

Area Code: 718

Post Office (nearest): Municipal Building Station, Municipal Building, 210 Joralemon Street, Brooklyn 11201, 875-1332.

Zip Codes: 11201, 11231

Police Precinct: Seventy-sixth, 191 Union Street between Hicks and Henry Streets, Brooklyn 11231, 834-3211.

Emergency Hospital: Long Island College Hospital, 340 Henry Street at Amity Street, Brooklyn 11201, 780-1000.

Library (nearest): Carroll Gardens, 396 Clinton Street at Union Street, Brooklyn 11231, 625-5838.

Public School Education: School District #15: Community School Board, 360 Smith Street, Brooklyn 11231, 330-9300.

Adult Education: See **Brooklyn Heights** and **Boerum Hill.**

Cultural Resources: See **Brooklyn Heights** and **Boerum Hill.**

Transportation—Subway: *Seventh Avenue IRT* (# 2, # 3) and *Lexington Avenue IRT* (# 4, # 5), Borough Hall; *Sixth Avenue IND* (F) and *Brooklyn-Queens Crosstown* (G) Bergen Street.

Transportation—Bus: Stop by the Brooklyn Transit Headquarters Information Center, 370 Jay Street, for a bus map of Brooklyn.

Carroll Gardens

Boundaries and Contiguous Areas: North: DeGraw Street and **Cobble Hill;** East: Gowanus Canal; South: Hamilton Avenue; West: Brooklyn-Queens Expressway.

In Carroll Gardens singularly deep and lushly planted gardens front the four- and five-story row houses so characteristic of Brooklyn's brownstone neighborhoods. These splendid yards, with trees as tall as the high-stooped townhouses, form part of an eleven-block tract laid out in the 1850s. Verdant blockfronts are, however, only part of the reason urban homesteaders began moving to Carroll Gardens in the 1970s. This predominantly Italian community has a lower crime rate than many other areas in Brooklyn. And furthermore, just like Cobble Hill, another "tight" neighborhood to the north, Carroll Gardens boasts better-than-average public elementary and secondary schools.

Other pluses? Great food shopping. Shiny eggplants, firm-fleshed peppers, snowy mushrooms — a veritable caponata — heap the Italian vegetable stands lining Court Street, where bulbous pecorino cheeses intersperse salamis and whole prosciuttos hanging from grocery store ceilings. Subway transportation to Manhattan by F Train is fast and direct, too.

Less expensive, and less gentrified than the Heights and Cobble Hill, Carroll Gardens has limited housing stock, although conversions become available now and then. The largest and most appealing of these is The Mill on President Street. Fifty-five condos, some of which should be available as rentals from their owners, are contained in the converted rope factory with exposed brick walls and massive red oak beams.

To be sure, Carroll Gardens isn't paradise. Those garden blocks exist only north of Fourth Place. Shanties and derelict buildings still border Red Hook to the south. Use a real estate agent to find an apartment here, if after a stroll of the park-like streets between Fourth and President you find the area appealing.

Area Code: 718

Post Office: Red Hook, 615 Clinton Street, Brooklyn 11231, 624-5632.

Zip Code: 11231

Police Precinct: Seventy-sixth, 191 Union Street, Brooklyn 11231, 834-3211.

Emergency Hospital (nearest): Long Island College Hospital, 340 Henry Street at Amity Street, Brooklyn 11201, 780-1000.

Library: Carroll Gardens, 396 Clinton Street at Union Street, Brooklyn 11231, 625-5838.

Public School Education: School District # 15: Community School Board, 360 Smith Street, Brooklyn 11231, 330-9300.

Adult Education: See **Brooklyn Heights** and **Boerum Hill**.

Cultural Resources: See **Brooklyn Heights** and **Boerum Hill**.

Transportation—Subway: *Sixth Avenue IND* (F) Carroll Street, Smith Street; *Brooklyn-Queens Crosstown* (G) Carroll Street, Smith Street.

Transportation—Bus: Stop by the Brooklyn Transit Headquarters Information Center, 370 Jay Street, for a bus map of Brooklyn.

Boerum Hill

Boundaries and Contiguous Areas: North: Schermerhorn Street; East: Third Avenue; South: Wyckoff Street; West: Court Street and **Cobble Hill.**

The Boerum Hill Historic District, bounded roughly by Hoyt and Nevins,

Pacific and Wyckoff Streets, contains an outstanding assemblage of pre-Civil War Italianate and Greek Revival row houses: a monument to the efforts of new homeowners who in the early 1960s fought off a city effort to tear down the then-dispirited rooming houses to make way for urban renewal. Boerum Hill's turnaround — from near-slum to tight residential community — was achieved by a dedicated band of pioneers sophisticated enough to see the area's potential.

Often referred to as the Golden Oak Capital of America, the Boerum Hill section of Atlantic Avenue is the city's prime source for oak furniture and Victorian bric-a-brac. It seems only fitting that the devoted homesteaders living nearby should have appropriate furnishings close at hand. Antique stores lining both sides of the avenue have made way for a French bistro and a deli or two — a sure sign that the middle class has moved in.

Area Code: 718

Post Office: Times Plaza Station, 542 Atlantic Avenue, Brooklyn 11217, 875-7882.

Zip Code: 11217

Police Precincts: Seventy-sixth, 191 Union Street between Hicks and Henry Streets, Brooklyn 11231, 834-3211; Seventy-eighth, 65 Sixth Avenue between 6th and Bergen Streets, Brooklyn 11217, 636-6411.

Emergency Hospital: Long Island College Hospital, 340 Henry Street at Amity Street, Brooklyn 11201, 834-3211.

Library: Pacific, 25 Fourth Avenue, Brooklyn 11217, 638-5180.

Public School Education: School District # 15: Community School Board, 360 Smith Street, Brooklyn 11231, 330-9300.

Adult Education: Brooklyn YWCA, 30 Third Avenue, Brooklyn 11217, 875-1190, offers a health program as well as a variety of adult classes.

Transportation—Subway: *Seventh Avenue IRT* (# 2, # 3) Hoyt Street, Nevins Street; *Lexington Avenue IRT* (# 4, # 5) Nevins Street; *Sixth Avenue IND* (F) Bergen Street; *Brooklyn-Queens Crosstown* (G) Bergen Street, Hoyt/Schermerhorn Streets; *Eighth Avenue IND* (A, C) Hoyt/Schermerhorn Streets.

Transportation—Bus: Stop by Brooklyn Transit Headquarters Information Center, 370 Jay Street, for a bus map of Brooklyn.

Park Slope

Boundaries and Contiguous Areas: North: Flatbush Avenue; East: Prospect Park West; South: Windsor Place; West: Fifth Avenue.

If Cobble Hill is the most homogeneous of Brooklyn's brownstone neighborhoods, Park Slope is the most heterogeneous, and proud of it. (It is also by far the largest of these communities.) The fact that the population is still economically, ethnically and racially mixed appears for a majority of residents to be the neighborhood's most attractive attribute. Second place is probably a tie between 526-acre Prospect Park, designed by Frederick Law Olmsted and Calvert Vaux, Central Park's architects, and Park Slope's proximity to Brooklyn's three imposing cultural bastions: the Brooklyn Museum, the Central Library at Grand Army Plaza and the Brooklyn Botanic Garden. A recent addition to Prospect Park is the re-opened Wildlife Conservation Center, a state of the art children's zoo with a restored 1912 carousel (50¢ rides).

Park Slope's development paralleled that of Prospect Park in the 1880s. Sites with a park view were most highly prized, and small Victorian mansions line Prospect Park West. Closeness to the park and Grand Army Plaza determined the quality and appointments also of the vigorously Victorian bow-fronted townhouses which march row upon stolid row down the sloping streets. North Park Slope, nearest Prospect Park West and the Plaza, is considered the classiest part of the neighborhood. South Park Slope, east of 9th Street, is the less expensive, still-developing section. Old industrial properties, such as the Ansonia Clock factory complex on 12th Street, once the country's largest clock works and now deluxe condominiums, have been converted to apartments and co-ops. Seventh Avenue, the principal shopping street and scene of a hugely successful fair each spring, reflects neighborhood needs: the boutiques, card shops and unisex hair cutters once found exclusively at the North Slope end of Seventh are now infiltrating blocks in South Park Slope as well.

Without qualification Park Slope, together with Brooklyn Heights, has arrived as a suitable address for middle class professionals, especially those with—or about to be with—families. P.S. 321, district 15's progressive, well-regarded elementary school, has served as an additional attraction to young families. But don't go looking for bargain basements; in real estate parlance, the neighborhood is "hot" (and has been for while), especially along the park. Prices are lower down the slope and in adjoining Windsor Terrace and Prospect Heights, two revitalizing communities nicely situated near Prospect Park.

Area Code: 718

Post Office: Van Brunt Station, 275 9th Street, Brooklyn 11215, 768-6284.

Zip Code: 11215, 11217

Police Precincts: Seventy-second, 830 Fourth Avenue between 29th and 30th Streets, Brooklyn 11230, 965-6311; Seventy-eighth, 65 Sixth Avenue between 6th and Bergen Streets, Brooklyn 11217, 636-6411.

Emergency Hospital: Methodist Hospital, 506 6th Street between Seventh and Eighth Avenues, Brooklyn 11215, 780-3000.

Library: Brooklyn Central Library, Grand Army Plaza at Flatbush Avenue, Brooklyn 11238, 780-7810.

Public School Education: School District # 13: Community School Board, 355 Park Place, Brooklyn 11238, 636-3204; and School District # 15: Community School Board, 360 Smith Street, Brooklyn 11231, 330-9300.

Adult Education: Brooklyn Museum Art School, 200 Eastern Parkway, Brooklyn 11238, 638-5000. Brooklyn Botanic Garden, 1000 Washington Avenue, Brooklyn 11225, 622-4433, holds classes for plant enthusiasts; you can also call 622-4440 1 to 2:30 p.m. Tuesday-Friday for answers to perplexing plant problems. Brooklyn Conservatory of Music, 58 Seventh Avenue, Brooklyn 11217, 622-3300. St. John-St. Matthew Emmanuel Lutheran Church Community Center, 415 Seventh Street between Sixth and Seventh Avenues, Brooklyn 11215, 768-0772, allocates space to community educational and cultural groups.

Cultural Resources: Brooklyn Museum, 200 Eastern Parkway at Washington Avenue, Brooklyn 11238, 638-5000. Behind the six Ionic columns of McKim, Mead and White's famed building are housed a number of exemplary collections as well as facilities for the cultural and educational programs sponsored daily by the museum.

Transportation—Subway: With the exception of the Eighth Avenue IND A and C trains, subways stop near one part of Park Slope or the other. Seventh Avenue and *Lexington Avenue IRT* trains stop at Grand Army Plaza; *Sixth Avenue IND* (F) stops at Fourth Avenue, Seventh Avenue and 15th Street; *Sixth Avenue IND* (D) stops at Seventh Avenue and Atlantic Avenue; *BMT* (N, R) stops along Fourth Avenue at Pacific Street, Union Street, 9th Street and Prospect Avenue.

Transportation—Bus: The Information Center at Brooklyn Transit Headquarters, 370 Jay Street, is the place to get a bus map of Brooklyn.

Fort Greene/Clinton Hill

Boundaries and Contiguous Areas: North: Myrtle Avenue; East: Classon Avenue; South: Atlantic Avenue; West: Flatbush Avenue and **Boerum Hill.**

"To the rear of the boisterous city hall quarter was Brooklyn's other fine residential district, the Hill. . . . Its elegant residences were fewer in number [than Brooklyn's Heights'] and their owners slightly further removed from the traditions of genteel respectability. It abounded in churches and middle class houses, the majority of whose owners worked in New York." So wrote a Brooklyn historian of late 19th century Fort Greene and Clinton Hill. Despite a decline in the intervening years, that description is valid once again. Except for the fringe areas, especially to the north and west. Today they are even fringier. What occasioned the turnabout? Historic designation and the brownstone revival, mainly.Revival came late, in the 1970s, to Fort Greene. Even the once-elegant brownstones on the choice streets nearest Fort Greene Park had become dilapidated wino rows. But beneath the grime and neglect the original detailing remained, awaiting the attention of gritty urban pioneers. Now, perfectly restored Anglo-Italianate brownstones line Washington Park, South Oxford and South Portland Streets. And sweeping 33-acre Fort Greene Park, the community's centerpiece designed by Olmsted and Vaux, has been restored to its rather English graciousness.

Homeowners are as likely to be black or Hispanic as they are white, as likely to be filmmakers or musicians as investment bankers. Fort Greene is integrated, both racially and socio-economically, and determined to stay that way. The throbbing cultural presence of the Brooklyn Academy of Music (BAM) helped stimulate the growth of a substantial community of black artists in Fort Greene. Yet a perception of crime persists, a perception which is greater than the reality, many residents insist. Besides, they say, with what you save on rent here, you can afford to take a cab from the subway station at 1 a.m.

Clinton Hill, like Fort Greene, which it borders and from which it is barely distinguishable, contains an astonishing treasury of late 19th century urban architecture. The key word in this neighborhood is Pratt. Kerosene magnate Charles Pratt built several handsome mansions on Clinton Avenue, including the present residence of the Bishop of Brooklyn. Charles Pratt also founded, built and, until his death in 1891, ran Pratt Institute, the focal point and cultural center of the community. And now it is the students, grads and faculty of Pratt (art, design, architecture, engineering, computer information and library sciences) who fill the streets and much of the local housing.

Clinton Hill has a few high rises and therefore a somewhat wider variety of housing than Fort Greene. But Clinton Hill has only one subway line. The G train, which stops at Clinton and Washington Streets and requires long waits as well as a transfer to reach Manhattan, is a definite minus. Fort Greene, on the other hand, is well tended by the subway system (see below) and offers easy on-street parking.

Both the Metrotech development to the west on Flatbush Avenue and the Atlantic Center mixed-use development recently begun on the southeast edge of Fort Greene should profoundly effect Fort Greene and Clinton Hill when completed in the mid-to-late-1990s. Expect the cost of housing to spiral. Meanwhile, apartment hunting here is best done through a knowledgeable real estate agent.

Area Code: 718

Post Offices: Pratt Station, 524 Myrtle Avenue, Brooklyn 11205, 622-8581; General Post Office, 271 Cadman Plaza East, Brooklyn 11201, 834-3000; Times Plaza Station, 542 Atlantic Avenue, Brooklyn 11217, 875-7882.

Zip Codes: 11201, 11205, 11217, 11238.

Police Precinct: Eighty-eighth, 298 Classon Avenue, Brooklyn 11205, 636-6511.

Emergency Hospital: Brooklyn Hospital, 121 DeKalb Avenue, Brooklyn 11201, 403-8000.

Libraries: Brooklyn Public Library, Clinton Hill Branch, 380 Washington Avenue, Brooklyn 11238, 857-8038; Walt Whitman Branch, 93 St. Edwards Street, Brooklyn 11205, 855-1508.

Public School Education: School District # 13, Community School Board, 355 Park Place, Brooklyn 11238, 636-3204.

Adult Education: Pratt Institute, Continuing Education, 200 Willoughby Avenue, Brooklyn 11205, 636-3453; Medgar Evers Community College, 1150 Carroll Street, Brooklyn 11225, 270-4900; St. Joseph's College, 265 Clinton Avenue, Brooklyn 11205, 622-4690.

Cultural Resources: Brooklyn Academy of Music (BAM), 30 Lafayette Avenue, Brooklyn 11217, 636-4100. The borough's premier cultural resource, BAM contains four theaters of differing sizes presenting a spectrum of performances by artists from all disciplines. Nearby: Long Island University, University Plaza, Flatbush at DeKalb Avenues, Brooklyn 11210, 834-6000.

Transportation—Subway: *Eighth Avenue IND* (A, C) Lafayette Street; *Sixth Avenue IND* (B, D) DeKalb Avenue; *BMT* (M, N, Q, R) DeKalb Avenue; *Seventh Avenue IRT* (# 2, # 3) Nevins Street; *Lexington Avenue IRT* (# 4, # 5) Nevins Street; Brooklyn-Queens Crosstown (G) Fulton Street, Clinton/Washington Avenues.

Transportation—Bus: The Information Center at Brooklyn Transit Headquarters, 370 Jay Street, is the place to get a bus map of Brooklyn.

QUEENS

Among the five boroughs, Queens is the acknowledged bastion of New York's middle class. As skyscrapers identify Manhattan and brownstones Brooklyn, so solid brick buildings — free-standing, Tudor-inspired houses, semi-detached, two-, three-and four-family dwellings and six-story apartment blocks — define a good part of the largest borough in the city.

Until 1909 and the completion of the Queensborough Bridge, semi-rural Queens was a backwater connected only by ferry boat to Manhattan across the East River. But the bridge, followed almost immediately by train and then by subway service through new tunnels under the East River, opened the way for commuters and commerce. Great parcels of land were snapped up by developers, and 1908 saw the beginning of a building spree that continued, with few pauses, until World War II. While some communities are architecturally noteworthy — Forest Hills Gardens, a carefully designed 1909 enclave planned down to its English rustic street signs, and Malba, a charming melange of lawns, leafy lanes and handsome, mostly 1920s homes nestled under the Whitestone Bridge — most of the housing is sturdy, unremarkable pre-World War II stock often laid out, suburban-style, in tracts.

Although many Queens neighborhoods are identified with various ethnic groups — Greeks gravitate to Astoria, Latin Americans to Jackson

Heights, Russians to Rego Park, Asians to Flushing — a multi-national mix of businessmen, engineers and other professionals continues to move into the area. Immediately across the river from Manhattan, new life is being breathed into Long Island City, not only by artists attracted by P.S. 1, a highly successful alternative art, dance and theater space, but also by the reestablishment of the enormous old Astoria movie studios, the new Silver Cup Studios, the Eaves-Brooks costume company and the gargantuan International Design Center, which contains more than 100 acres of showroom space. The 42-story, glass Citicorp spire, towering over these industrial surrounds like a giant among midgets, now dominates Long Island City. Forever discussed but not yet on its way: a major mixed-use project by the Port Authority of NY & NJ along the East River.

Long Island City may be evolving into what *New York* magazine has called "The New Hot Neighborhood," but not necessarily for the newcomer; although a number of artists are residents of this factory town, there is a paucity of houses and residential lofts. Astoria just to the north and Sunnyside to the southeast, both equally accessible to Manhattan, are moderately priced alternatives. Within subway reach, Rego Park, Forest Hills and Kew Gardens are popular established communities where one-bedroom apartments rent for the same amount as a Manhattan studio. Further east, the new condominium units renting in big Bayside high rises seem to have appeal for those who don't find the trip by express bus or Long Island Railroad too daunting.

Names of Queens real estate brokers will be found in the chapter on **Apartment Hunting.**

Astoria

Boundaries and Contiguous Areas: North: East River; East: Grand Central Parkway, Brooklyn-Queens Expressway and LaGuardia Airport; South: 35th Avenue and **Sunnyside;** West: East River.

You don't have to be Greek (or Italian, Yugoslavian, German or Bohemian either) to live in Astoria, but it can't hurt. With a population that is nearly 60% Greek or Hispanic, this community has a distinct Old World feel. With and without belly dancers, the tavernas on Ditmars

Boulevard and Broadway vibrate long and late to the keening of Greek dance music. The most recent wave of immigrants is a hodge-podge of Irish, South Americans, Slavs and Asians. The quintessential Astoria is on display at the Ethnic Music Festival, a food, music and dance marathon held each September at Bohemian Hall, a traditional mittel-European beer garden at 24th Avenue and 29th Street.

Urban professionals have discovered the apartments in the decently maintained but unprepossessing two-story houses and small apartment buildings bordering Astoria's relatively safe streets, in particular the area between Crescent and 35th Streets, which is within distance of the N line and a 20-minute commute from Midtown. (A caveat: presumably Astorians have no problem with the improbably numbered streets, drives and avenues here; outsiders find them incomprehensible.)

The Olympic-sized city pool in spacious Astoria Park, just beneath the Triborough Bridge on the East River, is free, as is the uncrowded running space around the park. Condo living, with a free health club and unobstructed view of the Manhattan skyline, came to Astoria with the opening of the 405-unit Shore Towers in 1990 at the southern end of the park.

Astoria was the home of Paramount Studios from 1919 until the 1930s, when the business moved — lock, stock and W.C. Fields — to Hollywood. The movies are back, however, sharing with television the enormous, refurbished Kaufman Astoria Studios on 35th Avenue between 34th and 37th Streets. The complex also houses the Museum of the Moving Image. Several production facilities have sprouted up nearby including Silvercup Studios, a maker of commercials and feature films. The revitalization of southern Astoria's movie and television industry has caused a new moniker for the area: Hollywood East.

Still, with the noteworthy exception of two extraordinary sculpture collections and the recent addition of a 750-seat public theater, Athens Square, cultural institutions and parks are in short supply in mainly blue-collar Astoria. Unlikely as it may seem, the prime showcase of Isamu Noguchi's sculpture — some 350 pieces by the famous artist — is located in the Noguchi Garden Museum on Vernon Boulevard at 33rd Road. And sculptor Mark Di Suvero organized the Socrates Sculpture Park, with a changing display of monumental works in a vacant East River lot just across Vernon Boulevard. Could a branch of Washington's Hirschhorn Gallery be next?

Area Code: 718

Post Offices: Astoria Station, 27-40 21st Street, Astoria 11102, 726-1005; Steinway Station, 43-04 Broadway, Astoria 11103, 726-1107; Woolsey Station, 22-68 31st Street, Astoria 11105, 274-5563; Broadway Station, 21-17 Broadway, Astoria 11106, 726-1007.

Zip Codes; 11102, 11103, 11105, 11106

Police Precinct: One Hundred Fourteenth, 34-16 Astoria Boulevard at 35th Street, Astoria 11102, 626-9311.

Emergency Hospital: Elmhurst Hospital Center, 79-01 Broadway, Elmhurst 11373, 334-4000.

Library: Astoria Branch, Queens Public Library, 14-01 Astor Boulevard, Astoria 11102, 278-0601; Steinway Branch, 21-45 31st Street, Long Island City 11105, 728-1965.

Public School Education: District # 30, Community School Board, 49-05 20th Avenue, Jackson Heights, 11106, 777-4600.

Cultural Resources: The Noguchi Garden Museum, 32-37 Vernon Boulevard, 204-7088, is open Wednesday and Saturday afternoons, April-November; Museum of the Moving Image, 36-01 35th Avenue, 784-4520.

Transportation—Subway: *BMT* (B, N) Broadway, 30th Avenue, Astoria Boulevard-Hoyt Avenue, Ditmars Boulevard; *BMT* (E, F) Steinway Street, 46th Street; *Brooklyn-Queens Crosstown* (G, R) Steinway Street and 46th Street.

Transportation—Bus: Stop by the Queens Transit Headquarters Information Center, 124-15 28th Avenue, Flushing, for a bus map of Queens.

Sunnyside

Boundaries and Contiguous Areas: North: Barnett Avenue and the Sunnyside Amtrak Yards; East: 52nd Street and New Calvary Cemetery; South: Long Island Expressway; West: 36th Street and Long Island City.

This traditionally blue-collar community bounded by railroad yards, industrial tracts, cemeteries and the legendary LIE (the Long Island Expressway, known, among other sobriquets, as the world's longest parking lot) won't be the next "in" New York neighborhood. But the sensible, mostly-brick homes and apartments lining Sunnyside's residential streets ten minutes by train from Manhattan do attract young professionals, as well as immigrants from overseas, with more space for lower-than-Manhattan rents.

Newcomers are especially drawn to Sunnyside Gardens. "The Gardens," the first U.S. development to be modeled on the English garden community, occupies 55 leafy acres north of bustling Queens Boulevard. Towering London plane trees shade the 650 one-, two-and three-family brick townhouses which enclose long, communal gardens. The effect is English village, with shrub-lined walks penetrating the landmarked blocks. "Like Greenwich Village and far more than Brooklyn Heights, it was a mixed community, in which one might mingle without undue intimacy with one's neighbors," recalls urban critic/historian Lewis Mumford, who lived in The Gardens from their inception in 1924 until 1936. They seem little changed.

There are private homes and rentals in greater Sunnyside as well, but most of the brick apartment blocks are non-rentable co-ops. The three main shopping thoroughfares are small-town Skillman Avenue at The Gardens' southern edge, Queens Boulevard in the shadow of the elevated IRT Flushing Line, and running diagonally southwest from the Boulevard, Greenpoint Avenue. There and on the side streets you can rent Korean movies, buy Irish imports, eat Italian, Middle European or Oriental, or lift a pint at Moriarty's Pub Restaurant. The city's only Spanish language theater, The Thalia on Greenpoint, plays to sellout crowds on weekends.

Thanks in large part to the efforts of the Sunnyside Foundation whose staff works on planning and preservation issues, Sunnyside is an appealingly cohesive community, for all its ethnic diversity. Stop by the Foundation's office at 41-13 47th Street (392-9139) for information, advice and a free copy of *The Sunnyside Herald* if you're thinking of moving here.

Area Code: 718

Post Office: Sunnyside Station, 45-15 44th Street, Sunnyside 11104, 729-1438.

Zip Code: 11104

Police Precinct: One Hundred Eighth, 5-47 50th Avenue, Long Island City 11104, 784-5411.

Emergency Hospital (nearest): Elmhurst Hospital Center, 79-01 Broadway, Elmhurst 11373, 334-4000..

Library: Sunnyside Branch, 43-02 Greenpoint Avenue, Sunnyside 11104, 784-3033.

Public School Education: School District # 2, Community School Board, 43-31 39th Street, Sunnyside 11104, 361-0750.

Transportation—Subway: Flushing Line (# 7) 40th Street, 46th Street, 52nd Street.

Transportation—Bus: Stop by the Queens Transit Headquarters Information Center, 124-15 28th Avenue, Flushing, for a bus map of Queens.

Rego Park

Boundaries and Contiguous Areas: North: Queens Boulevard; East: Yellowstone Boulevard and **Forest Hills;** Southwest: Woodhaven Boulevard.

What distinguishes Rego Park from neighboring Forest Hills and Kew Gardens, which it very much resembles, is the appreciably higher ratio of apartment buildings to private dwellings, slightly lower rents, somewhat older population and proportionately more recent immigrants. While the number of Indians, Pakistanis and Asians has been increasing throughout the three communities, Rego Park has also attracted a sizeable Russian population, a large Israeli group and a nucleus of Iranians.

One of the borough's largest malls, the metal-paneled Queens Center containing an A & S branch, among others, with Macy's nearby, is quartered on the Rego Park stretch of Queens Boulevard. Smaller, more intimate shops line 63rd Drive.

It should be noted that the imposition of a rigid grid pattern was foiled in this part of Queens by circuitous streets laid out in "crescents" by the original developers. Wherever possible, each numbered thoroughfare has an Avenue, Road and Drive to its credit. For example, 63rd Avenue, 63rd Road, 63rd Drive in that order. The streets tend to be named, not numbered. Rego Park was first developed in 1923 and named for the company that built it: the Rego (for Real Good) Construction Company.

Area Code: 718

Post Office: Rego Park, 92-24 Queens Boulevard, Rego Park, NY 11374, 429-2696.

Zip Code: 11374

Police Precinct: One Hundred and Twelfth, 68-40 Austin Street, Forest Hills, NY 11375, 520-9311.

Emergency Hospital: St. John's Hospital, 90-02 Queens Boulevard, Elmhurst, NY 11373, 457-1300.

Library: Rego Park, 91-41 63rd Drive, Rego Park, NY 11374, 459-5140.

Public School Education: Public School District # 28 (see **Forest Hills**).

Adult Education: Queens College (see **Kew Gardens**); St. John's University (see **Forest Hills**).

Transportation—Subway: *BMT* (R) Rego Park Station, 67th Avenue; *Brooklyn-Queens Crosstown* (G) Rego Park Station, 67th Avenue.

Transportation—Bus: Stop by the Queens Transit Headquarters Information Center, 124-15 28th Avenue, Flushing, for a bus map of Queens.

Forest Hills

Boundaries and Contiguous Areas: The neighborhood is shaped roughly like a lower case "d". North: Long Island Expressway; East: Grand Central Parkway and Corona Park; South: Union Turnpike and **Kew Gardens**; West: Yellowstone Boulevard and **Rego Park**.

Practical Queens Boulevard, a major shopping thoroughfare which sensibly separates curbside businesses from through traffic with narrow cement dividers, belies the charm of Forest Hills as it cuts through the heart of the neighborhood. Bordering Corona Park northwest of the boulevard, the "Cord Meyer" district consists of gracious, white-trimmed brick homes begun in 1904 and large apartment buildings constructed later by the Cord Meyer Development Co., which is still the largest landlord in the area. South a block just off Austin, considered one of the most enticing shopping streets in Queens, lies "The Gardens." Forest Hills Gardens, designed in the eclectic tradition by an architect of the Beaux Arts school and sponsored by the Russell Sage Foundation, has few peers in the half-timbered world of Victorian Tudor. Brick-fronted Cotswoldian houses face curving drives and landscaped plots originally planned by Frederick Law Olmsted, Jr. Instantly successful, the development spawned housing decorated with Tudor cliches throughout central Queens.

Until 1977, when the US Open Tennis Championships moved to Flushing, Forest Hills was the self-described "lawn tennis capital of the Western Hempishere." But the West Side Tennis Club, still occupying ten acres next to the Gardens, continues to add luster to the community by hosting the men's World Champion matches each spring, among other tournaments. Shopping and noshing opportunities also add allure.

In addition to the attractive Austin Street spots, appealing cafes, craft and antique stores are cropping up on Metropolitan Avenue.

Old, established, and mostly—about 90% according to the last census—white Forest Hills is becoming increasingly cosmopolitan. (A local real estate agent reports a Japanese language map of Forest Hills on sale in Tokyo bookstores.) And increasingly, its brick apartment buildings have gone co-op. The few six-to ten-story rental buildings congregating on either side of Queens Boulevard and the IND/BMT subway lines, as well as major arteries like Ascan, Metropolitan and 108th Street, are worth pursuing for their quality pre-war construction as well as convenience to public transportation. Semi-detached apartments and units in private homes may require a slightly longer walk but offer landscaped lots and winding streets as dividends.

Area Code: 718

Post Office: Forest Hills, 106-28 Queens Boulevard, Forest Hills, NY 11375, 268-1696.

Zip Code: 11375

Police Precinct: One Hundred and Twelfth, 68-40 Austin Street, Forest Hills, NY 11375, 520-9311.

Emergency Hospitals: LaGuardia Hospital, 102-01 66th Road, Forest Hills, NY 11375, 830-4000; Parkway Hospital, 70-35 113th Street, Forest Hills, NY 11375, 990-4119.

Library: Forest Hills, 108-19 71st Avenue, Forest Hills, NY 11375, 268-7934.

Public School Education: School District; # 28, 108-55 69th Avenue, Forest Hills, NY 11375, 830-8800.

Adult Education (nearest): St. John's University, Grand Central and Utopia Parkways, Jamaica, NY 11439, 990-6161.

Community Resources: West Side Tennis Club, 1 Tennis Place (bounded by Burns and Dartmouth Streets and 69th and 70th Avenues), 268-2300.

Transportation—Subway: *Eighth Avenue IND* (E), *Sixth Avenue IND* (F), *Brooklyn-Queens Crosstown* (G), *BMT* (R) all to 71st and Continental Avenues, Forest Hills.

Transportation—Bus: Stop by the Queens Transit Headquarters Information Center, 124-15 28th Avenue, Flushing, for a bus map of Queens.

Kew Gardens

Boundaries and Contiguous Areas: Northeast: Queens Boulevard; South: Metropolitan Avenue and Forest Park; West: Union Turnpike and **Forest Hills**.

Bracketed by LaGuardia Airport and John F. Kennedy International, Queens is home to thousands of airline employees. Kew Gardens in particular is popular with flight crews, who can spy their very own red-tiled roofs as the jets they man pass over the community en route to the airports. Real estate agents report more rentals available and more singles residing in Kew Gardens than in Forest Hills and Rego Park.

The neighborhood's oldest section dates to 1912, when the Kew Gardens Corporation was formed. The substantial Colonialand Tudor-accented private homes built on high, comparatively hilly ground between Maple Grove Cemetery and Forest Park have cachet even today. After some years heavy with co-op conversions, the blocks of red brick apartment buildings that ring Kew's center are becoming more affordable and turning co-op at a slower rate. Austin Street and Metropolitan Avenue together with Lefferts and Queens Boulevards make up Kew's main shopping area.

At its southeasternmost tip, Kew Gardens hosts not only the borough's newest commercial skyscraper, a tall, rectangular grey block with cutout circles at the corners, but also Queens Borough Hall just across the Van Wyck Expressway, a long bureaucratic brick and limestone structure usually filled with politicians and, occasionally, useful publications about the borough.

Area Code: 718

Post Office: Kew Gardens, 83-30 Austin Street, Kew Gardens, NY 11415, 847-1978.

Zip Codes: 11415, 11375, 11365

Police Precinct: One Hundred and Second, 87-34 118th Street, Richmond Hill, NY 11418, 805-3200.

Emergency Hospital (nearest): LaGuardia Hospital, 102-01 66th Road, Forest Hills, NY 11375, 830-4000.

Libraries: Lefferts, 103-34 Lefferts Boulevard, Richmond Hill, 843-5950; Glen Oaks, 25604 Union Turnpike, Forest Park, NY 11426, 347-8200.

Public School Education: Public School District # 28 (see **Forest Hills**).

Adult Education (nearest): Queens College, 65-30 Kissena Boulevard, Flushing, NY 11367, 520-7000.

Community Resources: Queens Borough Hall, 120-55 Queens Boulevard, Kew Gardens, NY 11424, 520-3220.

Transportation—Subway: *Eighth Avenue IND* (E) Kew Gardens/Union Turnpike; *Sixth Avenue IND* (F), Kew Gardens/Union Turnpike; *BMT* (R) Kew Gardens/Union Turnpike.

Transportation—Bus: Stop by the Queens Transit Headquarters Information Center, 124-15 28th Avenue, Flushing, for bus map of Queens.

Bayside

Boundaries and Contiguous Areas: North and East: Cross Island Parkway; South: Long Island Expressway; West: Francis Lewis Boulevard and Utopia Parkway.

The bright barn-red Long Island Railroad station, white-trimmed and snappy, differentiates Bayside from other Queens stops. So does the concentration of pubs and restaurants—some dim and glitzy, others homey-comfortable with fireplaces—that surround the station. These places attract singles and have a bubbling atmosphere after work and on weekend nights. North of this Bell Boulevard and 41st Avenue junction, one-and two-family homes reestablish that urban/suburban quiet which typifies residential Queens until you reach Bay Terrace. Here, newly constructed condominiums and co-oped garden apartment buildings again break the mold.

While the older, free-standing homes contain rental apartments, condominium rentals in the Bay Club, though expensive, are probably the biggest draw. The enormous development consists of 1,036 condominiums in two three-pronged towers, a glass-domed swim club, a health club and five tennis courts. The Bay Bridge condo development nearby, with some 2,000 luxury townhouses, is a shorefront village in itself. From the Bay Club windows, and from those in the older co-ops, you can see how the community got its name—Bayside is bounded on two sides by Little Bay and Little Neck Bay—and the Whitestone, Triborough and Throgs Neck Bridges connecting Queens to The Bronx as well.

Bayside has water views but no direct subway connection to Manhattan. Commuters have three public transportation choices: the Long Island Railroad, express buses, or Queens buses to Flushing's Main Street Station and the # 7 Flushing Line subway.

Area Code: 718

Post Office: Bayside, 212-35 42nd Avenue, Bayside, NY 11361, 229-0699.

Zip Codes: 11360, 11361, 11359

Police Precinct: One Hundred and Eleventh, 45-06 215th Street, Bayside, NY 11359, 279-5200.

Emergency Hospital: St. Mary's Hospital for Children, 29-01 216th Street, Bayside, NY 11360, 281-8800.

Library: Bayside, 214-20 Northern Boulevard, Bayside, NY 11361, 229-1834.

Public School Education: Public School District; # 26, 61-15 Oceania Street, Bayside, NY 11364, 631-6900.

Adult Education: Queensborough Community College, 222-05 56th Avenue, Bayside, NY 11364, 631-6262.

Community Resources: Crocheron Park, 33rd Avenue and Little Neck Parkway, 7225-2620, 45 acre park; Queensborough Community College Gallery, 222-05 56th Avenue, Bayside, call 631-6396 for information.

Transportation—Train: Regular LIRR service.

Transportation—Bus: Stop by the Queens Transit Headquarters Information Center, 124-15 28th Avenue, Flushing, for a bus map of Queens.

STATEN ISLAND

New York's least-populated borough is, for many, simply the turn-around point for New York's most beloved, and cheapest, boat ride. Not that Staten Islanders mind. The 400,000 residents would just as soon keep their 61-square-mile island off the coast of New Jersey to themselves. In fact, November 2, 1993 marked a red letter day when islanders voted overwhelmingly to secede from New York City. Final word rests with Albany and this question is not likely to be settled soon.

Dreams of remaining far from the madding New York crowd were, in fact, conclusively shattered when the austerely beautiful Verrazano-Narrows Bridge connecting Staten Island with Brooklyn was opened in 1964. The island's semirural isolation ended once and for all as Brooklynites flocked across the longest single-span bridge in the world to take up residence in dozens of new tract developments.

Giovanni da Verrazano discovered hillocky Staten Island in 1524 but, until the dedication of his namesake bridge 440 years later, the island remained something of a backwater. Henry Hudson claimed *Staaten Eylandt* for the Dutch East India Company in 1609; however, Britain acquired Staten Island when the British took over New Amsterdam in 1644. Farming, and then oystering, flourished. By the mid-1800s, a railroad, trolley cars and ferry service made the island's seashore and salubrious air accessible to the gentry.

The fickle fashionables had moved on though by the time Staten Island became part of New York City in 1898. Too bad, because the city improved the new borough's ferry service immeasurably: by 1904 there were a number of sturdy seaworthy boats running on schedule for the first time since young Cornelius Vanderbilt instituted ferry service to Manhattan around 1810. Today, three sunset-yellow ferries ply the choppy waters of the Upper Bay between St. George and the Battery during the rush hours. Off-peak, two just-modernized 1,200-passenger boats handle the immensely scenic 25-minute crossing. Now, not only do tracts and shopping malls flourish south of the Staten Island Expressway, straining the island's over-taxed infrastructure, but a modest renaissance is underway in communities within walking distance of the ferry landing. Wall Streeters cherish the office-to-ferry walk, as well as the uphill stroll home, almost as much as they cherish the 50¢ round-trip fare.

Hills—precipitous slopes reminiscent of San Francisco—and stunning views from the craggy ridge that rises between St. George and Richmondtown characterize that quarter of Staten Island nearest Manhattan. On leafy Todt, Emerson and Grymes Hills, million-dollar homes look over the tree tops to Brooklyn and Manhattan. Wood-frame Victorian houses, salted among the stucco mini-mansions and angular contemporary homes, are the darlings of homesteaders. You're more likely to find a rental apartment in a converted one-or two-family house than in an apartment building on Staten Island — although red brick apartment towers do exist.

The Staten Island Chamber of Commerce, 130 Bay Street, Staten Island, NY 10301, 727-1900, sells an excellent street map for $2; the MTA ' s Staten Island Bus Map (free at the Chamber) is equally useful. Rental classifieds in the *Staten Island Advance* are more numerous on Saturday and Sunday but this afternoon paper publishes real estate ads every day. In Manhattan, pick up a copy of the *Advance* at the newsstand located inside the ferry terminal. *The Village Voice* is also a good source for listings.

St. George

Boundaries and Contiguous Areas: North: Richmond Terrace; East: Bay Street; South: Victory Boulevard and **Stapleton;** West: Jersey Street.

Flags aflap, the beguiling limestone and brick Borough Hall caps a rise to the right of St. George's ferry terminal. This handsome landmark, steam cleaned and newly bright, is symbolic of St. George's struggle against blight. The ragtag downtown sector defies gentrification but uphill, within sight of the neo-Gothic spires of Curtis High School (between St. Mark's Place and Hamilton Avenue), you'll find restored Victorian, Tudor and 1920s-stucco houses as well as a few apartment buildings.

In contrast to the maple-shaded period homes, the three converted grain and coffee warehouses that comprise Bay Street Landing are very 1980s. Arguably the borough's trendiest housing, these waterside condominiums a five-minute walk east of the ferry terminal are the first stage in a projected harborfront revival. Here, black pines and juniper separate the public marina, esplanade and the glass-enclosed Landing Cafe from the access road. Shades of Sausalito. New rentals, rare in Staten Island, are to be found in moderately-priced waterfront mid rises at Harbor View. What's next? Development of the abandoned, park-like U.S. Coast Guard base which lies between the ferry terminal and The Landing.

Come spring, fishing enthusiasts flock to the charter boats tied up at The Landing's pristine new docks. The Joseph L. Lyons Pool, one of Staten Island's four municipal swimming pools, and the George Cromell Center, an indoor recreation center with tennis courts and a track situated on a pier, are both located near The Landing's complex.

Check the classifieds and our list of Staten Island real estate brokers in the **Apartment Hunting** chapter for rentals, and after filing off the ferry, walk through the gradually reviving community of St. George. Sustenance for your search? La Fosse aux Loups, a Belgian bistro wedged between City Hall and the court buildings at 11 Schuyler Street, serves imaginative (and inexpensive) lunches on weekdays. Moules, waterzooi, carbonnades flamandes and other Belgian specialties are featured at dinner six nights a week.

Area Code: 718

Post Office: St. George, 45 Bay Street, Staten Island, NY 10301, 981-1313.

Zip Code: 10301

Police Precinct: One Hundred Twentieth, 78 Richmond Terrace, Staten Island, NY 10301, 876-8500.

Emergency Hospitals (nearest): Bayley Seton Hospital, 75 Vanderbilt Avenue (at Bay Street), Staten Island, NY 10304, 390-6000; St. Vincent's Medical Center of Richmond, 355 Bard Avenue, Staten Island, NY 10301, 876-1234.

Library: St. George Library Center, 5 Central Avenue, Staten Island, NY 10301, 442-8560.

Public School Education: School District; # 31: Community School Board, 211 Daniel Low Terrace, Staten Island, NY 10301, 273-9559.

Adult Education: College of Staten Island, St. George campus (part of the City University of New York), 130 Stuyvesant Place, Staten Island, NY 10301, 982-2000.

Cultural Resources: Snug Harbor Cultural Center, 1000 Richmond Terrace, Staten Island, NY 10301, 448-2500, is located in a clutch of handsome Greek Revival buildings on 80 arboreous acres. Once a haven for indigent sailors, the colonnaded buildings are now the locus of Staten Island's cultural rebirth. Concerts, art exhibits and plays fill the high-ceilinged halls. Also on the grounds you'll find: The Staten Island Botanical Garden, 273-8200, and the Staten Island Children's Museum, 448-6557.

Transportation—Train: The Staten Island Rapid Transit train costs $1.25 one way and provides service between the St. George Ferry Terminal and Tottenville at the southern tip of the 13.9-mile-long island. The second stop, Tompkinsville Station, is used for Bay

Street Landing. Call 718-720-3545 for information.

Transportation—Bus: Local buses cost $1.25 one way. The #101, #102 and # 104 buses leave from and return to the ferry terminal after circling northwestern St. George. Take the # 109 bus for Bay Street Landing. Express buses to Manhattan via the Verrazano Bridge and Brooklyn Battery Tunnel cost $3.50 one way. Call 718-330-1234 for bus information.

Transportation—Ferry: Passenger ferries run every 15 or 20 minutes during rush hours, every half hour at other times, every hour from 11:30 p.m. to 6:30 a.m. Service is less frequent on holidays and weekends. The fare is 50¢ round trip. Car ferry service was suspended in 1991 after fire damaged the Whitehall terminal. According to ferry personnel, resumption of car service is "under consideration." Call 718-390-5253 for information.

Stapleton

Boundaries and Contiguous Areas: North: Victory Boulevard and **St. George**; East: Bay Street and Upper New York Bay; South: Canal and Broad Streets; West: Louis Street, Van Duzer Street and **Grymes Hill**.

Bordering Bay Street, Stapleton boasts a batch of more-collectibles-than-antiques stores and Staten Island's only glade of fern bars. These cafes, tarted up with Tiffany style lamps, polished brass and old-fashioned bottle vases, point to the presence of newcomers in Stapleton's craggy hills.

Located only two stops from the ferry terminal on the SIRT train, Stapleton for some time has attracted artists and young families looking for a third bedroom. Now, here come bankers and stockbrokers from Lower Manhattan. Sturdy 19th century homes characterize housing in Stapleton Heights and adjacent Ward Hill. Asphalt shingles sheath houses down on the flats near the gourmet takeout shops, the library and handsome Tappan Park. The Mud Lane Society, a group of community boosters, promotes Stapleton with an annual house tour.

Area Code: 718

Post Office: Stapleton, 514 Bay Street, Staten Island, NY 10304, 727-2207.

Zip Code: 10304

Police Precinct: One Hundred Twentieth, 78 Richmond Terrace, Staten Island, NY 10301, 876-8500.

Emergency Hospital (nearest): Bayley Seton Hospital, Bay Street and Vanderbilt Avenue, Staten Island, NY 10304, 390-6000.

Library: Stapleton, 132 Canal Street, Staten Island, NY 10304, 727-0427.

Public School Education: School District # 31 (see **St. George**).

Adult Education (nearby): St. John's University, 300 Howard Avenue, Staten Island, NY 10301, 390-4545.

Cultural Resources: The Jacques Marchais Center of Tibetan Art houses Tibetan monastery artifacts at 338 Lighthouse Avenue; call for an appointment, 987-3478.

Transportation—Train: The Stapleton Station is the third stop on the SIRT train. (Details under **St. George**.)

Transportation—Bus: The # 2, # 113, # 117 and #109 travel Bay Street as far as Canal; the # 103 runs along Van Duzer Street and St. Paul's Avenue in Stapleton Heights. (Details under **St. George**.)

Grymes Hill and Silver Lake

Boundaries and Contiguous Areas: North: Louis Avenue; East: **Stapleton,** Van Duzer Street, and Vanderbilt Avenue; South: Clove Road and the Staten Island Expressway; West: Victory Boulevard.

One blustery afternoon, a salty sea breeze rattled maple and birch branches, garnishing Grymes Hill with russet fall leaves. Save for the outline of Wall Street's mist-shrouded skyline, you could have been in Westchester. Interspersed with narrow blacktop lanes and imposing houses, the hills of Staten Island radiate a rustic sub-urbanity.

The higher you climb any one of the island's myriad hills, the more imposing the homes become. Four-hundred-foot high Todt Hill, the tallest of Staten Island's peaks, is the toniest. Grymes Hill, nearer the ferry terminal, is the most intellectual: St. John's University and Wagner College cluster its slopes, the College of Staten Island lies in an adjacent valley. Though 12-story Sunrise Tower is co-op, there are 475 two-and three-bedroom rental apartments in the Grymes Hill Apartments Complex, built by Donald Trump's father in the 1940s. In addition, rental apartments can be found in remodeled one-family homes.

Silver Lake combines with Clove Lakes Park to form a sylvan green-belt. There are tennis courts, bridle paths, ice skating rink and a municipal golf course laid out around the reservoir, and between Clove Road and Broadway a small, accessible zoo with a first-rate reptile collection.

Area Code: 718

Post Offices: St. George, 45 Bay Street, Staten Island, NY 10301, 981-1313; Stapleton, 514 Bay Street, Staten Island, NY 10304, 727-2207.

Zip Codes: 10301, 10304

Emergency Hospitals (nearest): Bayley Seton Hospital, Bay Street and Vanderbilt Avenue, Staten Island, NY 10304, 390-6000; St. Vincent's Medical Center of Richmond, 355 Bard Avenue, Staten Island, NY 10301, 876-1234.

Library (nearest): Stapleton, 132 Canal Street, Staten Island, NY 10304, 727-0427.

Adult Education: College of Staten Island, Sunnyside campus (nearby), 715 Ocean Terrace, Staten Island, NY 10301, 982-2000; St. John's University, 300 Howard Avenue, Staten Island, NY 10301, 390-4545; Wagner College (and Wagner College Planetarium), 631

Howard Avenue, Staten Island, NY 10301, 390-3100.

Cultural Resources: Staten Island Zoo, 614 Broadway, Staten Island, NY 10310, 442-3100.

Transportation—Train: A steep climb is required to reach Grymes Hill from Stapleton, the nearest stop on the SIRT line. (Details under **St. George**.)

Transportation—Bus: The # 113 and # 117 buses traverse Van Duzer Street along the base of Grymes Hill; the # 6, # 106, # 111 and # 112 traveling Victory Boulevard connect with the # 6S shuttle bus at Clove Road. The shuttle follows Howard Avenue as far as the St. John campus. (Details under **St. George**.)

NEW JERSEY

Hoboken

Boundaries and Contiguous Areas: North: Weehawken; East: Hudson River; South: **Jersey City**; West: **Jersey City** and Union City.

Physically, Hoboken hasn't changed much since the early 1900s. Until recently. Most of this tidy, small (population 45,000) "Mile Square City" sandwiched between the Hudson River and Jersey bluffs was built between 1860 and 1910. By 1900 Hoboken was famous as the first American port of call for tens of thousands of immigrants, many of whom stayed close by finding jobs in the city's numerous light manufacturing plants. Industrious working and middle-class citizens built the simple, unadorned brownstone and brick row houses that comprise most of Hoboken's real estate, although the patrician Stevens family, who bought what was to become Hoboken soon after the Revolution, lived in relative isolation and splendor in the Castle Point section of town. This tract is now occupied by the Stevens Institute of Technology, the engineering school founded by the family. (And it is here beside the Hudson that a state-of-the-art scientific research center will rise when a partner can be found for the joint venture.)

Laid out in a grid that encompasses several pleasant, leafy squares, Hoboken, with its workingman's bars and sizeable Hispanic population, still retains a blue collar tinge.

But with the closing of Maxwell House Coffee, the last employer of any size within Hoboken's boundaries, the housing here has increasingly been occupied by refugees from across the Hudson, who now gaze back at a Manhattan skyline visually afloat on the river, gleaming in the morning sun and ablaze with lights at night.

In the early 1970s a tide of disaffected New Yorkers, many of them singles, was attracted to this community just ten minutes from Manhattan by subway (PATH). Artists and rock musicians as well as young professionals discovered Hoboken, and the row house renovations, the cafes, interesting shops and galleries dotting the original downtown and Washington Street neighborhoods show it. Where homesteaders pioneer, serious developers almost always follow. Certainly, the conversion to condos of tenement blocks along Monroe, Adams and the other "presidential" streets west of Washington, as well as new apartment buildings rising on once heavily industrial land in the southwest quadrant, bear decided witness to *that* fact.

Yet to be determined is the fate of Hoboken's mile-long riverfront scrunched between the humongous harborside developments planned for Weehawken to the north and under construction in Jersey City to the south. The huge Erie-Lackawanna Terminal building has been spruced up to house commercial tenants and a handsome Art Deco waiting room. Now, after 22 years, the Hoboken Ferry, with three vessels, plies the Hudson between Hoboken and Battery Park. But the projected $600 million waterfront revitalization plan is stalled at this writing. No matter. The very *idea* of transformation jolted Hoboken's housing market, which is expanding. *The Hoboken Reporter*, available free at 1311 Washington Street, is an excellent source of rentals, which tend to run about 25% below comparable Manhattan dwellings. For names of local brokers and a shares agency, refer to the chapter on **Apartment Hunting**.

Area Code: 201 (North and Central New Jersey).

Post Offices: Main Office, 89 River Street, Hoboken 07030, 659-3220. All branches have the same telephone number and zip: Castle Point Station, Stevens Institute of Technology; Uptown

Station, 57 W. 14th Street; Washington Street Station, 734 Washington Street; and West Side Station, 502 Grand Street.

Zip Code: 07030 covers all of Hoboken.

Police Station: # 1 Police Plaza, 108 Newark Street, Hoboken, 07030, 420-2100.

Emergency Hospital: St. Mary's Hospital, 308 Willow Avenue, Hoboken, 07030 792-8100.

Library: Hoboken Public Library, 500 Park Avenue, Hoboken, 07030, 420-2346.

Public School Education: Hoboken Board of Education, 1115 Clinton Street, 420-2162.

Cultural Resources: The Hoboken Civic Theater troupe uses the Union Club for performances; the Hoboken Chamber Orchestra gives concerts at the Demarest Grammar School. Membership in the Hoboken-North Hudson YMCA, with its tiled pool, workout rooms and movement classes, is an inexpensive alternative to the health and fitness centers proliferating here. American rock reigns at a number of clubs on Washington Street like The Elysian Cafe, # 1001, 659-9344, and Maxwell's, # 1039, 656-9632.

Transportation—Subway: PATH trains, 212-435-7000, shuttle between the Hoboken Station next to the Conrail (old Erie and Lackawanna Railroad) Terminal and Manhattan every 10 minutes from about 6:30 a.m. to 8:30 p.m., every 15 minutes between 8:30 and 11:45 and from then on every 30 minutes until 6:30 a.m. A direct line runs between Hoboken and the World Trade Center, and another between Hoboken and West 33rd Street and Sixth Avenue, making stops at Christopher near Hudson Street, then at 9th, 14th and 23rd Streets, all on Sixth Avenue.

Transportation—Bus: Frequent commuter bus service on the # 126 line operated by New Jersey Transit, 212-564-8484 (and be prepared to wait) for schedules, and on buses operated by Red

Apple Transit, 201-420-9697 and 212-564-8484, connect Hoboken Terminal and Manhattan's Port Authority Bus Terminal at Eighth Avenue and 40th Street (the South Wing).

Transportation—Ferry: Service between Hoboken and Battery Park. Ferries run weekdays every 10 minutes between 4 a.m. and 7 p.m. and every 20 minutes between 7 p.m. and 9 p.m., with no weekend runs. Prices are $2 one way, $18 for ten trips, and $62 for a monthly pass. For information call 908-GO-FERRY.

Jersey City

Boundaries and Contiguous Areas: North: **Hoboken**; East: Hudson River; South: Bayonne; West: Brunswick Street.

Jersey City, directly across the Hudson River from the World Trade Center, is not yet New York's "sixth borough." If, however, comparatively inexpensive commercial office space, riverfront development and a large stock of 19th century brick and brownstone townhouses are requisites for boroughhood, then Jersey City may yet make its point.

New Jersey's first city—"settled in 1630" says the historical marker erected in Paulus Hook, the oldest section of town—has survived three and a half centuries largely as a working-class community. Today it has a population of 280,000 and an enviable position five minutes by PATH train under the Hudson from Lower Manhattan.

The arrival of brownstoners presaged the current Jersey City revival. Twenty years ago "New Yorkers," emboldened by the successful restorations in Hoboken, began buying and reclaiming townhouses in the historic districts bordering Hamilton and Van Vorst Parks. Today, co-ops and condominium conversions are popping up in these neighborhoods as well as in the adjoining Paulus Hook historic district. And once Banker's Trust leased space at the vast Harborside Financial Center (as the rehabilitated Pennsylvania Railroad warehouse is now called), it became clear that back-office operations of large Manhattan corporations would prove a boon to the local economy. Now, gleaming skyscrapers soar along wide boulevards that connect Harborside with Newport, the enormous, $10-billion apartment, mall and townhouse-marina complex across the Hudson River from Manhattan's Battery Park City.

The redoubtable LeFrak organization has four red brick apartment blocks up and renting at Newport, just one stop— the Pavonia-Newport station—from Manhattan by PATH train. The studio to two-bedroom apartments account for 1,504 of the 9,000 rental and condo units planned for completion by 1995 in this 300-acre waterside development. Newport's partially-opened, semi-circular mall adds a number of new retail outlets to the department stores and other shops found up the hill on Jersey City's Journal Square.

West of the harbor developments and 35 minutes from Manhattan by PATH, a 1,176-unit project rises, phoenix-like, from the ashes of the former home of the New Jersey Giants, Roosevelt Stadium. Society Hill, as the condominium community has been dubbed, offers middle-priced town houses and apartments, marina, tennis courts, and two pools. With other projects already in the works, this K. Hovnanian project has spurred the revitalization of this up-and-coming area.

The Jersey Journal published every day but Sunday is the best source for Hoboken or Jersey City classified rental ads. In Manhattan, buy *The Journal* at newsstands in the World Trade Center, the 14th Street Downtown PATH station and outside the 33rd Street PATH station. See **Apartment Hunting** chapter for names of brokers.

Area Code: 201 (North and Central New Jersey).

Post Office: The main Post Office, 69 Montgomery Street, 915-7000, is located in Downtown.

Zip Code: 07302 covers the Downtown area; Port Liberté, 07305; Newport, 07310.

Police Station: East District, 207 Seventh Street, 547-5408.

Emergency Hospital: St. Francis Hospital, 25 McWilliams Place, 714-8900.

Library: The main branch of the Jersey City Public Library, 472 Jersey Avenue, 547-4500, is located in Downtown.

Public School Education: Jersey City Board of Education, 241 Erie Street, 915-6000.

Adult Education: St. Peter's College, 2641 Kennedy Boulevard, 333-4400, Jersey City State, 2039 Kennedy Boulevard, 200-2000, and the Jersey City branches of Hudson County Community Colleges, headquartered at 168 Sip Avenue, 656-2020, all offer evening classes but most are held in campuses up in Jersey City Heights, not in the Downtown area.

Cultural Resources: The Jersey City Museum, fourth floor, Jersey City Public Library, 472 Jersey Avenue, 547-4514. Liberty Science Center, 25 Phillip Street, Jersey City, 07305.

Transportation—Subway: On PATH, 212-435-7000, the trip between the four stops in Jersey City (Journal Square, Grove Street, Exchange Place and Pavonia-Newport) and the World Trade Center takes 10 minutes at most and trains run at four to six minute intervals during rush hours, every 10 to 15 and 30 minutes at other times. It takes 20 minutes at most from Journal Square or Grove Street to 33rd Street in Manhattan (with stops at Sixth Avenue and Christopher, 9th, 14th and 23rd Streets in between). Service is almost as frequent on the 33rd Street line as on the World Trade Center line. PATH trains also run to Hoboken and Newark from all four Jersey City stations.

Transportation—Bus: The Hudson Bus Co., 212-564-8484 or 201-653-2220, operates frequent service between Jersey City and Wall Street or the Port Authority Bus Terminal in Manhattan.

Manhattan Address Locator

Formulas for finding street and avenue addresses above 14th Street are described below. Crosstown street numbers follow a more-or-less set pattern; not so, avenue street numbers. In a town where 950 Amsterdam Avenue is at 107th Street, 950 Broadway at 23rd, 950 Fifth at 76th and 950 Third at 57th, the somewhat elaborate system used to discover the location of an avenue address is worth knowing.

East and West Side Avenues

To determine the cross street for an address on an avenue, proceed as follows: first, take off the last digit of the building number; second, divide the remainder by two; third, add or subtract the number given in the column below.

AVENUES A, B, C, D	Add 3
1ST AVENUE	Add 3
2ND AVENUE	Add 3
3RD AVENUE	Add 10
4TH AVENUE	Add 8
5TH AVENUE	
Up to 200	Add 13
Up to 400	Add 16
Up to 600	Add 18
Up to 775	Add 20
From 775 to 1286	
(Cancel last figure)	Subtract 18
6TH AVENUE	
(Ave. of the Americas)	Subtract 12
7TH AVENUE	
Below 110th Street	Add 12
Above 110th Street	Add 20
8TH AVENUE	Add 10
9TH AVENUE	Add 13
10TH AVENUE	Add 14
AMSTERDAM AVENUE	Add 60
BROADWAY	
(Above 23rd Street)	Subtract 30
COLUMBUS AVENUE	Add 60
CONVENT AVENUE	Add 127
LENOX AVENUE	Add 110
LEXINGTON AVENUE	Add 22
MADISON AVENUE	Add 26
MANHATTAN AVENUE	Add 100
PARK AVENUE	Add 35
WEST END AVENUE	Add 60

Central Park West and Riverside Drive do not fit into this formula. Divide the house number by 10 and add 60 to find the cross street on Central Park West; for Riverside Drive, divide the house number by 10 and add 72.

East Side Crosstown Streets

Fifth to Madison & Park: 1 to 99
Park to Lexington: 100 to 140
Lexington to Third: 140 to 199
Third to Second: 200 to 299
Second to First: 300 to 399
First to York: 400 to 499

West Side Crosstown below 58th

Fifth to Avenue of Americas: 1 to 99
Ave. of Americas to Seventh: 100 to 199
Seventh to Eighth: 200 to 299
Eighth to Ninth: 300 to 399
Ninth to Tenth: 400 to 499
Tenth to Eleventh: 500 to 599

West Side Crosstown above 58th

Central Park West to Columbus: 100 to 199
Columbus to Amsterdam: 200 to 299
Amsterdam to West End: 300 to 399
West End to Riverside: 400 to 499

Apartment Hunting

Renting an apartment in New York City is not the impossible dream it once was. In fact, Manhattan's supply of rental apartments has expanded in recent years rather than contracted. Expanded, that is, at the high end of the rental market, where there is now a glut. Except in some special categories, prices are off their 1988 peak by about 30%, and landlords have been offering concessions for several years now. Most recently, however, the market has tightened slightly and landlords and brokers have become somewhat less negotiable. Unfortunately, less expensive apartments (the affordable one-or two-bedroom, hold the Jacuzzi) are still hard to find. Non-subsidized middle income housing starts in Manhattan are nil.

Between 1985 and 1989, the Real Estate Board of New York estimates, construction was completed on some 19,242 condominiums and 15,892 rental apartments. Since then, demand has dropped behind supply and in a weakened economy apartment completions have fallen off an estimated 74%.

A saturated condominium market, paradoxically, has helped increase the supply of rental apartments. Condominiums in considerable numbers entered the rental pool when they were purchased for investment purposes rather than for owner occupancy and when they failed to attract buyers. They are offered as rentals through the building sales office or through real estate agencies dealing in rentals. As this trend has accelerated, pressure is put on cooperative boards to liberalize their subletting provisions. This in turn facilitates the rental of owner-occupied co-op apartments, with the result that still more units are added to the city's rental stock.

A third factor influencing the availability of rental apartments is the decontrol of rent controlled apartments. Of 155,000 rent controlled apartments on the city rolls in 1987, 35,000 had been decontrolled by 1992.

So it is that rental prices have bottomed out and, on the whole, actually decreased. In Manhattan's established neighborhoods, location doesn't much influence price. One rental expert estimates that in Greenwich Village and the neighborhoods between 23rd Street and 96th Street (Chelsea, the Upper East and West Sides, Murray Hill, Gramercy Park), the price difference between comparable apartments is almost negligible. If price is an object then, it is best to search in the developing Manhattan neighborhoods and in the boroughs.

With pluck, imagination and fortitude you can and will find an adequate place in an appropriate neighborhood. Various strategies for doing so are listed below in order of conventionality and practicality, but to start, some golden generalities:

- **Don't panic.** Don't be immobilized by what you may have heard. Negativism will get you nowhere—to live. Take as much time as you can possibly manage and be as rigorous as possible and your search will in all probability yield a pleasing apartment.

- **Be prepared for high rents**. Newcomers, especially, are subject to shock at even today's more realistic rents. In the long run it may just be possible to find that charming, sun-drenched apartment in the neighborhood of your dreams for a reasonable sum, but such gems take time and contacts, so brace yourself.

- **Be adventuresome but prudent**. The housing squeeze of the 1980s intensified gentrification of neighborhoods throughout the city. The middle class was on the move, turning yesterday's marginal areas into meccas for today's trend-setters. Behind dusty facades from the Bowery to upper Broadway lurk attractive, cozy apartments, but before getting too carried away, realize that not all areas are suitable, most certainly not for single women.

- **Inquire about a neighborhood.** Local police precincts (see listings under **Neighborhoods**) can supply valuable safety information about a particular neighborhood, street or block within their boundaries. Stop by the precinct for candid and well-founded opinions about the characteristics and police problems of a particular area.

• **Consider subletting or sharing to start.** If you are in desperate need of a roof and have not discovered a feasible rental, seriously consider these alternatives. Subletting or sharing buys time to find the optimum situation in the most suitable neighborhood.

Generalities out of the way, on to ways of finding space.

Newspaper Classified Advertisements

Because individual landlords as well as brokers place ads, classifieds sometimes are a means of avoiding brokerage commissions. Chances are, however, you will end up using a broker. The classifieds provide a good way of finding one and of discovering which brokers are active in a particular neighborhood.

The Sunday *New York Times* Real Estate section, printed Friday night and delivered to dealers sometime on Saturday, contains the best rental listings in the city. *The Times* actively discourages sale of the Sunday edition before the multisectioned paper is completed Saturday evening. However, many outlets sell the sections they have on hand (for full newspaper price) Saturday morning. Search and you may find. While far fewer in number, daily ads in *The Times* are also worth checking.

The Village Voice is a good source of rental listings for Manhattan as well as other boroughs. Newsstand deliveries are made around 5 a.m. Wednesday morning; the newsstand on the island behind the Seventh Avenue IRT Uptown Christopher Street subway entrance at Sheridan Square is one of the first places to receive delivery. You can also get early copies Tuesday night at the Village newstand on Astor/Lafayette.

***The Wall Street Journal*'s** Friday edition lists apartments for rent in "The Mart" classified section.

***The New York Post*'s** rental classifieds are best consulted on Friday. The Friday edition is printed Thursday night and delivered to all-night newsstands in the mid-Manhattan area (try stands at Grand Central or Pennsylvania Stations Thursday night around midnight). *The Post* (once again, Rupert Murdoch's toy) is a particularly good source for apartments in Queens, Brooklyn and The Bronx.

The Daily News' Brooklyn and Queens editions carry numerous rental classifieds for those boroughs. Listings in the Manhattan edition are negligible.

New York Press is a free weekly distributed each Wednesday. Look for it in restaurants, stores and street boxes below 28th Street, sparsely uptown. A good source for sublets.

The Jersey Journal, published in Jersey City Monday through Saturday, is the paper to consult for rentals in Hoboken and Jersey City. *The Journal* can be purchased at the World Trade Center and at newsstands adjoining the 14th Street and 33rd Street PATH stations in Manhattan.

New York City neighborhood newspapers—*The Villager*, *Chelsea-Clinton News*, *The West Side Spirit* (Upper West Side), *Our Town* (East Side) and others—occasionally carry a rental ad or two but are not prime sources. In Brooklyn, however, two weeklies, the **Brooklyn Heights Press**, 129 Montague Street, second floor, and **The Phoenix**, 33 Flatbush Avenue, carry sublet and rental advertisements. First copies of the Press are delivered to the office around 2 p.m. Wednesday afternoon, and **The Phoenix** reaches Brooklyn newsstands early Thursday morning.

Real Estate Brokers

New York City's real estate brokers focus on sales rather than rentals. However, some agencies specialize in rentals, and many have brokers who handle nothing else. At the end of this section, we've listed the names of real estate brokers as a service. Their presence in this book indicates no endorsement. Rather, firms and the neighborhoods they cover are given as possible starting points for your search.

Real estate agencies tend to concentrate their efforts on one or a series of contiguous neighborhoods, for example: the Upper East Side;

Chelsea, the Village and SoHo; Gramercy Park and Murray Hill. If your heart is set on one location, it is important to discover the most savvy brokers in that area. If almost any neighborhood will do, make sure you list with several knowledgeable firms in order to get the coverage you need.

Count on spending some time and effort discovering a broker sympathetic to your needs and capable of showing you suitable places. In the long run, a broker may well be the best lead to a decent apartment.

Broker commissions for unfurnished apartments currently range between 10% and 15% of one year's rent, and in New Jersey, where rentals are more generally available, one month's rent or, in rare cases, no commission at all. But in the softer real estate market of the 1990s, brokers have eased up as well. It isn't unusual for brokers to reduce a fee or eliminate it all together. So be firm and negotiate.

Referral agencies that extract payment in return for a list of available apartments or require a registration fee are to be avoided. Under recently passed legislation, referral agencies are obligated to find an apartment for you if you pay their fee. Legislation or no, it is best to steer clear of them.

Recommendations for finding a real estate broker:

• Gather names from appealing classified listings.

• If your heart is set on one locale try some of the smaller firms whose storefronts you'll notice when pounding the pavements. These firms seldom advertise but are often good sources for listings in the immediate vicinity.

• Ask friends, firms and family for suggestions. As previously mentioned, not all capable agents with good lists advertise widely.

• As a start, we've compiled a list of brokers who handle rentals in Manhattan, parts of The Bronx, Brooklyn, Queens, and Hoboken and Jersey City, NJ.

Manhattan Real Estate Brokers
(Area Code 212)

- Ambrose-Mar Elia Co., 770 Lexington Avenue, NYC 10021, 752-7789: Upper East and West Sides. 137 Waverly Place, NYC 10004, 675-6980: Gramercy Park to the Battery.

- Brocor Realty, 1202 Lexington Avenue, NYC 10028, 996-1666. East Side from 96th Street to Gramercy Park.

- Douglas Elliman, 654 Madison Avenue, NYC 10021, 705-4700. Upper East and West Sides.

- Dwelling Quest Corp., 226 East 54th Street, Suite 400, NYC 10022, 754-3000. Upper East and West Sides.

- The Feathered Nest, 310 Madison Avenue, Suite 630, NYC 10017, 867-8500. All Manhattan.

- Selena Godeau, 88 University Place, NYC 10013, 645-1800. SoHo, Chelsea, East and West Village.

- Joseph H. Green Realty, 4310 Broadway, NYC 10033, 795-0144. Washington Heights and Inwood.

- Sandra Greer Real Estate, 201 East 77th Street, NYC 10021, 472-1878. Mostly East Side, Upper and Lower.

- Gumley-Haft Inc., 110 East 59th Street, NYC 10022, 371-2525. Luxury rentals, Upper East Side.

- Macklowe, 142 West 57th Street, NYC 10019, 265-5900. All Manhattan.

- Alice F. Mason, Ltd., 635 Madison Avenue, NYC 10022, 832-8870. Luxury rentals on the Upper East Side primarily.

- Moss Realty, 2508 Broadway, Suite 1-A, NYC 10025, 222-4040. All Manhattan.

- Prolific Realty, 202 Waverly Place, NYC 10014, 989-3012. Greenwich Village.

- Frederick M. Reed and Co., 405 Park Avenue, NYC 10022, 826-2150. Upper East Side.

- Eugene Rooney, 191 Avenue of the Americas, NYC 10013, 691-8380. Chelsea and West Village.

- Salon Realty Co., 316 East 89th Street, NYC 10128, 534-3131. Upper East Side.

- Schein Realty Co., 1425 Second Avenue, NYC 10021, 861-2400. Upper East Side, Upper West Side and Clinton primarily.

- J. I. Sopher & Co., 425 East 61st Street, NYC 10021, 303-4000. Upper East Side and Manhattan generally.

- Robert Stein, 827 West 181st Street, NYC 10033, 928-3805. Washington Heights.

- Stevens Co., 2350 Broadway, NYC 10024, 580-3737. Upper West Side.

- Wendy Walters & Associates, 201 West 77th Street, NYC 10024. Upper West Side.

The Bronx
(Area Code 718)

- E.R.A. Susan Goldy & Co., 6114 Riverdale Avenue, Bronx 10471, 549-4116. Riverdale.

- Trebach Realty, 3801 Greystone, Bronx 10463, 543-7174. Riverdale.

Brooklyn Real Estate Brokers
(Area Code 718)

- Heights Cranford Agency, 144 Montague Street, Brooklyn 11201, 624-7000. Brooklyn Heights, Cobble Hill, Boerum Hill, Park Slope.

- Kazeroid and Aberman Realty, 196 Seventh Avenue, Brooklyn 11215, 499-8200. Park Slope.

- William B. May Co., 150 Montague Street, Brooklyn 11201, 875-1289, Brooklyn Heights, Cobble Hill, Carroll Gardens; 397 Flatbush Avenue, Brooklyn 11238, 230-5500, Park Slope, Prospect Park.

- Naida McSherry, 275 Clinton Avenue, Brooklyn 11205, 230-0030. Fort Greene and Clinton Hill exclusively.

- Carl F. Peek, Inc., 174 Court Street, Brooklyn 11201, 935-9800. Brooklyn Heights, Cobble Hill and vicinity.

- Patricia Perlman, 32 Court Street, Brooklyn 11201, 855-8708. Brooklyn Heights, Park Slope, Cobble Hill, Boerum Hill, Carroll Gardens.

- Renaissance Properties, 102 Hoyt Street, Brooklyn 11217, 875-5650. Fort Greene and Clinton Hill.

Queens Real Estate Brokers
(Area Code 718)

- Crest Haven Realty, Inc., 28-17 Astoria Boulevard, Astoria 11102, 545-7666. Astoria.

- Roslyn Deller, 39-68 45th Street, Sunnyside 11104, 786-0995. Sunnyside.

- Green-Ways Realty, 2 Tennis Place, Forest Hills 11375, 544-1952. Forest Hills, Kew Gardens, Rego Park.

- Lane Realty, 107-40 Queens Boulevard, Forest Hills 11375, 268-3500. Forest Hills, Kew Gardens, Rego Park.

- H.K. Benjamen, 212-89 26th Avenue, Bay Terrace Shopping Center, Bayside 11360, 423-4330. Bayside.

- Nu Place Realty, 120-10 Queens Boulevard, Kew Gardens 11415, 793-9500. Forest Hills, Kew Gardens, Rego Park, Briarwood.

- Lois Schenck Real Estate, 46-15 Skillman Avenue, Sunnyside 11104, 706-0957. Sunnyside, Woodside.

- Terrace Realty, 16 Station Square, Forest Hills Gardens, Forest Hills 11375, 268-1045. Forest Hills, Rego Park, Kew Gardens.

Staten Island Real Estate Brokers
(Area Code 718)

- Appleseed Agency—Century 21, 2043 Richmond Avenue, New Springville 10314, 698-9797. North Shore.

- St. George Realty-Century 21, 531 Forest Avenue, St. George 10310, 273-6200. Grymes Hill, St. George, Stapleton. Sublets.

New Jersey Real Estate Brokers
(Area Code 201)

- Boyne Real Estate, 303 Grove Street, Jersey City 07302, 451-0950. Jersey City.

- Eileen Cappock, 115 Washington Street, Hoboken 07030, 792-5200. Hoboken.

- Severino Realty, 920 Washington Street, Hoboken 07030, 653-1800. Hoboken.

- Singleton and Galman, 1106 Washington Street, Hoboken 07030, 656-5400.

- West Bank Realty, Inc., 313 First Street, Hoboken 07030, 792-0100. Hoboken.

New Buildings

Renovated factories, warehouses and other commercial buildings occasionally add new rental units to the city's supply. Apartments in reconstructed or totally new buildings command top dollar. However, it is often possible to avoid brokers' commissions in these buildings when landlords and managers pay on-site rental agents to fill the buildings as quickly as possible. The agents, as employees of the landlord, charge no commission.

Direct Action

In a town where intrepid apartment hunters used to read the obituary columns with as much intensity as the real estate classifieds, no one need feel self-conscious about tackling landlords, managing agents, superintendents or local merchants in order to locate a place in a particular neighborhood or building.

Consider trying some of these alternatives:

• **Call the managing agent of a likely building.** The firm's or agent's name is usually posted near a building's entrance. If no telephone number is given, check the phone book.

• **Speak with the superintendent directly.** To find him, check the building directory, buzzer listings or, in the case of the smaller brownstones with shared part-time supers, your man could be the person sweeping the steps or putting garbage cans out on the sidewalk.

If an apartment is available, the super or manager will sometimes send you to a broker to gain access. If a vacant apartment is found through independent efforts, you are not liable for the broker's fee. However, since reasonable apartments are in short supply, need usually overrides the fine points of the legal situation; most people prefer to pay the commission rather than go without the apartment. Once secure in your nest, if you want redress, file a complaint with the Division of Licenses, New York Department of State, 270 Broadway, NYC 10007, 212-417-5747. This may eventually result in a settlement.

- **Pavement pounding** accompanied by incessant querying of merchants, stoop sitters, dog walkers, postmen—indeed anyone who looks like a resident of the neighborhood— can yield results as well as blisters.

- For those intrepid souls determined to find an apartment in a specific building or block there is always **Cole's Metropolitan Householders Directory**, known familiarly as "Cole's Directory" or the "criss cross directory." This reverse telephone book lists addresses first and residents second. The names and telephone numbers of those living at any given address are listed by building, block by block.

     Cole's does not note building owners per se, but it does carry the building's phone number if there is one. If the place is small, you can gamble on finding the owner by dialing the residents listed at the given address. Reference copies of Cole's Directories for all five boroughs are available in the North Central Reading Room of the New York Public Library, 42nd Street and Fifth Avenue. The Business Section of the Mid-Manhattan Library, across the street at 455 Fifth Avenue at 40th Street, has the annual Manhattan edition of Cole's in its reference stacks.

- For the record, some but not all apartment buildings are listed in each borough's **Yellow Pages** by street and number under the alphabetical heading "Apartments and Apartment Houses." Others are listed alphabetically by name.

Word of Mouth

The grapevine approach—broadcasting your need through a network of local friends—is often an effective means to a desired apartment. However, when you're new to town the chances of having such a network are probably slim. But do use any contacts available. Parents can call old college chums. Who knows, their children may be leaving a desirable place. Your college friends may have a lead; their in-laws may, too. Nine phone calls may an apartment produce— but may not either. In any case, personal contacts are often a shot at the type of place that never makes it as far as *The Times* or a broker's office.

Bulletin Boards

Certain neighborhoods, particularly the newer, more homogeneous communities such as SoHo and Tribeca, as well as some large buildings, have bulletin boards (or blank wall space—cork isn't a prerequisite) where an occasional apartment turns up among the sheets offering children's skis, a ride to California and opportunities for self-improvement. Inquire locally to find out which bar, supermarket or grocery store serves this neighborhood function. Bulletin boards in university areas also include valuable information, notably New York University, Columbia, and Hunter College.

House Organs

Many corporations and organizations publish newsletters or magazines for their personnel that print employee advertisements (Time-Warner's *F.Y.I.* comes to mind).

Sublets and the occasional rental turn up in these columns, and it is worth asking friends working for likely concerns to check their in-house publication for leads.

College-Related Associations

Various New York alumni associations are addressing the difficulty graduates have settling or relocating in the city. Contact your alumni office or local group to see if they can help. Some university clubs also offer advice and an occasional lead.

Employers

Increasingly, larger companies are using, and paying for, the services of relocation firms to find suitable long-and short-term apartment rentals for their executives and to help solve the various problems associated with moving and settling in. The fortunate employee is saved money and headaches in the bargain. Presumably you'll be informed by the company for which you are working whether it is prepared to offer help with your search for living quarters.

Some 25 major companies belong to the Open Housing Center, Inc., a nonprofit organization located at 594 Broadway, 212-941-6101, which specializes in resettlement counselling and locating housing for employees. Undoubtedly, you will be told if your employer is a subscriber. We mention the center because it also publishes a number of useful pamphlets for sale to the public at large about New York City housing.

Sublets

Most brokers offer long-term sublets and advertise them, together with regular rentals, in local newspapers. Leaseholders of rent stabilized or exceptionally reasonable apartments have been known to ask for fixture fees or key money in a sublet situation. While some people do pour money and energy into rehabilitating an inexpensive rental apartment and may deserve compensation for their efforts when they move, fixture fees that reflect no real value are tantamount to key money, which is illegal.

Consider the furnished sublet as a useful interim measure. Available long or short term, sublets often provide the time needed to discover the optimum rental apartment. Then, too, there is always the possibility that the original tenant will decide not to return, et voila, no need to move until the original lease runs out.

Prime sources for sublets include:

- *The Village Voice* with its special "Sublets" classified section.

- *The New York Times*, which lists sublets under "Apartments—Furnished" and "Apartments—Unfurnished," # 1501 to # 1516.

- *New York Press* is a free weekly distributed each Wednesday. Look for it in restaurants, stores and street boxes below 28th Street, sparsely uptown. Good source for sublets.

- **Brokers** A number of sublet specialists advertise in the *Voice* and *New York Times*. Typically, commissions on furnished rentals run between one-half and one month's rent for periods of less than nine months. Most agencies charge 15% for longer sublets.

Four brokers currently specializing in sublets:

• The Feathered Nest, 310 Madison Avenue, NYC 10017, 212-867-8500. Call for appointment.

• J. Senter, 211 East 51st Street, Suite 4E, NYC 10022, 212-935-8730. Call for appointment.

• Short Term Housing, 862 Lexington Avenue, NYC 10021, 212-570-2288. Call for appointment.

• Urban Ventures, 38 West 32nd Street, NYC 10018, 212-594-5650. Call for appointment.

• **Bulletin boards** in large buildings, bars or other neighborhood locations. Large apartment complexes have lists for rental apartments the proverbial block long. However, leaseholders arrange sublets directly and occasionally post notices on community bulletin boards. Check with the management of these big units to see if they have a central sublet source.

• In-house publications tend to be a better source of sublets than of rentals.

Sharing

One of the best solutions to cutting high housing costs, particularly for young, single people, is an apartment share. But if you are just arriving in the city and don't know anyone, you may not have anyone to share with. If networking with old college buddies fails to turn up anything, your best bet is probably the newspapers or a roommate-finding service.

To find a room or bed in someone else's apartment check the *Times* ads under "Apartments to Share," # 1696, and the *Voice*'s "Shares." Some leaseholders prefer to have roommates pre-screened and list with agencies that arrange apartment shares for a flat fee up front.

Reputations ebb and flow; we can't guarantee satisfaction. But if you want to investigate this option, two of the firms in Manhattan are:

- Roommates—Apartment Placement Services, 212-288-9825 or 212-724-2800 ext. 271. Elizabeth Greer specializes in placing college graduates and young professionals in shared apartments throughout the city. The $350 fee covers an in-depth, hour-long interview and as many listings—over as long a period as necessary—to find the best situation. Roommates also handles rentals and sublets for a $450 fee.

- Roommate Finders, 250 West 57th Street, Suite 1629, NYC 10019, 212-489-6862, open Monday-Friday noon to 8, Saturday and Sunday noon to 6. For the $175 fee the client, after filling out a registration sheet covering personal habits and preferences and discussing specifications in a half-hour interview, is given copies of the information sheets on prospective apartments and/or roommates. You can call daily for new listings, and if you find your own roommate or apartment, you are entitled to a 50% refund. Listing is free.

A Tenant's Guide to Subletting and Apartment Sharing, published by The New York State Tenant and Neighborhood Coalition, 198 Broadway, Room 1000, New York, NY 10038, 212-695-8922, has recently been updated. Well worth $10 (join the Coalition for $20 and get a tenants' rights newsletter as well as the pamphlet free), this invaluable 22-page guide details the practical and legal ramifications of apartment sharing and the ins and outs of subletting to, as well as from, another individual.

Money Matters

Even though this book begins by describing New York's neighborhoods and how to hunt for an apartment, the fact is that opening a bank account and establishing credit will undoubtedly be a newcomer's first order of business. High time, then, for information about personal savings and checking accounts, credit cards and, for your edification come April 15, New York State and City income tax procedures.

Bank Accounts

While it is still probably true that most people choose their bank for its location, not its logo, innovative services, differing interest rates and minimum account requirements can be important determinants in where you decide to put your money. If the range and quality of services a bank offers is more important to you than convenience, shop around. The city's 3 biggest retail banks, **Citibank**, **Chase** and **Chemical**—which includes the old Manufacturer's Hanover have over 50 branches each in Manhattan alone.

Traditional distinctions between commercial banks, savings banks and brokerage houses have become blurred. As one bank officer commented, "There are no set rules anymore. The situation is completely fluid." Says another: "It's a consumer's market today. Our bank's strategy is to establish a relationship with each customer." That's why you'll now find special windows for particularly affluent customers and business clients commonplace, savings banks offering checking accounts, and fee-free regular checking accounts that require a $1,500 minimum balance at one bank, $3,000 at another.

What's next? Anything that will make it easier for customers "to access their money with speed, efficiency and convenience." This means do-your-own-banking programs for computer owners, traveler's checks and cash advances on VISA and MasterCard at multilingual ATM machines in airports, bus terminals and train stations, and being able to use your New York bank card at a network of affiliated banks anywhere in the country.

• **Checking accounts** Obtain an application blank and take it, filled out—two references are required, usually the name of your current, or previous, bank and that of your employer— to the branch where you intend to bank, together with two signed pieces of identification: a driver's license, credit card, draft card, student ID with photo are all acceptable. Some banks require a minimum start-up deposit, some don't. Your account can be opened immediately, but checks and deposit slips won't be issued until your signature is verified. Some firms arrange for employees to open accounts at their own banks, which facilitates the process and may allow you to obtain fee-free checking regardless of your balance. Check with your employer's benefits person.

"Regular" or non-interest-earning personal checking accounts that eliminate service charges as long as a minimum daily balance is maintained are standard today. Another way to obtain fee-free checking is to link a money market, certificate of deposit or savings account kept in the same bank to your regular checking account. Bank charges currently run between $9 and $15 for any month the balance drops below the specified minimum. Similar charges are levied on interest-earning "NOW" checking accounts if they fall below required minimum balances.

• **Savings accounts** Follow the procedures detailed above for checking accounts to apply for a "statement" savings account that provides monthly statements of all transactions and can be linked to your checking account. At this writing, statement accounts generally pay no more than 3% interest, reflecting the long term drop in interest rates. Most banks require an average minimum balance of $1,500 a month; fall below that amount and you'll have to pay maintenance charges.

After establishing good banking and credit relationships, you can apply for a mortgage, an auto, personal or education loan and credit cards. Bank cards for use in cash machines are issued automatically to new customers.

Credit Cards

On the off chance that your mailbox hasn't been filled with credit card applications you can call to request one. A recent twist to consider: frequent-flyer miles earned as you use your card. Shop around for the one best suited to your travel needs.

- **American Express**, 800-528-4800. A Green Card costs $55 per year and requires proof of an income of $15,000 or over. A Gold Card costs $75 a year, entitles the holder to a line of credit, and requires proof of $20,000 or more in income. The Platinum Card costs $300 a year and you don't call American Express, they call you. If, after being deemed credit worthy and, not so incidentally, you have charged at least $10,000 a year on your Green or Gold Card in the past, then you're invited to join the Platinum set.

- **Diner's Club**, 800-525-9135. Diner's issues one card, which costs $80 a year and requires proof of an annual income of $25,000 or more.

- **Discover Cards**, 800-347-2683, are issued by Dean Witter Financial. There is no annual fee for the basic Discover Card, and minimum income is judged on a case-by-case basis, e.g., college students can apply and face different credit criteria.

   Discover also issues a Private Issue Card, which carries a $40 annual fee and requires higher income.

With both cards, you get cash back at the end of each anniversary year. The basic card refunds up to 1 percent of your total purchases after the first $3,000 of use, and the Private Issue refunds 1.5 percent after the first $3,000.

Report lost or stolen cards by calling the toll-free number.

- **VISA and MasterCard** can be obtained from a variety of financial service organizations, usually banks, but nowadays everyone seems to be offering their own version. There used to be little difference between various VISA and MasterCard options; today, however, annual fees may be waived, interest rates vary and many cards offer frequent flyer miles. It pays to shop around especially if you don't pay off your balance every month.

• **Department stores** Most accept personal checks for the amount of the purchase, but with qualifications: two forms of identification, your driver's license and a major credit card or department store charge card, are usually required. In addition, some stores accept only checks printed with the customer's name and address. Out-of-state checks and third-party checks may be refused altogether.

Virtually all the major New York City department stores now accept American Express and/or MasterCard and VISA. (See chapter on **Shopping** for specifics on who accepts what.) However, store charge accounts do offer advantages: advance notice of sales, mail or phone orders, no annual fee, and at Bloomingdale's and Macy's, the option of spreading payments over a period of time for an added finance charge. Fill out the store's application form, which asks for personal statistics, bank and credit information, and recent employment history. Accounts are approved within three to eight weeks, depending on how long verification takes.

Macy's offers instant store charge account privileges to credit card holders who apply in person with two pieces of identification. Brooks Brothers accepts all major credit cards. Apply in person and they will open an account for you on the spot.

If you don't like wasting hours dialing 800 numbers after a credit card theft or loss, register your cards with an agency that will cancel them for you. For instance, Hotline Credit Card Bureau of America, 800-327-1284, charges a yearly fee for the service and guarantees card replacement. Major banks offer a similar service to their VISA customers for an annual fee.

Income Taxes

Heralded by freshly painted H&R Block signs and black-bordered boxes in the newspapers warning "Only 10 more days to file your income tax returns," April 15 arrives every 365 days. In New York City, the Internal Revenue Service and NewYork Department of Taxation and Finance provide literature and telephone taxpayer information services designed to answer your tax questions year round.

- **Federal** income tax forms can be obtained by calling 800-829-3676, or call 212-732-0100 (for residents of Manhattan). Call 718-596-3770 to obtain explanatory literature as well as answers to specific questions, such as which of the three tax forms—1040EZ, 1040A or 1040—you should use. The staff at the Internal Revenue Service office, open 7:30 a.m. to 5 p.m. downtown at 120 Church Street, provides instruction in the fine art of calculating your Federal income tax but won't do it for you.

- **New York State and New York City** use a combined income tax form. Call 800-462-8100 to receive forms: if you use either IRS 1040EZ or 1040A, choose the IT 100, which you fill in and let the State tax people calculate for you, or the IT 200, which you calculate yourself; if you file the Federal 1040 long form, you'll need the IT 201. The number for taxpayer assistance is 800-C-A-L-L-T-A-X.

    Your Federal Adjusted Gross Income is the tax base for state and city taxes. New York State Taxable Income is calculated by adding and subtracting various New York State "modifications." The New York City Resident's Income Tax is based on New York State taxable income. Residents pay a percentage of the State category into which their income falls.

Deposits and Leases

Once theory has been put into practice and an apartment found, be prepared to sign the lease and a check or two. But before you do, we suggest you read *Rent Smart*, a 37-page booklet that untangles lease legalese and describes tenants' rights in New York State. Call 518-474-1471 or write to the State Consumer Protection Board, 99 Washington Avenue, Albany, NY 12210, for a free copy.

Deposits

Your first check will undoubtedly be a deposit held by the broker or landlord while credit references are being researched. Don't go apartment hunting without money in the bank and checkbook in hand. The first person to put down a deposit (customarily one month's rent) with the landlord or broker stands the best chance of signing the lease. The credit investigation should take no more than a couple of days if you are already employed or can substantiate a reasonable gross annual income through bank and savings accounts. You may be charged $50 for the credit check in a co-op sublet.

Once you are pronounced creditworthy, the deposit check should be accepted as your first month's rent, two months in advance for some short-term rentals. The interest-earning security deposit, one month's rent generally, will be refunded at the end of your lease, providing the apartment is left in the same condition in which it was found. If a real estate broker is involved, your third payment will be the broker's fee, which currently averages about 15% of the first year's rent. In some cases, the owner will pay all or part of the fee.

Leases

Read the lease carefully before signing it and all those checks. Married couples should have both names on the lease; unmarried couples should try to get both names on the lease, though the landlord is not legally obliged to do so. A standard form is customary. Be familiar with the content of the entire lease, but pay special attention to the end of the form where the qualifying clauses are typed. Clauses should specify any agreements made with the landlord about alterations, repairs, painting and new appliances. They will undoubtedly include any restrictions the landlord cares to impose. If you have a dog, be sure the lease states that dogs are allowed to inhabit the apartment.

Determine how the building is heated and who pays the bills. If the landlord is responsible, there must be a clause in the lease to this effect. Traditionally, landlords pay for steam heat and gas heat. Tenants customarily pay for exceedingly costly electrical heat. In some buildings gas and electricity charges for stoves and ovens are included in the rent, but, in general, count on being billed directly by Con Edison for all utilities in the apartment proper.

Since 1982 **smoke detectors**, essentially one per sleeping area, have been mandatory in New York apartments. Tenants are responsible for the repair and maintenance of these alarms.

The landlord is legally responsible for ridding apartments of **cockroaches**. Some provide routine exterminator services; others simply take care of the matter as it crops up. Obviously, the ounce of prevention method is preferable and you should know in advance if regular service is included in your lease.

Check for a sublet clause. Subletting is allowed "with the landlord's permission." This means he can say no. To avoid permission being withheld capriciously, the clause should mention that the apartment can be sublet with written permission from the landlord "which permission shall not be *unreasonably* withheld."

Conversely, if you are subletting an apartment from the original leasee, determine whether or not you have a legal right to be there. If you have questions about the propriety of a subtenancy and the apartment falls under city or state-enforced guidelines, try calling one of the organizations listed below (the Rent Stabilization Association, DHCR office or the New York Loft Tenants) with your concerns.

Subletting a cooperative apartment can be daunting. Not only is it necessary to prove yourself to the landlord but you must pass the scrutiny of the building's board of directors, too. However, the traditionally restrictive subletting practices of many cooperative buildings are slowly being liberalized. Free from boards of directors, individually-owned condominium apartments can be sublet at the owner's discretion.

Rent Stabilization and Rent Control

Many—950,000 is a ballpark figure—apartments on the market today are *rent stabilized*. Few if any of the estimated 120,000 *rent controlled* apartments ever reach the market. They either are passed among qualifying members of one family like heirlooms or, once vacant, automatically become rent stabilized (apartments in large buildings) or decontrolled (apartments in buildings with five units or less). Buildings constructed before February 1, 1947, come under rent control. Instituted in 1969, rent stabilization covers apartments in buildings constructed between February 1, 1947, and December 31, 1973.

Rents for apartments built after January 1, 1974, are not bound by any laws except for those special few where real estate tax abatements or rehabilitation laws apply. Buildings with less than six apartments are free from any rent restrictions unless they contain rent controlled units. Rents in condominiums and cooperative apartments are left to the owner's discretion.

Stabilized rents negotiated each June under the aegis of the New York Rent Guidelines Board go into effect the following October 1. A rent stabilized landlord in New York City is not obligated to sign a lease for more than one year the first time around. However, when it comes time to renew, he must offer tenants the right to sign a one-or two-year lease. A three-year lease may be requested but the landlord is not required to provide one.

The Rent Stabilization Association (the *landlord* group), 1500 Broadway, NYC 10036, will answer questions about tenants' rights under rent stabilization. Call 212-944-4700. The New York Division of Housing and Community Renewal (DHCR), 92-31 Union Hall Street, Jamaica 11433, 718-739-6400, handles complaints from both *rent stabilized* and *rent controlled* tenants. Complaints as well as inquiries about *co-op conversions* can be addressed *in writing* only to the New York State Attorney General, 120 Broadway, NYC 10271.

If your apartment is rent controlled or rent stabilized, call the State DHCR office in your borough with any questions or problems: Upper Manhattan, above 110th Street, 163 West 125th Street, 212-870-8930; Lower Manhattan, below 110th Street, 156 William Street, 212-240-6010; The Bronx, 1 Fordham Plaza, The Bronx, 718-519-5700; Brooklyn, 91 Lawrence Street, Brooklyn, 718-643-4141; Queens, 164-19 Hillside Avenue, Jamaica, 718-739-6400; Staten Island, 350 St. Mark's Place, 718-816-0277.

Tenants of any stripe can call 212-960-4800, the Central Complaint Bureau of the New York City Department of Housing and Preservation, 215 West 125th Street, NYC 10027, 24 hours a day, seven days a week. Bureau operators answer questions and pass along housing complaints to the appropriate New York City agency.

Lofts

During the 1960s the trickle of hardy artists working and living illegally in industrial lofts located in zoned-for-manufacturing-only districts became a proper stream. Pressure to rectify the situation resulted in the legalization of lofts for Artists in Residence during the Lindsay administration. An applicant had to prove working artist status to qualify for AIR space. Plenty of prospective tenants didn't qualify though—alternative life style enthusiasts flocked to Lower Manhattan, Jill Clayburgh led thousands of divorcees who would be painters to SoHo—and illegal loft tenancies proliferated.

The problem was readdressed and in 1982, Article 7-C was added to New York State's Multiple Dwelling Law. Loft living was legalized in manufacturing buildings (buildings that did not have residential Certificates of Occupancy) containing three or more rental units. Some parts of the city—sections of the Garment District and the Washington meat market in the way-West Village, for example—were exempted, but in Chelsea and Lower Manhattan, in the Fulton Ferry area of Brooklyn and Long Island City in Queens, numerous loft dwellers finally found themselves enfranchised.

The loft law did not, however, create complete order out of chaos, and the legality of some loft-living situations is still in doubt. Anyone considering renting or subletting a loft is well advised to check with one of the three loft groups currently active in Manhattan before signing the lease:

- **Lower Manhattan Loft Tenants, Inc.**, 200 Broadway, 212-344-8866. An educational and informational, not-for-profit organization concerned with all aspects of residential lofts. The Loft Tenants willingly counsel prospective loft dwellers—renters and purchasers alike. They hold free weekly clinics Tuesdays 5:30—7 p.m. and will answer questions regarding recent updates to the loft law.

- **The New York City Loft Board**, 116 Nassau Street, 11th Floor, 212-788-4636, is the city agency charged with overseeing the legalization of residential lofts.

- **The New York State Tenant and Neighborhood Coalition, Inc.** is, in their own words, "a statewide membership organization dedicated to passage of stronger tenant protection laws, stronger enforcement of existing laws, and creation of decent, affordable housing". They publish a concise and exceedingly useful pamphlet entitled *A Tenant's Guide to Subletting and Apartment Sharing* ($9 and available from the Coalition at 198 Broadway, Room 1000, New York, NY 10038). Other booklets for tenants are planned.

Getting Settled

Let's see. You've opened a bank account and established credit and have finally found an apartment. So now, keys and lease in hand, it's time to have utilities connected and the telephone installed. You can really make yourself at home once you can cook and call; really settle in once you possess a library card and can vote. The how-to's follow.

Consolidated Edison

Call Customer Service, 212-614-2100, to have utilities turned on. A personal visit from Con Ed is not necessary unless the prior tenant's service was cut off for non-payment. Expect to wait at least one business day before service commences. Deposits are no longer required for residential accounts.

Telephone Service

The three most readily apparent results of the historic 1984 breakup of AT&T have been lower long distance rates as a result of competition from newly-organized long distance carriers, cheaper prices for a burgeoning selection of telephone equipment, and higher charges for local telephone service, thanks to the fact that now-independent regional companies such as NYNEX (the new name for New York Telephone) lost that profitable long distance business which once subsidized local rates.

To institute new service, call the appropriate business office: Manhattan, 212-890-2350; Bronx, 718-890-2450; Brooklyn, 718-890-1450; Queens, 718-389-9940; Staten Island, 718-890-1450. If you can answer three out of six credit questions positively, no deposit is required. If you flunk the test, the company requests a deposit, which accumulates interest and is refunded in a year's time.

Telephones can be rented from AT&T, call 800-555-8111, but most people prefer to buy their telephones outright from either AT&T, a department store (Macy's has a particularly good selection) or specialty shops such as the Fone Booth, 12 East 53rd Street, NYC 10022, 212-751-8310.

Long distance service is provided by AT&T, 800-222-0300, and other carriers, which quote cheaper residential rates. These companies include GTE Sprint, 800-877-4646; ITT Longer Distance, 800-526-3000; MCI Execunet, 800-624-2222; RCI, 800-458-7000; and Western Union, 800-257-4900. Variables, other than rates, include volume discounts, monthly minimums and the fact that AT&T may offer slightly more comprehensive overseas service. Check around. But remember, a few New York City exchanges are still unequipped to give alternate carriers the same direct access AT&T gets; you must dial an extra five digits from some exchanges to obtain non-AT&T long distance service.

Newcomers or not, most New Yorkers aren't aware of how much good information can be found in the city's telephone books. The White Pages includes an extensive listing of community service numbers as well as government listings and an emergency care guide. The Yellow Pages is almost in itself a guide to New York City. Seek it as a reference for historical sites and landmarks, public transportation maps, a yearly calendar of events, and sports stadiums and concert hall seating charts! The Business to Business Yellow Pages, which lists all wholesalers and manufacturers, is free of charge and can be obtained by calling your local telephone office. Call 800-426-8686 to purchase consumer and business-to-business 800 directories.

To the familiar toll-free 800 numbers, which are proliferating as a means of delivering information, help and merchandising services, have been added a bewildering array of "Dial-It" numbers for the use of which the *caller* is billed. Want to know your horoscope, the Spanish lottery results, the Dow Jones closing, who won the third race at Hialeah this afternoon, last night's wrestling match, or the time? You can dial a 976 number to find out. For more money, sometimes, you can dial-a-prayer or an insult, get a tarot card reading, enter a joke contest, answer a trivia question, get a soap opera update or make a date by calling a 540 number. Consult the NYNEX FYI Pages in the Yellow Pages to keep track of these constantly changing numbers. New York Telephone's *Calling Guide* is perhaps more universally useful, offering details on the various telephone services offered by the company and useful numbers for transportation, cultural institutions, hot lines and educational resources. If it doesn't come with your telephone, call 212-269-7777 or your local telephone office to get it.

Television Stations

So that you may tune in your favorite show immediately upon arrival, we list national television networks (and local independents) and their New York channels: **Channel 2**—WCBS; **Channel 4**—WNBC; **Channel 5**—WNYW (Fox); **Channel 7**—WABC; **Channel 9**—WOR (an independent New Jersey-based station); **Channel 11**—WPIX (independent community station serving the tri-state area); **Channel 13**—WNET (Public Broadcasting System). Note that an Ultra High Frequency station, **Channel 21**—WLIW (Long Island's public network channel), broadcasts many of the public network TV series ("Masterpiece Theater" and the like) carried on Channel 13 but at different times. When you miss an episode on Channel 13, you can usually catch it a night or two later on Channel 21. City-owned UHF **Channel 31**—WNYC—also carries PBS reruns, in addition to other independent programming.

You'll find weekly programs for the broadcast channels as well as cable channels (including HBO, Showtime and the like) printed in TV Guide and the Sunday New York Times' "Television". This supplement also carries a complete "Station Guide" detailing the ownership and/or focus of broadcast and cable stations.

Cable Television

Expanded programming and famous skyscrapers make cable an attractive and often necessary option in New York City. Service in Manhattan is monopolistic: one company has exclusive rights to the northern half of the borough, another company to the southern half. The situation is more fluid in outlying areas, where several firms vie for customers. With a few exceptions, both Manhattan distributors offer the same services: Home Box Office (HBO) for movies, MTV (music videos and rock/pop concerts), Nickelodeon for children, sports on Sportschannel (for events blacked out in the metropolitan area), Madison Square Garden Cable Network and ESPN, as well as channels broadcasting news, weather, health and stock market reports and entertainment. Manhattan Cable offers Cinemax for still more movies, while Paragon has Showtime (also movies) and Uptown (R-rated movies from 9 p.m. to 1 a.m.) for its upper Manhattan subscribers.

If your building isn't already wired, the owner or manager must request hookup, which has been known to take anywhere from several months to a year. If you're living below 79th Street on the West Side or below 86th Street on the East Side, contact Time Warner Cable of New York City, formerly Manhattan Cable TV, 120 East 23rd Street, NYC 10010, 212-674-9100. Brooklyn and Queens residents should call Time Warner at 718-358-0900. In Manhattan above 79th Street on the West Side or 86th Street on the East Side, contact Paragon Cable, 5120 Broadway, NYC 10034, 212-304-3000.

Radio Stations

Music lovers are best served by their FM dials; news and talk shows dominate the AM band. However, on either broadcast frequency most stations specialize further still, emphasizing one format or one sound. Check below to find your station. For program particulars, consult **The New York Times** daily radio listings and **New York** magazine's Cue entertainment guide, which publishes classical music "Highlights" weekly.

- **AM News:** CBS 880—"Newsradio"; WINS 1010—"Give Us 22 Minutes and We'll Give You the World."

- **AM Talk:** WABC 770; WMCA 570—"The Voice of New York"; WNYC 830—the city's own station features cultural and consumer-oriented broadcasts and National Public Radio's "All Things Considered"; WOR 710—insomniac radio (talk around the clock).

- **AM Classical:** WQXR 1560—*The New York Times'* station throws in hourly newsbreaks, too.

- **AM Sports:** WFAN 660.

- **FM Classical:** WKCR 89.9—classical when it isn't jazz, country or talk; WNYC 93.9—classical, swing and jazz interspersed with PBS programs including "All Things Considered" and "Prairie Home Companion"; WQXR 96.3—*The Times'* mostly-music but some-news-too format.

- **FM Jazz:** WBGO 88.3—contemporary jazz from Newark; WKCR 89.9—about half the time Columbia University's station plays jazz.

- **FM Listener Sponsored Radio:** WBAI 99.5—just like the populace that supports it, this talk and music station is invigorating, maddening and appealing all at the same time.

- **FM Country:** WYNY 103.5.

In hot pursuit of the booming 20-to 35-year-old market, most New York FM stations feature "Top 40 Radio" and are fiercely competitive. According to a knowledgeable radio staffer, New York's contemporary FM music stations currently fall into the following trade categories:

- **Urban Contemporary** (dance music with a driving beat): WBLS 107.5 and WRKS (KISS) 98.7.

- **Album Oriented Rock**: WNEW 102.7 and WXRK 92.3.

- **Current Hit Radio:** WPLJ (Power 95) 95.5.

- **Hot Hits** (slightly wilder than Current Hit Radio; more novelties): WHTZ (Z100)100.3.
- **Adult Contemporary** (soft sounds aimed at the 24-to 54-year-olds): WLTW 106.7 and WNSR 105.

- **Golden Oldies** (rock and roll from the 1950s and 1960s): WCBS 101.1.

• **Middle of the Road** ("easy listening" for over-35-year-olds; Sinatra triumphant): WPAT 93.

Driver's Licenses and Automobile Registration

New residents with valid foreign or out-of-state licenses have 30 days to apply for a New York State Driver's License and to register their cars and motorcycles. Licenses and vehicle registrations are issued by the District Office of the New York State Department of Motor Vehicles, 141 Worth Street, corner Centre Street, NYC 10013, open Monday through Friday 9 to 4:30, Tuesday until 7 p.m. Pick up a license application, Driver's Manual and, if necessary, an Automobile Registration form at the District Office or have them sent by calling 212-645-5550. A valid out-of-state license exempts you from the road test, but you must pass the vision, road sign and written tests.

Unless you get lucky, happening by when the examiner has a time slot open, you must make an appointment in advance to take the written test. Write to the Preliminary Test Office of the Department of Motor Vehicles in whichever borough you live, or stop by in person. No appointment can be made by phone. The written tests, based on the Driver's Manual, are given from 8 a.m. to 2 p.m.

Because tests are scored there and then, you are issued a temporary license which allows you to drive immediately if you pass. Your official license, the one with the photograph, is mailed to you. You must have the completed application form, current license and $32.25, which includes the written test fee, license validation fee and picture, taken at the time your license is issued. New York State licenses are valid for four years.

If your license has lapsed or this is your first, pick up the materials and take the vision, road sign and written tests noted above. You'll then be eligible for a learner's permit. With this in hand, after a three-hour course at a licensed driving school, it is possible to take the road test, the ultimate qualification for the New York Driver's License. Examiners can be finicky, but the most frustrating aspect of the road test is getting an appointment to take it. If you can arrange to take the test out of town, or at least out of Manhattan, do so.

You need the following documents to register your car or motorcycle: Registration Application or Title completely filled out, proof of ownership, proof of insurance, proof of vehicle inspection, sales tax clearance, and proof of your identity and birth. Read the back of the Application for Registration to determine what "proofs" are acceptable. The registration fee depends on vehicle weight.

Long lines are a Department of Motor Vehicles tradition. Best time to go is early in the week. Fridays are particularly busy. The last workday of any month can find the line spilling out onto Worth Street's sidewalk and is to be avoided, period.

Parking Your Car

You may have a very helpful helpmate, willing to spend long hours switching a car from one side of the street to another in order to conform with New York's alternate side of the street parking laws, or you may derive pleasure from driving through lonely streets at night looking for a legal spot. Either way, you had better be informed about alternate side of the street parking regulations. Call 212-566-4121 to find out if regulations are in effect on any given day or, better yet, get a free copy of the Department of Transportation's calendar showing the days your car doesn't have to be moved. Send a stamped, self-addressed envelope to Calendar, NYC Department of Transportation, 40 Worth Street, NYC 10013.

Most people working full time must find private parking for their cars. Monthly garage rates keep rising. In any of Manhattan's prime areas, count on paying between $200 and $400 a month. There are alternatives, however, to be found in garages around the fringe of town, on the Lower East Side, south of Greenwich Village along the West Side Highway and north of Morningside Heights. A favorite for the budget-conscious below 14th Street is Pier 40, West and Houston Streets. The problem here is that Pier 40 is not close to a subway line, and the buses that pass nearby (the # 13 and # 10) do so only seldom. Open lots are cheaper and some are better guarded than others. Again, however, the more reasonably priced lots tend to be on the periphery of town.

If you use a car only occasionally, consider a private garage in a nearby community that is easily accessible by public transportation. See page 187 for information about car rentals.

Traffic Tickets and Towing

What's the price if you get caught? To help you decide whether to take that parking chance or not, here is what tickets currently cost below 96th Street in Manhattan (tickets in the boroughs are sometimes cheaper): $40 if the meter has expired; $50 if you're parked on the wrong side of the street in an alternate-side-parking zone; $55 for double parking or parking within 15 feet of a fire hydrant, in a No Parking or No Standing zone. No ticket costs more than $55, though fines increase by $10 per day after 30 days and by $20 per day after 45 days. If you are going to pay your fines, do it immediately.

But tickets are only a part of the penalty. The real deterrent to joining the ranks of New York's scofflaws is the threat of having your automobile towed. It costs $150 to retrieve your car from the pound on Pier 76 (Twelfth Avenue and 38th Street) in Manhattan, plus $15 a day (not including the day your car was towed) for storage. You must produce the car's registration and your driver's license to get the automobile back. If your name is on the registration papers, you can pay by check—that is, if your name is printed on the check. Otherwise, or if you have accumulated unpaid traffic tickets, you must produce cash, certified check or traveler's check for payment. The pound is open 7 a.m. to 6 a.m., seven days a week. Call 212-TOW-AWAY to determine whether your car has been towed; if it isn't in the pound (and you haven't misplaced it), your car has been stolen or the marshall has towed it away for nonpayment of tickets.

To find out if you have an accumulation of tickets (they often blow off the windshield; then, too, other drivers swipe them to put under their windshield wipers in order to fool the cops) call the Parking Violations Bureau's Help Hot Line, 212-477-4430. All five boroughs have Help Centers where you can get a free computer printout of your tickets: One Centre Street, Manhattan; 1400 Williamsbridge Road, 1st floor, The Bronx; 89-61 162nd Street, Jamaica, Queens; 210 Joralemon Street, 9th floor Brooklyn; 350 St. Mark's Place, 3rd floor, Staten Island.

Don't Even Think of Parking Here! by Paul Trapido and Barbara Ensor covers just about every topic a car owner in New York needs to know (published by Simon & Schuster).

Voter Registration

Registering to vote is as simple as calling the Manhattan Board of Elections, 212-886-3800, and requesting an Application for Registration and Enrollment by Mail, completing the form and returning it to the board. If you live in another borough, the Manhattan Board will pass the completed application along to the appropriate borough board: Bronx, 718-299-9017; Brooklyn, 718-522-3116; Manhattan, 212-868-3788; Queens, 718-392-8989; and Staten Island, 718-727-4300. If you enroll in a political party, the form must be received by the Board of Elections 25 days before the primary or general election. You can also register in person during specific central registration periods at Election Board headquarters, 131 Varick Street, 9th Floor, NYC 10013.

Further questions about voting procedures? The candidates? The offices to be filled? Issues? The **League of Women Voters** addresses these questions and will help you answer them either by telephone, 212-677-5050, or through the materials they publish. You can stop by their offices at 817 Broadway corner of East 12th Street, 6th floor, for a copy of their useful guide, *What Makes New York City Run*, $4, or have it sent by mail for an extra dollar. Also, good to have is *The Green Book* ($12.99, Citybooks Store, 61 Chambers Street) which lists numerous elected officials as well as all city departments and offices. If you have a government related problem, the telephone listings in this guide can be a powerful tool.

Library Cards

The New York Public Library, with four research libraries, numerous special divisions for various disciplines, famous reference collections and over 80 branches in Manhattan, The Bronx and Staten Island, is one of the city's great treasures. Residents of Brooklyn and Queens, however, aren't bookless: the Brooklyn Public Library has 59 branches, the Queens Borough Public Library, 60.

Library cards are free and entitle you to borrow or request circulating books from any branch in the system. To obtain a card, give your name, address and proof of residence to the staffer at the return desk of the nearest branch library. Call 930-0800 for library hours—which vary widely from branch to branch.

One wonderful resource is the library's Telephone Reference Service, 212-340-0849. Library researchers try to answer all viable questions and, if they cannot, will refer you to the department most likely to have the required data. If the Manhattan number is too busy, try the Brooklyn, 718-780-7700, or Queens, 718-990-0714, Telephone Reference Service numbers.

Passports

The process of getting a passport in New York City can be more than a little taxing. First, call 212-399-5290 to obtain recorded factual information. With luck, the recording will answer all your questions. You can call the Washington Passport Information Office, 202-647-0518, where they not only answer the phone but your questions, too. Furthermore, one of New York's most ignominious experiences, one that ranks right up there with standing in line for a driver's license at the Department of Motor Vehicles on Worth Street, consists of queuing at the Passport Agency in Rockefeller Center during vacation periods. The following information is meant to save you both a phone call and a trip to Rockefeller Center and, should a visit prove unavoidable, some tips about the best times to go.

If you are applying for a passport for the first time, you must have 1) proof of citizenship: an original, or copy, of your birth certificate with a raised seal, or naturalization papers, and 2) proof of your identity: a driver's license or other ID with a photograph. (If you don't have these papers, call the Passport Agency for alternatives.) You will need two passport photos (there's a photographer two flights below the Passport Agency at 630 Fifth Avenue) and $65 if you are over age 18, $40 for minors. You will find the necessary forms at all of the addresses listed below, and you must appear in person to get your first passport. But you needn't go to the Passport Agency. There are three centers that can process your application:

- **Clerks of the State Supreme Court:** (Manhattan) Court House, 60 Centre Street, 10007; (Brooklyn) New Supreme Court, 60 Adams Street, 11201; (Bronx) County Building, 851 Grand Concourse, 10451.

- **Post Offices:** (Manhattan) General Post Office, 8th Avenue and 33rd Street; Ansonia Station, 1990 Broadway; Church Street Station, 90 Church Street; Cooper Station, 93 Fourth Avenue; Franklin D. Roosevelt Station, 909 Third Avenue; and Manhattanville Station, 365 West 125th Street. (Call the General Post Office for stations with passport windows in the other boroughs.)

- **Passport Agency,** 630 Fifth Avenue, Room 230, NYC 10111, 212-399-5290, open 7:30 to 4, Monday through Friday.

To renew a passport, pick up form DSP-82 (or, if you were under 18 when you obtained your previous passport, form DSP-11) at any of the addresses listed above and mail it to the New York Passport Agency, accompanied by two passport pictures, $55 and your expired passport. Allow six to eight weeks, more if you're applying in high summer season, or mention the date of your departure on the form; passports are processed on the basis of departure date.

If you must leave the country in a hurry, it is possible to obtain a passport in one day by going to the Passport Agency with your ticket and other necessary papers. In high season (April through June, just before Christmas, Easter and other school holidays) the line forms 45 minutes to an hour before the doors open at 8 a.m. Buy a cup of coffee, take a book or the newspaper and prepare to wait. After you make application, you'll have to return around 4 in the afternoon to get the new passport.

Off-season, the Passport Office offers reasonable service early in the morning and later in the afternoon. Its infamous reputation is based on agency handling of the spring and pre-Christmas crush.

Suppose you've got to go to Botswana on short notice, you don't even know what documents and shots you need, and you're too busy to get it together. What to do? For a fee (up to $150 for a same-day passport renewal) a knowledgeable staff at Passport Plus, 677 Fifth Avenue at 53rd Street, 212-759-5540, will handle it for you.

Recycling

Like it or not, recycling has become a necessary part of life in New York City and everywhere else. In most areas, residents are used to placing newspapers, magazines and corrugated cardboard neatly tied with string on the curb on appointed days. (To find out the pickup days for your neighborhood call the New York City Department of Sanitation at 212-219-8090.) If you're in an area where official recycling is in effect, you leave your separated garbage (i.e. washed cans, plastic and glass bottles, and aluminum foil) curbside in the blue drums provided by the Sanitation Department. Newspapers, magazines and cardboard should be secured with twine in stacks of 18 inches or less. Returnable bottles and cans should be redeemed. For those without an ecological conscience, fines start at $25 for the first offense and go up with each succeeding violation.

If your area hasn't jumped on the bandwagon and you want to do a little conservation of your own, there are two recycling centers in Manhattan. Several mobile drop-off centers are operated by the Department of Sanitation; call the Sanitation Action Center, 212-219-8090, for their locations and hours.

- **The Village Green Recycling Team**, Avenue of the Americas at West 4th Street, 777-1422, open 5 to 7 Monday, 11 to 2 Wednesday, 8 to 11 Friday, 10 to 3 Saturday. Accepts newspapers, office papers, aluminum and tin cans, plastics, bottles and glass.

- **Upper West Side Recycling Center**, 1047 Amsterdam Avenue at the Cathedral of St. John the Divine, 316-7540. Accepts office paper, aluminum cans and foil, tin cans, plastic bottles and glass.

Building Staff

New Yorkers rely on the staff of their buildings in ways that are unique to the city—and they reward their staff in an equally unique manner.

Most multi-unit residences have a superintendent (the "super") who is responsible for the maintenance and day-to-day operation of the building. Many Superintendents may be assisted by porters and hallmen. There are also doormen (and today, doorwomen) in many buildings. In luxury buildings, perhaps a concierge.

Because most New Yorkers do not rely on their cars to accomplish their daily tasks, many goods and services are delivered by businesses to the consumer's home even when they are not there. Thus the importance of the building staff. Other staff duties may include hailing cabs, providing important building information, directing repair people, door holding and—in some buildings—even mail delivery. Most of all, your staff (particularly the doorman) is the first line of security in your building, making certain that anyone who desires entrance truly belongs there.

In addition to the generally higher rents found in staffed buildings, there is an unspoken cost associated with the extra service. It is widely expected that a building's residents tip the staff at Christmas-time for general services rendered throughout the year. (Anything beyond a general service, such as pet-walking or heavy lifting, is best attended to at the time the service is performed.) The tip is by no means mandatory but individual service has been known to decline precipitously for those more Scrooge-like residents. The custom varies widely from building to building both in terms of cost and how the money is dispersed. It is a good idea to find out what is customary in your building and budget for the holiday season accordingly.

Safety in New York City

Although many American urban areas have higher crime rates than New York City, an important part of getting settled in New York *is* learning to live safely. What follows are some basic guidelines:

- Walk like a native by moving briskly and with a sense of purpose.

- *Always* remain alert to what is around you (in front and in back); if you don't pay attention to your surroundings—for example, by walking and listening to a Walkman—you make yourself a target for a crime.

- Stay clear of deserted areas such as empty streets, uninhabited subway cars or platforms and lonely automatic teller machines.

- If you must take the subway late at night, always get in the car that houses the brakeman (generally one of the middle cars). Typically, there is a black and white "zebra" sign marking the spot where the brakeman's car stops—ask the token seller where it is.

- Look for children playing outside or women walking on their own as signs that an area is safe.

- If you do find yourself on an ominous-looking block, avoid the sidewalk and walk directly in the street to be in view of traffic.

- If you feel you are being followed, walk into the nearest restaurant or store.

- Conceal your valuables, and if you wear a diamond ring turn it around so only the band is showing. Cover watches and necklaces.

- Hold your handbag close to you, wearing the strap across your chest. Don't hang a purse on a restaurant chair or restroom hook.

- Do not count your money in public or use big bills.

- Be discreet when using your phone card at a public phone; onlookers may read your calling card number by watching how you hit the phone pad.

- Avoid the temptation to play three-card monte on the street; *you won't win.*

- Beware of operators working as a team: someone who tells you she just dropped her contact lens might well have a friend who is reaching in your handbag.

- Remember: you do not owe a response to anyone who asks for one. This may seem callous but it is better to err on the side of bad manners rather than bad judgement.

The New York City Police Department publishes free brochures on safety. These booklets include safety precautions addressed to men, women, children, the elderly—even to runners. Brochure topics also include how to safeguard your apartment, car and small business. See the final section of this book for emergency phone numbers.

Finally, become involved in your neighborhood. Community is New York City's new buzzword. All over town, people are organizing block associations to monitor crime. To find out if a block association exists in your neighborhood, or to set one up, call Citizen's Committee for New York City at 212-684-6767.

Helpful Services

It should come as no surprise that the international service capital is as energetic in supplying the needs of New Yorkers as it is of those the world over. Multitudinous talents and supremely innovative minds combine to provide a mind-boggling array of services, for individuals as well as for industry. Shelter magazines and newspapers seldom let a month or week go by without feature articles about umbrella repair specialists, third-generation tapestry reweavers, or the pair of clever Upper East Side women now available to reorganize your closets. We'll leave these summaries of the city's more recherche services to the press and provide instead the names of a few representative firms and organizations which supply basics such as baby sitters, cleaning men and women and television rentals.

Baby Sitters

When it comes to sitters, New York's no different than the suburbs. Neighborhoods are stocked with reliable teen-agers looking for jobs. But it takes time to meet them and, occasionally, local kids aren't available on short notice or for New Year's Eve. So we've listed a number of alternatives. Some of the agencies also provide full-time, sleep-in or live-out help.

Agencies

- **Avalon Nurses Registry,** 162 West 56th Street, 212-245-0250. Rate is $7 per hour for a child over seven months; four-hour minimum. Travel is $3 during the day, $6 after 8 p.m. Each additional child over seven months is $1 per hour. You can call them 24 hours a day, seven days a week. Fees include the agency commission.

- **Baby Sitter's Guild**, 60 East 42nd Street, 212-682-0227. The hourly fee for one child is $8.50 to $12, with an additional 50¢ per hour for each sibling and $3/hour for a visiting friend. With enough advance notice a sitter with a nursing background is provided for children under six months. There is a four-hour minimum plus $4.50 to $7.00 for travel depending on time of day. Fee includes the agency's commission. Call between 9 a.m. and 9 p.m. seven days a week. While requests made during the day for that evening can usually be filled, it is better to call a day ahead.

- **Town & Country's Gilbert Child Care**, 157 West 57th Street, Suite 303, 212-245-8400. The hourly rate is $7.25 for children over nine months ($8 - $9 under nine months) with a four-hour minimum; add $1/hour per sibling; $2/hour per visiting child. Daytime carfare is $4, nighttime carfare is $8. Call Monday through Friday 9 to 5. Same-day service is possible but plan a few days ahead for weekends.

- **Hand-in-Hand Agency**, 116-55 Queens Boulevard, Forest Hills, Queens, 718-268-6666. They provide sitters city-wide. $7 per hour, with a four-hour minimum. Call Monday through Friday, 9 to 5. A machine will take your number and someone will call back. Allow one or two days' notice.

Non-profit

- **Parents League,** 115 East 82nd Street, 212-737-7385. The League's baby-sitting service is just one of several benefits included in the $35 annual membership fee. Sitters are students, ages 13 to 18, who attend League member schools or who are the children of members. Riffle through the sitter files, arranged by neighborhood, in the League's office between 9 and 4 Monday through Wednesday, 9 - 7 on Thursday or until noon on Friday.

Schools

- **Barnard College Babysitting Service**, 606 West 120th Street, 212-854-2035. To pre-register, call in your name, address, phone number and name of your pediatrician. Once you are in their file, call Monday through Friday between 10 and 5, two days in advance of your needs. The student will call you back. Rates are $6 per hour. There is also a $15 annual fee.

- **St. Francis College,** 180 Remsen Street, Brooklyn, 718-522-2300, ext. 260. If you live in the Brooklyn Heights area, phone in your needs; minimal information is posted and the student who wants the job goes to the Student Placement Office for details. Rates are up to the individual.

- **St. Vincent's Hospital School of Nursing**, 27 Christopher Street, don't call. Mail or bring a notice to Re: Tina to be posted on the school's bulletin board. Negotiate a rate with the student who calls you.

Furniture, TV, VCR, Computer, Air Conditioner Rentals

Anyone arriving in New York unburdened by furniture can remain that way by renting. This option is great if you're in a state of flux or want to postpone paying for an apartment's worth of furnishings all at once. Monthly charges for the mainly contemporary styles stocked by our representative sampling of rental companies are usually pro-rated on the basis of a one-year lease. Most firms will credit rental charges already paid if you decide to purchase your furniture outright.

Prices quoted below for a one-bedroom apartment would include: bed, night stand, dresser, lamp, mirror, sofa, occasional chair, end table, cocktail table, lamp, dining table and four chairs. Be sure to take your floor plan; most showrooms provide decorator service. Delivery takes two to five days. Add 8.25% sales tax and 5% fire insurance to the monthly rates.

In addition, we queried several video and computer rental firms about the equipment and services they provide as well as their (1994) rates. Most companies require deposits but the amounts fluctuate. Make sure to check.

Furniture Rentals

- **AFR The Furniture Rental People**, 711 Third Avenue at 44th Street, 212-867-2800, open 9 to 6, closed Sunday. While AFR prices each piece individually, the items listed above would cost a minimum of $300 a month for three months, and $150 a month for six months to a year. Delivery is $150 round-trip, and a deposit of one month's rent plus a two-month security fee is required.

- **I.S. Furniture Rentals**, 49 West 23rd Street, 212-924-4800 or 800-255-6651, 9 to 5, closed Saturday and Sunday. Rentals here are by the piece. Our selection would cost between $100 and $200 a month, depending on the items chosen and the length of the contract. First month's rental in advance plus two months' security. There is a one-time fee of $95 for delivery and pickup.

- **International Furniture Rentals**, 345 Park Avenue, entrance on Lexington Avenue between 51st and 52nd Streets, 212-421-0340, open 9 to 6, 10 to 2 Saturday, closed Sunday. The price spread quoted for our one-bedroom apartment reflects quality differences: from $119 to $500 a month. Delivery is $80 each way. One-and-a-half month's rent required as a deposit.

Television and VCR Rentals

- **ABC TV Rentals**, 131 East 31st Street, 212-532-6728. Rental fees are $45 per month and up, including pick-up and delivery. Installation is generally available within two hours, as is repair service. No deposit required if you have a home telephone listed in your name and can provide the name of a current employer.

- **Audiovision**, 1221 Second Avenue, 212-988-5756. Several brands—Panasonic, RCA, Sharp—of VHS video cassette recorders rent here for $50 per month, $20 per week. The fee for installation, delivery and pickup in Manhattan is $25.

- **Columbus TV and Video Center**, 529 Columbus Avenue, 212-496-2626. A variety of video cassette recorders rented by the day, the week or the month; $55 for one month, $35 per month for six months, with a $10 installation fee.

- **Federal Rent-A-TV Corp.**, 1588 York Avenue between 83rd and 84th Streets, 212-734-5777. The cost is $55 for the first month, $22 for each additional month for a 13" color TV; $40 and $35 for each additional month for a 19" set. Cash deposit, or an American Express, MasterCard or VISA balance equal to the value of the set, is required. Delivery is included. Federal also rents video equipment.

- **Granada TV Rentals**, 171 Milbar Boulevard, Farmingdale, NY 800-281-3151. There is a three-month minimum for both televisions and VCRs, but after that you can rent by the month. After three months, Granada offers a buy option. A 13" RCA color TV or a 19" set rents for $24.95. Delivery costs $15 and takes two days; $35 security deposit is collected with the first month's rent. Free service included. VCRs cost $24.95 a month for the first three months (the minimum rental period). The security deposit is $35, delivery and installation $15.

Computer Rentals

- **Computer Software Center**, 575 Eighth Avenue at 38th Street, 212-564-9088. You can use an IBMs or Compaqs at the Center's 19th-floor showroom for $35 a day. The company also rents IBMs and Compaqs for $95 a week, $150 a month. Delivery and pickup charges vary. Printers are available for rent as well. You supply your own software.

- **PC Computer Rentals**, 360 West 31st Street, 9th floor 212-532-2222. One of the biggest firms in the rather limited computer rental business, PC Computer rents primarily IBM-compatible systems. Rates are $200 a month and up.

- **PCR Personal Computer Rentals**, 257 West 29th Street, 212-268-0200, or 800-922-8646 from outside the tri-state area, open 24 hours a day, seven days a week. By-the-week or monthly rental rates fluctuate depending on the make or model of computer rented. This IBM-authorized nationwide chain specializes in IBM, Compaq and Apple computers, HP and QMS laser printers. Lotus software available. Delivery, set-up and pickup cost $50, service is free. AE, MC, V.

Air Conditioner Rentals

- **A A B C O Amber Corp.**, 1594 York Avenue, 212-535-9578 or 212-734-5777. Average cost per unit for the hot season (May through mid-October) is $200, service included. Specifics depend on room size and BTU requirements. AE, MC, V.

- **Ace Air Conditioning Service Corp.**, 24-81 47th Street, Astoria, Queens, 212-406-2256 from Manhattan. Room size determines the cost of the unit: approximately $175 for a bedroom, $245 for a living room. Price includes delivery, removal and service, if required. MC, V.

- **Columbus Air Conditioning Center**, 529 Columbus Avenue, 212-496-2626. Rentals run $145 to $300 depending on the BTUs required, May through mid-October. Service and delivery are included. AE, MC, V.

House Cleaning

Word of mouth is your best bet for finding a cleaning person (women have no monopoly on the profession here). Ask friends and neighbors if they know of someone with a few hours available. If this doesn't work, you might try one of the services. The hourly rates quoted include dusting, changing linens, mopping, vacuuming, laundry, cleaning bathrooms and washing dishes. The same firms provide specialists to handle floor waxing, washing walls and other heavy duty jobs at higher fees.

- **Lend-A-Hand, Inc.**, 200 West 72nd Street, 212-362-8200. Housecleaning is one of the many services provided by this agency's actors, musicians and dancers. The rate is $14 per hour, plus a $15 finder's fee , for one person, whose references are checked before going out on a job.

- **Maid in N.Y.**, 200 Park Avenue South, 212-777-6000. Homes as well as industrial sites and business offices are serviced by some 100 employees, who currently work for $12 an hour (four-hour minimum) plus $2.50 for transportation. Times and schedules are arranged to suit the client: weekly, bi-weekly or just once for a thorough spring cleaning.

- **Maids Unlimited, Flatiron Services**, 230 East 93rd Street, 212-369-9100. $54 for four-hour minimum, $13.50 each additional hour in Manhattan. For regular service, the same person would be sent if possible. One or two days' notice required. Help is bonded. Maid uses your supplies.

Mail and Telephone

You haven't found an apartment yet, or are out of town frequently and want to keep in touch. Telephone answering services either answer your own phone or assign you a number. Mail receiving agencies or "mail centers" hold or forward mail, receive and ship packages.

Your telephone equipment must be connected to that of the answering firm to use your own phone number. NYNEX levies a monthly carrying charge of $5.19 and a $52.70 one-shot installation fee as long as the answering service is nearby or handles your exchange. Allow two or more business days to be connected with a service. Using a service-provided number, you avoid installation and carrying charges and can begin receiving messages the day you sign up.

Elect service 24 hours a day, seven days a week or during business hours only (9 to 5 or 8 to 6, Monday through Friday). Monthly fees include a specified number of messages; additional messages cost around 50¢ each.

Call Forwarding is less expensive for residential customers who want to use their own number rather than a 24-hour telephone service. NYNEX's Call Forwarding enables you to connect your phone to an answering service by dialing 72 plus the service number. To disconnect when you return, dial 73. The NYNEX one-shot installation charge is $16; the carrying charge is $4.15 a month. (Businesses pay $56 and $6.23 monthly for Call Forwarding.) Expect to pay the answering company about $60 a month for 24-hour service and $50 for service during business hours only.

Many firms offer telephone or mail service, or both. The following companies, arranged alphabetically, are illustrative. Check the Yellow

Pages under "Mail Receiving Services" and "Telephone Answering Services" for more comprehensive lists.

- **Copy/Com**, 70A Greenwich Avenue (near Seventh Avenue), 212-924-4180. Mailboxes rent from $82.27 (including tax and $10 key deposit) for a standard size for four months to $214.33 total for a large box for 12 months. Copy/Com also ships and receives packages, makes copies of printed materials and cassettes, and takes orders for printed stationery and business cards.

- **Messengers Plus**, 1317 Third Avenue, 212-879-8383. $67.50 per month for business hours and $79.50 a month for 24-hour service to answer your phone; each service includes 70 messages. Pay for one month to start—the full amount is credited to your account. Answering N.Y. provides service to customers with exchanges concentrated on the Upper East Side from about 68th to 90th Streets.

- **Proxy Message Center**, 210 East 86th Street, Suite 600, 212-472-1233. This company covers all of Manhattan, charging, for commercial use, $72.95 with 90 free calls (additional calls are 55} each); for residential use, $34.95 for 35 calls (additional calls are $1 each). Mail service is $30 a month, two month's payment in advance.

- **Village Answering Service**, 204 West 20th Street, 212-924-8406. Daytime service (9 to 5 weekdays) costs $49.50, 24-hour service $59.50 and with either you are charged 35} for each call over the allotted 100 calls a month. Covering exchanges between 30th Street and Canal Street downtown, this group also will wake you up for a monthly charge of $22.50, provide you with a beeper for $18 a month and 40} each time you are beeped plus a one-time deposit of $50 and insurance of $20 and, if you're a telephone client, make their mail address available to you for $36 a month.

- As a relatively new alternative to the answering service and the answering machine, NYNEX is offering **Call Answering**. Once the service is activated on your touch-tone phone ($20.15 installation charge for a residence), it is on 24 hours a day, cutting in after, say, the third ring and recording up to 40 messages of up to two minutes.

Messages are retrievable from any touch-tone phone. Cost for a residence is $6.23 per month, plus two call charges to record and retrieve each message, billed on your monthly statement. Call 800-637-7243, Operator 224, for the service.

Moving and Storage

Disagreeable moving experiences aren't obligatory but they do happen, and it's difficult to know where to begin listing moving companies. So, with the exception of a couple of storage companies and a few mini-warehouses that might be helpful to know about, we've dispensed with listing names in this section. The State Department of Transportation says most people use the Yellow Pages to find a mover; you can consult the *Village Voice* classified for short hauls. Whoever you use, make sure they are certified.

Instead of a list of moving companies, we'll begin by describing what two government regulatory agencies, the New York State Department of Transportation and the Federal Interstate Commerce Commission, can do for you.

Interstate movers are licensed by the ICC, intrastate companies by the DOT. Neither agency gives out names, but if you call the ICC, 212-264-1072, or the DOT Motor Carrier Investigations Bureau, 718-732-4810, they'll tell you if the mover is licensed.

Before a move takes place, the Interstate Commerce Commission requires interstate movers to furnish clients with a copy of When You Move, Your Rights and Responsibilities prepared by the Commission. To receive these guidelines before hiring a mover, call the New York Office of the ICC, 212-264-1072, and they'll send you one.

After the move, if there has been a problem, call the appropriate agency to find out how to proceed. The ICC and the DOT can provide assistance only when you use a certified mover. Hire an unlicensed firm and you're on your own in case of damage or loss.

Storage facilities may be required when you have to ship your furniture without an apartment to receive it or if your apartment is too small for all your belongings. The New York City Department of Consumer Affairs licenses storage—but not self-storage—warehouses. Dissatisfied? Call the city's all-purpose complaint number, 212-487-4398.

Storage Warehouses

- **Central Moving and Storage**, 718-622-2660, has a fireproof warehouse in Brooklyn. Charges are 30¢ a cubic foot per month, plus a one-shot warehouse handling charge that amounts to one month's storage. Estimates are based on the number of rooms of furniture and household goods you'll be storing.

- **The Seven Santini Bros.**, 201-340-8210, has a warehouse for the storage of household goods at 141 Lanza Avenue, Garfield, NJ 07026. The Manhattan warehouse is for fine arts storage only.

Self-Storage Companies

The ability to rent anything from 3 foot by 3 foot lockers to small storage rooms is a great boon to urban dwellers. Collectors, people with old clothes they can't bear to give to thrift shops and those with possessions that won't fit in a sublet or shared apartment all find mini-warehouses a solution to too-small living spaces.

Rates for space in Manhattan self-storage (you or your mover get the goods there) facilities are competitive: expect to pay about $55 a month for a locker 4' by 4' by 7', $90 a month for an 8' by 8' by 8' space, and so on. If you're looking for lower rates, check the prices for storage units located in the suburbs and boroughs other than Manhattan.

- **Keepers III**, 212-924-8484, has locations at 43 Clarkson Street near Houston Street, 444 East 10th Street between Avenues C and D, and at 2577 Forest Avenue on Staten Island. Prices at the East Side location are slightly less than those on the West Side and Staten Island.

- **Manhattan Mini Storage**, 212-757-4700 and 212-255-0482, with locations at 520 West 17th Street corner of Tenth Avenue, 600 West 58th Street corner of Eleventh Avenue and 570 Riverside Drive corner of 134th Street, offer private storage rooms from 5' by 5' to 10' by 25' (the size of some NYC studio apartments).

- **U-Haul Moving and Storage** has a mini-warehouse located at 562

West 23rd Street, 212-620-4177, with rooms 4' by 8' for $40 and 8' by 12' for $120, as well as facilities in Brooklyn, The Bronx and Queens.

For other names and addresses in the burgeoning self-storage field, check the Yellow Pages under "Moving & Storage —Self Service."

Shopping for the Home

Big city living encourages idiosyncratic life styles. The idea of proximity breeding privacy seems contradictory, but in New York City that's the way it works. Freed from small-community pressures to pay token respect to values not necessarily shared, New Yorkers pursue their interests and goals singularly unencumbered by considerations as to "what the neighbors might think." Home decoration is a striking case in point. Anything (within the terms of the lease) goes, and while stingy with space, when it comes to providing all the goods and services necessary for us to feather our wildly divergent, albeit mainly minuscule, nests, the city really comes through for its residents. Generally speaking, there are at least three approaches to shopping in Manhattan: 1) largish, fairly priced, standard sources; 2) famous signature shops and upscale boutiques; and 3) discounters and/or alternative resources such as wholesale districts and sample sales.

Unless otherwise noted, all stores mentioned accept American Express, MasterCard and VISA. One last caveat. If the idea of shopping is appalling, there's always furniture rental. See the chapter on Helpful Services for a list of firms.

Full Service Department Stores

As designer boutiques fragment row upon heretofore sensibly labeled row of merchandise into seemingly hundreds of glass-sheathed cubicles, one-stop shopping the full service store has lost cohesiveness but still beats 15 stops in a 20-block neighborhood. Although more difficult than it once was, it's comforting to take a 15-item list, silk pins through box springs, and pass the afternoon under one roof. So, we lead off with the queens of New York's merchandise scene, listed alphabetically, before splintering into our own smaller sections.

- **A & S** (Abraham and Straus), 420 Fulton Street, Brooklyn, 718-875-7200, open 9:45 to 6, to 7 Monday, to 9 Thursday, noon to 5 Sunday. AE, MC, V, A & S charge. Talk about full service! Lucky Brooklyn residents need travel no further than the Hoyt Street stop on the Seventh Avenue IRT #2 or #3 train for practically any nicety or necessity. A & S has both an optometrist and a chiropodist on duty, counters for shfl repair and dry cleaning, and a fur storage and restyling service. From TVs and electronics on the Lower Level to fabric on Six and furniture on Seven, this rather reserved no-non-sense institution also heeds the latest fashions with up-to-theminute styles from leading designers on Three.

- **A & S**, Avenue of the Americas at 33rd Street, 212-594-8500, open 9:45 to 8:30 Monday, to 6:45 Tuesday and Wednesday, to 8:45 Thursday, 10 to 6:45 Saturday, 11 to 6 Sunday. AE, MC, V and A & S card. You can't get your eyes tested or your shfls soled at *this* A & S, but the At Your Service Desk on Two will check your coat and bags while you shop, get you tickets to a Broadway show, make your dinner reservations, give you a subway map or call you a cab. Bucking a tide of department store closings, in 1989 A & S moved *into* Manhattan as the anchor store in A & S Plaza, a gleaming chrome-and-glass vertical mall a block square in midtown. Float up to Seven in a theatrically-lit glass bubble elevator at the edge of the soaring mall atrium, choose from a gaggle of fast-food eateries for lunch, and drift down from electronics and home furnishings on Six through wearing apparel and jewelry to running shfls below ground level. It's not chic, but the clothes are au courant and reasonably priced. Adjoining boutiques stacked around the mall offer books to records to toys to ski equipment as the bubbles rise and fall. It's Trump Tower downtown (and downscale).

- **Barneys New York**, Seventh Avenue at 17th Street, 929-9000, open 10 to 9, to 8 Friday, to 7 Saturday, noon to 6 Sunday. AE, MC, V, Barneys card. Free parking. The suavest department store in town is bandbox bright and shiny but nowhere near full service. Why then include this elegant bazaar when we overlook equally fashionable Bendel's and Bergdorf's? Because Barneys is a pioneer, that's why: the first distinguished multi-floor store for men, women and chic kids below 23rd Street since the turn of the century. Downtowners have long been accustomed to Barneys fine men's furnishings but still have trouble remembering that they don't have to travel to 57th Street to find Norma Kamali, Azzedine Alaia, Armani, Hermes, Issey Miyake, Jean-Paul Gaultier and many other top designers. Truly tasteful new and antique jewelry, china, linens, tabletop accessories and gifts are lodged on Barneys smart first floor. Le Cafe, open on the lower level for light breakfasts, snappy buffet lunches and dinners has already become one of the most popular stops on the city shopper's route. Funky December window displays provide an alternative to more traditional holiday storefronts at Lord & Taylor and Saks Fifth Avenue.

The downtown Barneys now has an uptown cousin, **Barneys New York,** at Madison and 61st Street, 826-8900. This store challenges the other uptown mega-merchants with its 3 restaurants, long hours (10 to 8 weekdays) and 8 floors of merchandise including newly discovered designers, exclusive Barneys lines and the trinkets and treasures that are Barneys hallmarks. As with the Seventh Avenue store, this is not a place for bargain hunting. The merchandise, however, is exquisite and the service is first-rate. You haven't lived until you've been fitted for a suit by one of the store's excellent staff. These people know what they are doing.

• **Bloomingdale's**, Third Avenue at 59th Street, 355-5900, open 10 to 6:30, to 9 Thursday, 11 to 6 Sunday. AE, DC, MC, V, Bloomingdale's charge. It wouldn't be surprising to see all eight stories of block-square Bloomingdale's swathed in Blackglama and grinning from *The New Yorker*'s slick pages one of these days. Along with other mink-wrapped legends, the store has worked hard to achieve entertainer status and like all top stars, not content to rest on laurels, sets trends and discards old routines as it tears along. But for all the NOWness, zap and glitter, Bloomie's has a sturdy core; you can leave your watch for repair, order Christmas cards, shop the best white sales in town January and August, buy a TV, a mattress and sweatsocks as well as try out glittery red Dorothy of Oz shoes to a disco beat, arrange an assignation over Izod shirts or nosh the food of the moment at one of five chic cafes.

Services include Beatrice Dale personal shoppers (705-2380) and translators, a bridal registry, decorators, and 24-hour telephone order service.

- **Lord & Taylor**, Fifth Avenue at 39th Street, 391-3344, open 10 to 8:30 Monday through Thursday, to 6:30 Friday and Saturday, noon to 6 Sunday. AE, Lord & Taylor's charge. The trim, self-confident customers here, dressed in "updated contemporary classics" and often found around the Soup Bar on Ten sipping vichyssoise in summer, Scotch broth in winter, tend to mirror the American look championed by the store. "Young American" designers on Six and the model rooms on Eight displaying a substantial collection of contemporary American furnishings are among the current darlings. Multilingual, the "Red Rose" personal shopping staff on Three handles international mail orders and, for an extra fee, a fashion adviser is available for counseling.

- **Macy's**, Broadway at 34th Street, 695-4400, open 10 to 8:30 Monday, Thursday and Friday, to 7 Tuesday, Wednesday and Saturday, 11 to 6 Sunday. AE, MC, V, Macy's charge. Enormous! Complete! And can it be overwhelming! First-timers take advantage of the multilingual information booths and descriptive giveaway location maps at first floor information booths. Others use Macy's Buy Appointment, the personal shopping service, and the 24-hour telephone ordering service, 800-528-6602. A total revamp of the beloved behemoth began at the basement level with the creation of the superb Cellar, a bazaar-like warren of individual food and homewares shops, and moved skyward as each floor was completely redone with pizzaz and flair. A merchandising tour de force and, equally miraculous, the sales help's attitude and quality of service has improved beyond belief.

- **Saks Fifth Avenue**, 611 Fifth Avenue at Rockefeller Center, 753-4000, open 10 to 6:30, to 8 Thursday, noon to 6 Sunday. AE, DC, MC, V, Saks charge. Carefully coiffed customers, self-assured and tan, and elaborate bouquets spraying nonchalantly into the glowing, wood-paneled aisles characterize Saks Fifth Avenue. So do the most refined escalators in New York. They Float you silently past eight well-lit shopping floors against a backdrop of perfectly placed plants, mirrors and pinky-beige marble Luxurious Saks exudes well-being from every tasteful counter. Faced with the largest selection of Vuitton luggage in town, a Revillon fur boutique and the stylish men's department on Six, you may forget that Saks harbors a useful set of shops along 49th and 50th Streets. Housewares, luggage, bathing suits and sportswear,the bath and linen shop and the art gallery all have private entrances. Recently, the store has made a fetish of personalized service. The Fifth Avenue Club, 753-4000, ext. 4200, on Three shelters five personal shopping services, among them the Executive Service for women executives.

Discount Stores

- **Century 21**, 22 Cortlandt Street (in lower Manhattan), 227-9092 and 472 86th Street, Bay Ridge, Brooklyn, 718-748-3266, open 9 to 7 Monday through Friday, 10 to 5 Saturday and Sunday. Not the nationwide real estate broker but something that is unique to New York City—a full service department store where *everything* is discounted. There are many real bargains here and the service is pleasant and no-nonsense.

Appliances, Electronics, Cameras

These three categories have been lumped together because many of the stores listed below cross merchandise lines.

- **Macy's** and **A & S** are the only full service department stores which sell washing machines, stoves and other major appliances.

- **Willoughby's Camera Store**, 110 West 32nd Street, 564-1600, open 9 to 7, to 8 Thursday, 10 to 6 Sunday. Phone quotes. Complete rental and service departments complement the most extensive photographic stock in the city. Willoughby's also has a computer department.

Specialty Shops

- **Alkit Camera Shop**, 866 Third Avenue between 52nd and 53rd Streets, 832-2101, open 7:30 to 6:30, 9 to 5 Saturday. "Generally" gives phone quotes. Full video and stereo line but fame rests on the quality and quantity of the professional and amateur cameras and other photographic equipment offered, as well as Alkit's custom order department and rental and repair services.

- **Lyric High Fidelity**, 1221 Lexington Avenue at 83rd Street, 535-5710, open 10 to 6, noon to 5 Sunday. "Only the finest stereo components." A strong selection of speakers.

- **Sound by Singer,** 18 East 16th Street, 924-8600, open 10 to 6, to 8 Tuesday and Thursday, noon to 5 Sunday. High-end audio equipment and an extremely knowledgeable sales staff. Specializes in American brands.

Discount Stores

The Lower East Side dflsn't have an exclusive on good buys. Appliances and electronics are sold all over the city at less than retail. A few of the many discounters in Manhattan:

- **ABC Trading Co.**, 31 Canal Street near Essex, 228-5080, open 10 to 6, to 1 p.m. Friday, closed Saturday. No credit cards. No phone quotes. Photographic equipment, small as well as major appliances, audio equipment and supplies, TVs and VCRs. ABC's special department for merchandise adapted to cycles and broadcast standards found throughout the world is a favorite of UN personnel and others living overseas.

- **Cambridge Camera Exchange**, Seventh Avenue and West 13th Street, 675-8600, open 9 to 6, 10 to 3 Sunday, closed Saturday. MC, V, Discover. No phone quotes. Complete photographic line, mostly mail order (free catalog) but good buys available to the walk-in trade.

- **47th Street Photo**, 67 West 47th Street, 921-1287, open 9:30 to 6, to 2 p.m. Friday, closed Saturday, 10 to 5 Sunday. Phone quotes. Expert advice and good prices keep multitudes flocking up the tired-looking stairs here for TVs, video cameras, recorders and games, typewriters, radios, stereos, computers, and a large stock of new and used cameras and photographic equipment. A second store is located at 115 West 45th Street, 398-1410.

- **Goodman Electronics**, 37 Essex Street near Grand, 673-3220, open 9:30 to 5:30, closed Saturday. AE, MC, V. No phone quotes. Name-brand luggage, dishes, calculators, hair dryers, TVs, radios and lots, lots more.

- **The Wiz**, 12 West 45th Street, 302-2000, and 404 Sixth Avenue, 677-2100, are two of the many city locations. Open 10 to 10, to 8 Saturday, 11 to 5 Sunday. No phone quotes. The newest competitor in the discount shopping game promises that "no one gfls lower" on stereo equipment, small electronics and TV prices.

- **Uncle Steve**, 343 Canal Street near Church, 226-4010, open 10 to 7 every day. Stereos, TVs, camcorders, radios, car sound systems.

- **Vendome**, 77 West 23rd Street off Sixth Avenue, 691-7500, open 8:30 to 5:30, 11 to 3 Saturday, closed Sunday. All major credit cards. Phone quotes. A member of a cooperative buying group that has its own warehouse, Vendome sells air conditioners, washing machines and other major, as well as small, appliances, computers, TVs and stereos. Major credit cards on small appliances but not on electronic equipment.

Alternative Sources

Head to **First Avenue between First and 12th Streets** for discounts on brand name appliances. Try both **Gringer & Sons** at 29 First Avenue at Second Street, 475-0600, and **Bloom & Krup**, 206 First Avenue at 12th Street, 673-2760, for bargain prices on dishwashers, freezers, refrigerators and stoves. Garland, SubZero, Traulsen, GE, KitchenAid and European manufacturers like Gaggenau and Miele, among others, are in stock or can be ordered.

Beds and Bedding

Department stores, and **Conran's** too, can take care of all your bedding needs under one roof. Lay in supplies during January and August, traditional White Sale months. **Bloomingdale's** becomes particularly generous at these times, stocking irregular Martex towels and name brand sheets at great savings.

Specialty Shops

- **Ad Hoc Softwares**, 410 West Broadway at Spring Street, 925-2652, open 11:30 to 7, to 6 Sunday. The high tech bed and bathroom furnishings displayed in this lightstruck corner store are softened by the inclusion of a few more traditional, even old fashioned, lines. Pale blue and rose French Jacquard handtowels, napkins and placemats and Carpe Diem lace curtains and lampshades add a little romance to Ad Hoc's own somber, rather austere collection of all-cotton sheets and to bed linens by international manufacturers including Wamsutta, Palais Royale and Castelini.

- **Arise Futon**, 415 Amsterdam Avenue at 79th Street, 212-362-2206, 265 West 72nd Street, 212-496-8410, and 57 Green Street, 212-925-0310, open 11-7 Monday to Saturday, until 8 on Thursday, 12-5 on Sunday. You'll find a large and reasonably priced selection of futons, frames, pillows and covers.

- **Bed & Bath & Beyond**, 620 Sixth Avenue, 255-3550, as the name declares, this popular (and affordable) newcomer to the Manhattan bedding scene, has almost everything for your household needs.

- **Castro Convertibles**, main store, 43 West 23rd Street, 255-7000, open 10 to 7, to 9 Monday and Thursday, to 7 Saturday, 11 to 6 Sunday; branch, 51 East 34th Street, 679-6099, open 10 to 6 seven days a week. First major distributor of the time-honored (since WWII anyhow) sofa bed solution for a one-room apartment.

- **Dixie Foam**, 611 Avenue of the Americas at 18th Street, 645-8999, open 10 to 6, closed Sunday. In this light-filled factory/showroom, 4" and 5 1/2"thick foam mattresses are the forte. Choose standard sizes or have irregular sizes cut and covered to order.

- **Jennifer Convertibles**, largest store, 1530 Second Avenue at 79th Street, 535-1242; other stores: 1014 Second Avenue at 54th Street, 751-1720; 404 Park Avenue South at 28th Street, 532-4697; 750 Broadway at 8th Street, 677-1539; 1770 Broadway at 57th Street, 581-1559; 2424 Broadway at 89th Street, 787-8507; and 206 Eighth Avenue at 20th Street, 924-8828; also in Brooklyn at 142 Montague Street, 718-852-3400, 280 Livingston Street at Bond Street, 718-643-8581, and 498 Fifth Avenue at 12th Street, 718-788-8119; and in Jersey City, Hudson Mall at Route 440, 201-451-2211; open 10 to 9, to 6 Saturday, noon to 5 Sunday. AE, MC, V. No question, stores in this chain, which bills itself "America's largest sofabed specialist", have the city's biggest selection of relatively inexpensive convertible sofas, including Sealy and Simmons models.

Alternative Sources

Household linens on the Lower East Side are squooshed into two blocks on Grand Street between Allen and Forsyth. An uptown look has intruded on the cramjammed bargain basement fustiness always considered de riguer in the city's most raffish bazaar area. The uninitiated will find comparatively sleek Harris Levy, 278 Grand, 226-3102, and Homeworks Design (this trendy name would have been unthinkable a few years ago), 281 Grand, 226-4644, easier to take, but the same Laura Ashley, Marimekko, Martex, Wamsutta, Cannon and Stevens lines are handled by Ezra Cohen, 307 Grand, 925-7800, and other unreconstructed firms along Grand. All closed Saturday, open Sunday. Department store White Sale prices match those you're likely to find on the Lower East Side but, if you avoid the Sunday crush, you'll discover sales personnel often more knowledgeable and helpful than their uptown counterparts.

- **ABC Carpet Co.**, 888 Broadway at East 19th Street, 473-3000, open 10 to 7, to 8 Monday and Thursday, to 6 Saturday, 11 to 6 Sunday. On Three, above the rugs, uptown imported and domestic designer lines, spreads and towelings are sold at downtown prices, along with a fetching array of folk art objects, decorative pieces and scatter pillows.

- **Kleinsleep,** 176 Avenue of the Americas between Spring and Prince Streets, 226-0900, open 10 to 7, 11 to 6 Sunday. Remainders from the six-store chain's extensive line of innerspring and foam mattresses and beds of all shapes and sizes are sold in the clearance center downstairs.

- **J. Schacter Corp.**, 85 Ludlow Street, 533-1150, open 9 to 5:30, to 4:30 Friday and Sunday, closed Saturday. AE. New York's leading feather merchants, famous for standard and custom-made pillows and comforters in various mixes of feathers and down and for reprocessing and cleaning already fabricated down bedding and garments.

Carpets and Rugs

For an overview, check the department stores, in particular **Macy's** for broadlooms and **Bloomingdale's** for imports.

- **Einstein Moomjy Inc.**, 150 East 58th Street, 758-0900, open 9:30 to 6:30, to 8 Monday and Thursday, noon to 5 Sunday. At this self-described "Rug Department Store" located in the Architects and Designers Building, the very best broadlooms share floor space with luminous Orientals as well as domestic and imported carpets of all kinds. Don't worry about missing an Einstein Moomjy sale: newspapers and TV are flooded with ads.

Specialty Shops

Oriental rug dealers are concentrated on, but by no means limited to, **Madison Avenue from 57th Street up past the Carlyle Hotel as far as 86th Street**. Oriental rug specialists here include **Dildarian Inc.**, 595 Madison near 57th, third floor, 288-4948, and **Marvin Kagan, Inc.**, 625 Madison at 59th, 535-9000. **A. Beshar & Co. Inc.**, 611 Broadway, Room 405, 529-7300, not only sells Orientals but is a cleaning specialist of top repute. For good buys on needlepoint rugs, among original handpainted or tapestry pillows, try **The Winthrop Collection**, 501 Lexington Avenue, at 47th Street, 212-593-3621.

- **Beyond the Bosphorous**, 79 Sullivan Street near Spring Street, 212-219-8257, open noon to 6 p.m. Tuesday through Sunday. *New York* magazine says "Kilim with Kindness" after landing great deals on Turkish Kilim runners, floor and scatter rugs.

- **Tribeca Rugs**, 90 Hudson Street near Harrison Street, 274-0376, open noon to 8, 2:30 to 5:30 Sunday. Here Kilim remnants are used to cover pillows mountained in the middle of the piles and piles of jewel-toned, flat-woven tribal Kilim rugs from Turkey and Pakistan.

Discount Stores

- **ABC Carpet Co**., carpets at 881 Broadway at East 19th Street, rugs across the street at 888 Broadway, 473-3000, open 10 to 7, to 8 Monday and Thursday, to 6 Saturday, 11 to 6 Sunday. An overwhelming selection of broadlooms from all the mills. The rug store carries new imports and, down in the basement, an in-depth stock of carpet remnants at bargain prices.

- **Carpet Fashions**, 111 Fourth Avenue at 12th Street, 677-1717, open 9 to 6, 10 to 6 Saturday, noon to 5 Sunday. This tidy discount emporium features over 20,000 kinds of carpet as well as ceramic tiles, parquet and other wood floor materials.

- **Central Carpet Cleaning Co**., 426 Columbus Avenue between 80th and 81st Streets, 787-8813, open 9 to 6, 10 to 7:30 Thursday, 9 to 5 Saturday, 11 to 5 Sunday. For over 50 years, Central has been supplying New Yorkers with antique and semi-antique Oriental rugs—from earthy Kilims to elegant Kashans. Go upstairs for more mundane mill ends and discounted broadlooms.

- **The Rug Warehouse, Inc.**, 2222 Broadway at 79th Street, 787-6665, open 10 to 6, to 8 Thursday, 11 to 5 Sunday. Discounted semi-antique and antique rugs fill a barn-like space above Woolworth's on the Upper West Side.

Alternative Sources

Carpets and rugs also turn up at thrift shops, auctions and flea markets. See **Home Furnishings** for details.

Computers

Personal computers are sold in slick manufacturers' showrooms designed for the 21st century as well as in comparatively cozy neighborhood centers and barn-like discount warehouses. Many outlets offer courses as well as literature on the subject. For an overview of current prices and trends, check the Science section of the Tuesday edition of *The New York Times*, where the weekly computer columns are flanked by ads for hardware, software and allied services.

- **Computerland**, 730 Third Avenue at 45th Street, 212-972-5099, open 9 to 5:30 Monday through Friday. An extensive line of IBM, Compaq, Epson, Hewlett-Packard, NEC, Toshiba and Macintosh desk-tops and laptops plus a variety of printers. There are classes as well.

- **Personal Computer Power Center**, 1650 Broadway at 51st Street, 212-727-8250, by appointment. Writers and other professional computer users who need occasional hand-holding, or at least guidance, with their systems swear by this SoHo outfit, which went from full retail to selling and consulting. For $75 to $100 a consultation they'll advise you on what you need, help you build a system and, if you like, sell you what you need. They also offer a consumers' guide course and a bookkeeping conversion course.

- **Radio Shack Computer Center**, 1134 Avenue of the Americas at 44th Street, 212-221-7435, open 9 to 7 weekdays, 10 to 6 Saturday, and 11 to 5 Sunday. The Radio Shack center stocks Tandy computers, printers and peripherals as well as thousands of software programs.

- **User Friendly**, 128 West 72nd Street, 580-4433; 200 East 83rd Street, 535-4100; and 401 Sixth Avenue at 8th Street, 675-2255, open 9 to 10 Monday through Thursday, 9 to 6 Friday, 11 to 7 Saturday, noon to 8 Sunday. Is your computer on the blink? Computer illiterates and literati can rent personal computers equipped with laser printers, scanners, modems, and graphic capabilities. Rates are calculated by the hour and functions used. A knowledgeable sales staff is on hand to lead you through any unfamiliar terrain with audio tutorials and advice, or, for a per-page rate, do the work for you.

Discount Stores

- **47th Street Photo**, 67 West 47th Street and 115 West 45th Street, 212-921-1287, open 9:30 to 6 Monday and Tuesday, 9:30 to 7:30 Wednesday and Thursday, 9:30 to 2 Friday, 10 to 5 Sunday, closed Saturday. This celebrated camera and electronic appliance firm, a stalwart of the discount scene, stocks a huge range of computer hardware and software at highly competitive prices.

- **J&R Computer World**, 15 Park Row across from City Hall, 212-349-4727, open 9 to 6:30 Monday through Saturday. This respected outlet sells IBM, Apple, Leading Edge, Wang, Canon, and a full line of printers, laptops, software and accessories, all discounted. They're big, but salesmen on the floor will talk to you if you don't know what you want. If you do know, you can phone your order, 800-221-8180.

Fabric—Decorating

Ringed around the Decoration & Design Building, 979 Third Avenue between 59th and 60th Streets, wholesale fabric showrooms marked "To The Trade Only" usually require shoppers to be accompanied by a decorator or to possess a decorator's card. No entree? Try the department stores or the retail fabric importers or discount merchants listed below, all of whom stock dress goods as well as slipcover, curtain and upholstery fabrics.

Specialty Shops

Retail Imports Fabrics identified with a specific nation form the basis for some of Manhattan's most enchanting retail outlets. You can buy yardage as well as decorative accents, clothes and accessories made from the goods featured at the following shops: **China Seas**, 979 Third Avenue, 752-5555, has few direct imports but a wide array of Orient-inspired patterns; **Handblock**, 487 Columbus Avenue between 83rd and 84th Streets, 799-4342, with hand-stamped and handwoven Indian cottons and an outstanding Dhurrie rug selection; **Island Trading**, 15 East 4th Street, 353-0297, open 11 to 7 Tuesday through Saturday, takes orders for hand-customed, Caribbean blocked batik fabric in their home-decorating department; **Laura Ashley**, 714 Madison Avenue at 63rd Street, 735-5000, displays three floors of furnishings, accessories and yardage in sprigged Victorian-style cottons; and that other British flower bower, **Liberty of London**, Fifth Avenue at 51st Street, 459-0080, stocks soothing Viyellas, silks and fine voiles in traditional florals, as well as newer geometric designs.

Discount Stores

- **K Trimming & Zippers**, 519 Broadway, 431-8929, open 9:30 to 6. Dig through boxes stuffed with grommets, braids and hundreds of buttons for low, low prices on all the trimmings.

- **Samuel Beckenstein**, 125 Orchard Street, 475-4525, open 9 to 5:30, closed Saturday. Big selection, low prices for decorating fabrics, men's suiting, and dress fabrics.

- **The Fabric Warehouse**, 406 Broadway at Canal Street, 431-9510, open 9 to 6, to 7:30 Thursday, 10 to 5 Saturday and Sunday. MC, V. Right in the heart of the fabric jobbing district between SoHo and City Hall, this ramshackle three-story outlet houses notable bargains.

- **Silk Surplus, Inc.**, 1147 Madison Avenue, 794-9373, and 223 East 58th Street, 753-6511, open 10 to 5:30, 11 to 4 Saturday, closed Sunday. MC, V. While noted for Scalamandre seconds, crewel-work, heavy embroideries and other elegant coverings, including silks, are stocked at both locations.

Alternative Sources

Mecca to home decorators and seamstresses are the Lower East Side fabric shops clustered on **Grand Street at the Eldridge Street intersection** (between Forsyth and Allen). These discount stores, like the household linen outlets adjacent, are open Sunday through Friday, closed on Saturday. Prices for the curtain, upholstery and slipcover fabrics in stock are almost always a better bargain than materials you select from the sample books. But these too are discounted. About half the stores have workshop facilities on premises. You'll find stellar names printed on the selvages of velvets, embroideries, cottons and tapestries: Brunschwig & Fils, Givenchy, Schumacher, and Stroheim & Roman were sighted. **Interiors by Royale**, 289 Grand Street, 431-0170; **Martin Albert Interiors**, 288 Grand Street, 226-4047; **Richard's Interior Design**, 317 Grand Street, 966-3606; and **Harry Zarin Company**, 292 Grand Street, 925-6112, are among the shops to investigate.

Furniture

Antique furniture dealers (at least in their shops) tend to cluster. Rare pieces from the 17th, 18th and 19th centuries, the quality found at the Winter Antiques Show held late each January at the Seventh Regiment Armory, are most likely to be found in elegant shops along Madison Avenue north of 63rd Street. Increasingly, retail outlets for less prestigious pieces are infiltrating the wholesale "To The Trade Only" antique district located in the quadrant formed by University Place, Broadway, East 9th and East 12th Streets in the Village. Art Deco dealers and those specializing in the Depression era, in Retro furniture and the now-fashionable Fifties clump together in SoHo. A handful of good sources can also be found in Greenwich Village. The more upscale antique stores, dealing mostly in Early American and French country furniture, line Bleecker west of Seventh Avenue. And try Hudson between Horatio and Barrow for chunky oak furniture of varying quality—everything from mirrored dressers and chests to large, heavy din-ing tables.

Look for furniture sales post-Christmas. Those held by New York department stores at their warehouses in the boroughs and suburbs offer especially large savings for anyone with a car and enough stami-na to brave the stampede.

- **Bon Marche**, main store, 55 West 13th Street between Fifth and Sixth Avenues, sixth floor, 620-5550; uptown store, 1060 Third Avenue between 62nd and 63rd Streets, 620-5591; both open 10:30 to 6:30, closed Sunday. MC, V. Good buys in upholstered chairs and sofas, laminate-and veneer-covered particle board book-cases and bureaus, and glass, chrome and marble-topped tables. Extensive, inexpensive, modern lighting fixtures are found on Seven at the 13th Street store.

- **Conran's**, main store, 160 East 54th Street at Third Avenue in Citicorp Center, 371-2225; downtown store, 2-8 Astor Place between Broadway and Lafayette Street, 505-1515; both open 10 to 9, to 7 Saturday, noon to 6 Sunday. AE, MC, V and Conran's charge card. Sensibly priced international selection of uncommonly attractive modern furnishings including Scandinavian bedding, Indian carpets, French and Finnish glassware and dishes, German lamps, and upholstered and tubular metal furniture from Canada and the US sold, at both spacious two-story locations.

- **The Door Store**, 1 Park Avenue at 33rd Street, 679-9700; other stores: 1201 Third Avenue at 70th Street, 772-1110; 123 West 17th Street west of Sixth Avenue, 627-1515; 130 Cedar Street off West Street, 267-1250; all open 9:30 or 10 to 5:45 or 6, later Monday and Thursday, noon to 4:45 or 5 Sunday; 1 Carlton Avenue, Brooklyn, 718-596-1938, open 9 to 4:30, noon to 4 Sunday. AE, MC, V. An excellent source of reasonably priced contemporary furniture, espe-cially desks, wall units, chairs and tables in oak, teak and pine—but no doors. Their sales are well worth watching for.

- **IKEA**, 1000 Center Street, Elizabeth, NJ, 908-289-4488, open 10 to 9 Monday through Saturday, 10 to 6 Sunday; Broadway Mall, Hicksville, Long Island, 516-681-4532, same hours as NJ, except on

Sundays when it is open 11 to 7. Those without a vehicle can take the LIRR from Penn Station and get off at the Hicksville station, for those going to the Elizabeth location, call 800-287-4532 for details about the bus service from Mid-town. IKEA fans will tell you that the trek to this 270,000 square-foot Swedish furniture store is a must for first apartment dwellers. So borrow a car if you can, and stock up on pine dressers for $68, kitchen tables for $59, all designed Swedish-style with clean lines and natural materials. Pick up sheets, glasses, wallpaper, lamps and more—for less. If you're in the New Jersey store, have a Swedish meatball lunch for less than $4 in IKEA's spacious, clean (if slightly antiseptic) cafeteria, also open for breakfast and dinner. IKEA does not accept American Express but they do accept Visa, MasterCard, Discover as well as personal checks. Delivery is available.

- **Jensen-Lewis**, 89 Seventh Avenue at 15th Street, 929-4880, and 1496 Third Avenue at 84th Street, 439-6440, open 10 to 7, to 8 Thursday, noon to 5 Sunday. Famous for deck chairs, satchels, backpacks and other canvas products in lots of zippy colors. In big, bright quarters, casual furniture and an expanding housewares department will be found, but canvas is still Jensen-Lewis' bag.

- **Maurice Villency**, 200 Madison Avenue at 35th Street, 725-4840, open 10 to 6, to 9 Monday and Thursday, noon to 5 Sunday. If sleek and modern, embellished with glass and brass, is the look you favor, then head for this sparkling showroom where furniture lines exclusive to Maurice Villency are displayed.

- **Workbench**, main store, 470 Park Avenue South at 32nd Street, 481-5454; other stores: 161 Avenue of the Americas at Spring Street, 675-7775; 336 East 86th Street between First and Second Avenues, 794-4418; 2091 Broadway off 72nd Street, 724-3670; 130 Clinton Street, Brooklyn Heights, 718-625-1616; all open 10 to 6:30, to 8 Thursday, to 6 Saturday, noon to 5 Sunday. Excellent resource for clean-lined wood and tubular steel furniture, platform beds, lamps and all sorts of desks.

- **Zona**, 97 Greene Street between Spring and Prince Streets, 925-6750, open 11:30 to 6, to 7 Thursday, noon to 5 Sunday.

Oh-so-tasteful, handcrafted Southwestern furniture, antique and contemporary, plus Navajo rugs, wood and clay artifacts. It's Santa Fe in SoHo.

Alternative Sources

- **Salvation Army**, main store, 536 West 46th Street between Tenth and Eleventh Avenues, 757-2311, and seven other outlets, open 9 to 4:45, closed Sunday. MC, V for purchases over $50. With great pride, the Army explains that the two huge warehouse floors on 46th Street contain everything a homemaker needs to set up housekeeping.

- **Thrift Shops** Charities and hospital research programs benefit from the proceeds of these stores, just as donors benefit from the tax deductions and buyers benefit from the bargains in designer clothes to silver pitchers to down sofas. Head to Third Avenue between 80th and 86th Streets and east to Second Avenue for new and gently used goods. **Spence-Chapin Corner Shop**, 1430 Third Avenue, 737-8448; **Irvington House Thrift Shop**, 1534 Second Avenue, 879-4555; and **Memorial Sloan-Kettering Cancer Center Thrift Shop**, 1440 Third Avenue, 535-1250 are just three among many thrift stores concentrated in this neighborhood.

- **Atlantic Avenue, Brooklyn** *The Village Voice* describes this as the best strip in the five boroughs for vintage furniture above the junk category. Beware of pricey delivery costs, the *Voice* warns, and think about renting a van. Atlantic Avenue between Nevins and Bond Streets.

- **Auction Houses** Diverting, and occasionally rewarding, auctions are another way of obtaining basic necessities such as mattresses, as well as moth-eaten mooseheads, which, in fact, make poor hatracks. Check the auction pages at the back of the Arts and Leisure section of the Sunday *Times* for sale descriptions and viewing hours. The big three, **Christie's**, 502 Park Avenue, 546-1000; **Phillips**, 406 East 79th Street, 570-4830; and **Sotheby Parke Bernet**, 1334 York Avenue, 606-7000, hold specialty auctions of interest to collectors and connoisseurs (and voyeurs) once or twice a week in season. The second tier, including **Christie's East**, 219 East 67th Street, 570-4141 (weekly); **William Doyle Galleries**, 175 East 87th Street, 427-2730 (every other Wednesday); and **Sotheby's Arcade Auctions**, 1334 York Avenue, 606-7000, usually auction off a varied selection of household goods in a single session. Note: Interior designers prowl the tag sale operation where Doyle's disposes of high-class flotsam from the adjacent gallery 8:30 to 4:30 Monday through Friday, 10 to 5 Saturday; you can too. For erratic quality, more fun and lower prices try: **Greenwich Auction Room**, 114 East 13th Street, 533-5550 (every third Wednesday or so); **Lubin Galleries**, 30 West 26th Street, 924-3777 (alternate Saturdays); and **Tepper Galleries**, 110 East 25th Street, 677-5300 (alternate Saturdays).

• **Flea Markets** This raffish country custom adapts well to New York's jostling sidewalks. Check the "Antiques" classified column near the back of the Weekend section in the Friday *Times* for flea market listings. All but the hardiest markets (and those held indoors) shut down from late fall until spring. The **Annex Antiques Fair**, Avenue of the Americas at 26th Street, 243-5343, 9 to 5 Saturday and Sunday, levies a $1 admission charge, but 80 to 100 dealers make it the largest and best of the lot. On Sundays, also, the same management runs the **Annex Flea Market** two blocks south at 24th Street, where new and used clothing and housewares are sold. These two markets have now been joined by **The Garage** on 112 West 25th Street, Manhattan's largest indoor flea market. All three markets are run by Alan Boss, and they are the closest thing in New York to a European flea market a la London's Portobello Road or Paris' Marche aux Puces.

• **Public school PTAs** sometimes sponsor flea markets on school grounds in order to raise funds. These are rain-or-shine affairs; sometimes they take place on Saturdays and Sundays and sometimes they don't. The most consistent markets include the one held in the Greenwich Avenue school yard of PS 41 between Seventh Avenue and 10th Street and in the Columbus Avenue yard of JHS 44 between 77th and 78th Streets. Also, at PS 321 on Seventh Avenue between 2nd and 3rd Streets. Other markets include the **SoHo-Canal Street Flea Market**, at Broadway and Grand and the

Indoor Antiques Fair, 122 West 26th Street.

• **The Street** A *New York Times* Home section featured the apartment of a dedicated young middle-class scrounger who furnished
his two rooms with street finds. The comfortable living room looked
just like home in the heartlands, traditional with overstuffed chairs, a
coffee table and standing lamp. Resourcefulness, a strong back and
willing cabbies are all that's required for street shopping—well, that
and a knowledge of the Sanitation Department's bulk collection day
for whatever area you're combing. It's legal to put large items on the
sidewalk after dark the evening before the appropriate Sanitation
Section's assigned day for bulk pickups. Days vary. Because bulk is
collected Wednesday on much of the Upper East Side, Tuesday
night is the best time to scout this fertile territory. Try Wednesday
nights in the West Village, where pickups are scheduled for
Thursdays. If found furniture is your style, call Manhattan East Bulk
Collection, 289-1800, or Manhattan West Bulk Collection, 265-7550,
for pickup days in sections near your apartment.

Hardware, Paints and Wallpaper

On Saturdays, slow-moving lines as long as the lists new residents
clutch make local hardware stores as good a way of meeting people as
local bars later that night. But once you've made new friends along with
those seemingly endless purchases, you may require more than the
good old all-purpose neighborhood reliable to fill decorating needs.
Some specialty resources, then.

• **Janovic Plaza**, main store, 1150 Third Avenue at 67th Street,
772-1400, open 9:30 to 6, 9:30 to 5:30 Saturday, 11 to 4:30
Sunday; other stores: 159 West 72nd Street between Broadway and
Columbus Avenue, 595-2500, open 7:30 to 6, to 8 Thursday, 9 to 6
Saturday, 11 to 5 Sunday; 213 Seventh Avenue between 22nd and
23rd Streets, 645-5454, and 161 Avenue of the Americas at Spring
Street, 627-1100, open 7:30 to 6:30, 9 to 6 Saturday, 11 to 5
Sunday. MC, V. The Bloomingdale's of the paint-and-wallpaper
scene, Janovic's image is as glossy as its enamels and printed foil
papers. At the Third Avenue store, they can computer-match any

color you bring in. For the latest colors and trends, as well as an overall view of what's available, Janovic can't be beat.

- **Simon Hardware**, 421 Third Avenue near 30th Street, 532-9220, open 8 to 5:30, 10 to 5 Saturday. AE, MC, V. Take a number and join the inevitable throng of contractors and decorators shopping Simon's first-rate stock of brass, bronze, pewter, plastic, wood, steel—whatever!—decorative hardware.

Discount Store

- **Pintchik,** 22nd Street and Third Avenue, 777-3030; 87th Street and Third Avenue, 289-6300; and 2475 Broadway at 92nd Street, 769-1440; open 8:30 to 6:50, 9 to 6 Saturday, 11 to 6 Sunday. Whether you select from books or open stock, all wallpapers are discounted here and so is the rest of the color-coordinated merchandise, which includes name-brand floor tiles, linoleum, paint, window shades and blinds.

Alternative Sources

Hardware and plastics—nuts and bolts made dingy by neighboring bright, bouncing baubles—overflow rows of cutdown cardboard boxes that alternate with the racks of surplus and flea market clothing lining Canal Street between West Broadway and Broadway. Most of this sidewalk hardware and pretty plastic bric-a-brac is useful only to the professional, handyman or collagist, but inside, generalists revel in complete selections of quality merchandise at exceptionally fair prices. Try any of the three stores sitting side by grey dilapidated side on Canal west of Broadway: Reliable Hardware, 303 Canal, 966-4166, AE, DC, MC, V; Canal Hardware, 305 Canal, 226-0825, particularly for machinists, plumbers, and do-it-yourself tools, all kinds of tools! AE, DC; and C. K. and L. Surplus, 307 Canal, 966-1745, MC, V.

- **Pearl Paint Co.**, 308 Canal Street, 431-7932, open 9 to 5:30, Thursday to 7, 10 to 5:30 Sunday. Listed here because of the discounted house paints, including Benjamin Moore, sold on One,

Pearl Paint is in fact renowned for art-related materials and accessories and its four upper floors are usually swamped with an international array of fine artists.

Housewares

- **Bazaar Stores** are a six-store chain easily identified by bright yellow plastic signs with bold blue letters: **Broadway Bazaar**, 2025 Broadway at 69th Street, 873-9153; **First Avenue Bazaar**, 1453 First at 75th, 737-2003; **Second Avenue Bazaar**, 501 Second at 28th, 683-2293; **Third Avenue Bazaar** at 1145 Third at 67th, 988-7600, and 1362 Third at 77th, 861-5999; and the **Third Street Bazaar**, 125 West Third off Sixth Avenue, 673-4138, open 10 to 6:30, 11 to 5:30 Sunday. All-purpose emporiums with adequately tasteful, moderately priced rattan chairs, painted glasses, curly plastic cords, greeting cards, black pressboard stacking tables, aluminum and enamel pots, etc. etc. etc.

- **Pottery Barn**, 117 East 59th Street between Lexington and Park, 753-5424; 250 West 57th Street at Eighth Avenue, 315-1855; 51 Greenwich Avenue between Sixth and Seventh Avenues, 807-6321; 700 Broadway at 4th Street, 505-6377; Pier 17 Pavilion, 89 South Street, 233-2141; 1451 Second Avenue at 76th Street, 988-4228; 2109 Broadway between 73rd and 74th Streets, 595-5573; 1292 Lexington Avenue between 87th and 88th Streets, 289-2477, open 11 to 9, noon to 7 Sunday. Pottery Barn keeps growing, so look for a new outlet in your neighborhood. It's not all pottery, for sure. There's a definitive selection of inexpensive to moderately-priced imported glassware, china and table settings, augmented by quality cookware, sometimes below list price, occasional gourmet items, well-priced chairs, cotton rugs, decorative items—whatever meets their sharp-eyed buyers' high standards for good design. Their periodic sales of specific merchandise are worth catching, and see Williams-Sonoma for savings on remainders at the store on Tenth Avenue.

- **Zabar's,** 2245 Broadway at 80th Street, 787-2000. Housewares department on the mezzanine open 8 to 6 daily. Food shops downstairs open 8 to 7:30, to midnight on Saturday and 6 on Sunday.

Expansive Zabar's, mecca to millions for unequalled edibles, houses an equally esteemed and often bargain-priced selection of supplies for the home and kitchen in four rooms on the mezzanine.

Specialty Shops

- **Bridge Kitchenware**, 214 East 52nd Street off Third Avenue, 688-4220, 9 to 5:30, 10 to 4:30 Saturday, closed Sunday. MC, V. Purveyors of durable, professional, high quality kitchen equipment— for example, chrome-topped glass shakers found on every luncheonette counter worth its salt, an enviable selection of French tin-lined copper pots, huge Hobart dough mixers—to the city's food establishment and serious cooks the world over.

- **Broadway Panhandler**, 520 Broadway at Spring Street, 966-3434, open 10:30 to 6, 11 to 6 Saturday, noon to 5 Sunday. AE, MC, V, $20 minimum. Discounted cookware (Calphalon, All Clad, Le Creuset) and quality kitchen tools for the serious cook. Hit Dean & Deluca a block north for your ingredients.

- **Fishs Eddy**, 889 Broadway at 19th Street, 420-9020; 551 Hudson Street at Perry, 627-3956, open 10 to 8 Monday through Saturday and 11 to 7 on Sunday. Surplus restaurant china where you can buy just one piece. Everything guaranteed chip and crack-free.

- **Hammacher Schlemmer**, 147 East 57th Street, 421-9000, open 10 to 6, closed Sunday. Accordian-like, the size of this establishment stalwart seems to expand and contract. Like its growing catalog business, Hammacher's features a collection of premier quality kitchen and barware, electronic products and gadgets galore.

- **D. F. Sanders and Co.**, 386 West Broadway, 925-9040, open 10:30 to 7, noon to 5:30 Sunday, and 952 Madison Avenue at 75th Street, 879-6161, open 10 to 6, noon to 5 Sunday. Uptown shoppers no longer need travel to SoHo for housewares with the hard-edged and hip industrial look so favored by loft dwellers. Softened by the rounded curves and bright colors of equally stylish Deco ware, Sanders' merchandise is now available in a smaller and slightly more refined shop across from the Whitney Museum as well as in the original downtown warehouse space.

- **Koto**, 71 West Houston Street, 533-8601, open daily 12 to 7. Sushi dishes and other Japanese kitchenware including animal chopstick rests.

- **Tiffany and Co.**, 727 Fifth Avenue at 57th Street, 755-8000, open 10 to 5:30, closed Sunday. Something a bit more upscale than rainbow plastic dinnerware from the Third Avenue Bazaar? Head past the world famous array of jewels and jewelry on Tiffany's high-ceilinged hallowed first floor and up to Three where, against shimmering ivory walls, plates by Picasso nudge Royal Crown Derby place settings. Tired of jelly glasses? Crystal's to your right.

- **Williams-Sonoma**, 20 East 60th Street, 980-5155; 110 Seventh Avenue, 633-2203; 1309 Second Avenue, 288-8404; 1175 Madison Avenue, 289-6832. Known through their appealing catalogue to serious cooks nationwide, this California-based firm specializes in quality cookware, handsome glassware, and mostly imported, country-style tableware. The familiar pieces, and then some, are available here, along with gourmet food items and cookbooks. For lovers of blue and color-coordinated kitchens it's a treasure trove. Where else would you find a red Kitchen Aid mixer? Their 15,000-square foot outlet location, 231 Tenth Avenue at 23rd Street, offers great discounts on remainder items from Williams-Sonoma and their other three stores: **Chambers Gardener's Eden**, **Hold Everything**, and **Pottery Barn**.

Alternative Sources

- **The Restaurant Supply District** As the use of professional kitchenware in the home increases, the wholesale restaurant strip along the seedy **Bowery between West Houston and Broome Streets** has become an accepted destination for retail shoppers in spite of its derelict state. Pots, pans, butcher block, Robot Coupes, Garland ranges, barware and thick, nigh on to unbreakable, dishes are available from most stores at less than uptown retail. Outlets include **Bari Restaurant Equipment Corp.**, 240 Bowery, 925-3845, for a grand assortment of pots, pans, strainers, stirrers and such must-haves as pizza ovens and gigantic wooden pizza spatulas.

- **Secaucus Outlet Center**, Secaucus, NJ and Flemington, NJ. Don't go around Christmas without armor plate. At other times, values obtained in these two discount meccas may well be worth the shlep. To get to **Secaucus**, about 15 minutes from the Lincoln Tunnel, follow signs to Route 3 West continuing about 6 miles to the "Meadowlands Parking" exit, take the down ramp to the light, then a left and continue past two more sets of lights to American Way, take another left and you will be confronted by a number of warehouses. Bring boxes for your gleanings and a companion to watch them as you gather. Get a booklet containing a map and brand names by merchandise category from the first warehouse. Mikasa and Copco both have large outlets here. While you're at it, if you've the stamina, load up on discount Gucci shoes, Liz Claiborne goodies, Oleg Cassini and the like. It takes an hour or so to reach **Flemington** and Dansk, Mikasa and an interminable number of other housewares outlets, but if quality doesn't give you the vapors, the quaint Victorian houses (filled with discount operations) lining the main street make shopping here less onerous. Fastest route is via NJ Turnpike South to Exit 10 "Methuen," picking up I 287 North to Exit 10 (again), marked "22 West," and "202/206" continuing 2 1/2 miles to a circle exiting on Route 202, to "Flemington/Princeton."

Lamps and Light Fixtures

You can't beat the department stores for variety and choice. But if you want better prices, or the newest imports, shop some of the sources below.

Specialty Shops

- **George Kovacs Inc.**, 330 East 59th Street, 838-3400, open 10 to 6:30, to 6 Saturday, noon to 5 Sunday. A striking line of contemporary battery-operated wall clocks has been added to the modern lighting fixtures Kovacs manufactures. You'll also find Noguchi-designed Akari lamps and European imports.

- **Just Bulbs Ltd.**, 938 Broadway, 228-7820. An eclectic and funky mix of bulbs (and more bulbs!).

- **The Lighting Center**, 1097 Second Avenue between 57th and 58th Streets, 888-8383, open 10 to 6, 11 to 5:30 Saturday, closed Sunday. Although a large selection of mainly American contemporary lighting fixtures crams the center's small, grey-walled retail shop, the specialty is track lighting. Have a system custom designed or choose from the Halo, Lightolier, Lighting Services or Altalite lines already on hand.

- **Lightforms**, 168 Eighth Avenue, 255-4664; 510 Amsterdam Avenue, 496-2090. Moderate to expensively-priced contemporary light fixtures; service.

- **Rosetta Electric**, 73 Murray Street off West Broadway, 233-9088, open 8:30 to 5:30, 9:30 to 4:30 Saturday, closed Sunday. A wide variety of lighting fixtures, more traditional than chic or high tech, at reasonable prices makes this a source worth investigating, especially if you live or work downtown. "You've never seen a lighting store quite like this," says a four-year Tribeca resident.

Alternative Sources

The Lamp and Light Fixture District concentrated on **The Bowery between Broome and Canal Streets** abuts wholesale restaurant supply stores that begin at Broome and end a few blocks north at Houston. If you know what you want, don't be daunted by lurid window displays of fantasy fixtures. Push on past high kitsch, find a salesman and describe your product. Chances are the fixture can be ordered or will be in stock at less than retail. But don't count on tender loving care. That's reserved for large wholesale buyers. Try **Bowery Lighting Corp.**, 132 Bowery, 966-4034, one of the largest stores in the district; **Harem Lites**, 139 Bowery, 226-3042, track lighting specialists stocking the Halo line; and **Paris Lighting Fixture Co.**, 134 Bowery, 941-8887, featuring fluorescent lighting and Lightolier track fixtures. **Just Shades**, 21 Spring Street, 966-2757, covers the gamut from burlaps to fine pleated ivory silks in all sizes; and **Grand Brass Lamp Parts**, 221 Grand Street, 226-2567, just around the corner from the lamp stores, is the place to go for findings.

Greenmarkets/Farmer's Markets

One of the surprises and joys of New York shopping has the been the great success of the many greenmarkets that now take place throughout the city. The Council of the Environment of New York City sponsors these affairs by arranging for farmers and bakers from the tri-state area to sell their produce and goods at various outdoor locations within Manhattan, Brooklyn and the Bronx. In addition to fruit and vegetable growers, the Council invites suppliers of beef, pork, lamb, poultry, eggs, honey, dairy, wine, flowers, maple syrup and other delectable items. Prices are competitive and the offerings are fresher than anything else except homegrown. All this and a general air of festivity is the reason why so many urbane New Yorkers have made greenmarkets a regular part of their shopping routine. Keep in mind that because the produce does come from the tri-state area, the warmer months are the most bountiful time to shop the markets. Unless otherwise noted, market hours are from 8 to 6.

Manhattan

City Hall	Tuesday	Year round
Park Row	Friday	Year round
World Trade Center	Tuesday	June-December
Church & Fulton Streets	Thursday	Year round
Federal Plaza	Friday	Year round
Broadway/Thomas St.	Friday	Year round
Washington Park	Wednesday (8-3)	Year round
Greenwich & Reade	Saturday (8-3)	Year round
St. Mark's Church	Tuesday	June-November
West Village	Saturday (8-1)	June-November
Gansevoort & Hudson	Saturday (8-1)	June-November
Union Square (17th & B'way)	Monday, Wednesday Friday and Saturday	Year round

Sheffield Plaza ....Wednesday ....Year round

57th St./9th Ave. ....Saturday ....Year round

W. 70th Street ....Saturday (8-3) ....July-November

I.S. 44
(77th & Columbus) ....Sunday ....Year round

West 102nd Street
(at Amsterdam Ave.) ....Friday (8-2) ....June-November

Harlem Hospital
(Lenox Ave. & 136th St.) ....Tuesday (8-3) ....July-November

West 175th Street
(at Broadway) ....Thursday ....June-December

The Bronx

Lincoln Hospital
(149th St. & Park Ave.)...........Friday (8-3) ....July-November

Poe Park (Grand
Concourse & E. 192nd) ....Tuesday...........................June-November

Brooklyn

Borough Hall..........................Tuesday...........................Year round

Montague Street....................Saturday ....Year round

Grand Army Plaza
(Prospect Park entrance) ....Saturday (8-4) ....Year round

Albee Square
(Fulton St. & DeKalb Ave.) .....Wednesday (8-3)..............July-November

Personal tours may be arranged of the **Union Square** greenmarket, the acknowledged granddaddy of them all. These tours take place on Wednesdays, Fridays and Saturdays and take about 1 1/2 hours. Call the Council on the Environment of New York City at 212-477-3220 for more information.

Sample Sales

Being new to New York, you're probably not familiar with a great New York amenity: sample sales. These are special sales of a designer's left-over inventory (from jewelry to furniture to whirlpools). Typically, designers do not advertise their sample sales, but predominant sale months are November, December, April and May. Scan *New York* magazine's "Sales & Bargains" section for some sale times and locations. Better yet, subscribe to the **S&B Report,** 212-679-5400, a monthly publication stating every major designer showroom sale in the city. A one-year subscription is $50.

Day Care

Child care for New York City's young molds itself to parental needs much as the Plasticine wedged and shaped on countless low tables responds to the pressure of small pre-school fingers. The search for acceptable day care solutions intensifies as the demand for flexible quality care accelerates. Non-profit agencies which act as go-betweens for parents and day care providers are proliferating. Some corporations have begun to distribute day care information to their employees while others have gone so far as to add on-premises facilities. Nursery schools which used to start with three-year-olds now have toddlers' groups for twos.

Still, quality day care is hard to find and more expensive in New York than anywhere else in the country, thanks to the tremendous cost of real estate and the need for stringent standards governing the operation of day care centers. Asked what is required to open a day care center here, Frances Alston, program director of the not-for-profit Day Care Council, says, "First thing is, rob a bank. You can't start a day care center in New York for less than a quarter million dollars."

Listed below you'll find thumbnail descriptions of the kinds of pre-school care (and education) available in New York City. Arranged chronologically by ages covered—from birth through six years—these categories are followed by the names of organizations which provide specific day care recommendations.

It should be noted that New York State establishes the eligibility requirements for publicly funded day care, be it Family Day Care in a private home or Group Care at a center. To be eligible, a family of two must have a combined income of less than $27,084, a family of three less than $29,460, a family of four less than $31,224, and so on. Almost all those entitled to assistance still pay something; currently fees range from a low of $2 per week per child up to $85 per week.

Resources

Infant Care

Formal programs for the two-month-old to two-year-old set are almost all publicly funded and appended to day care centers. Call the New York City Health Department's Division of Day Care, 212-334-7803, for the names of city-licensed facilities. Infants can also be placed in Family Day Care homes.

Family Day Care

More and more middle-class parents are electing family care for their toddlers. Said to be the most widely used form of day care in the country, here in New York City the Health Department and/or other agencies involved in the field certify and supervise individuals caring for infants and toddlers in their apartments. These "providers," often mothers of young children drawn to child care as a means of remaining at home with their own youngsters, are allowed to oversee up to six children—no more than two of whom can be infants—in their dwelling at one time. Typically, parents who do not qualify for assistance pay between $30 and $40 per child for a six-to eight-hour day.

Group Day Care Centers

These city-licensed facilities, be they in the private or public sector, offer educational as well as caretaking programs for groups of children primarily, but not exclusively, between the ages of two and six years for an extended (beyond normal nursery school hours) or a full eight-hour day.

- **Publicly funded day care centers** are usually found in, or contiguous to, neighborhoods with the greatest economic need. Even with an income above the maximum allowed by the state (see introduction for specifics) parents proving "social" need—those working full time qualify—can apply to publicly funded day care centers if they are prepared to pay the full cost for their child's care, currently between $80 and $217 a week, depending on the facility.

- **Private centers** tend to be either nursery schools which have

added all-daycare to the regular school curriculum or centers established to supply day care which also offer education.

Playgroups

Neighborhood parents often band together informally, usually in cooperative fashion, to care for a small group of pre-schoolers for a half-day or
so, one, two or three times a week.

Toddlers' Groups

Formal groups with a paid trained professional in command cater to the
18-to 36-month-old set. Groups with more than five children must be
licensed by the Department of Health. Toddlers' groups are also
appended to nursery schools and even a few private elementary and
secondary schools.

Nursery Schools

In New York they are usually private and, while geared to three-, four-
and five-year-olds, often include toddlers' groups and sometimes all-day
care as well.

Information Sources

Two books which are especially useful to parents of young children in
the city may also save considerable calling time. *New York Parents'
Book* by Lois Gilman (Penguin) covers everything from having the baby
to care to entertainment. *The Manhattan Directory of Private Nursery
Schools* by Linda Faulhaber (SoHo Press) is a detailed listing of more
than 150 nursery and all-day programs plus other useful information.

Several non-profit organizations as well as the Agency for Child
Development, jointly sponsored by the city, state and Federal govern-
ments, provide accurate information about local facilities. To determine
the most suitable day care solution for your family's needs you should
consult these sources while pursuing the other leads suggested at the
end of this chapter, if necessary.

- **Agency for Child Development**, 30 Main Street, Brooklyn 11201, call 718-260-6000 for pre-school information and referrals from the ACD's Vacancy Information Service. Their staff provides names and addresses of private as well as publicly funded and Head Start child care facilities located in the five boroughs. This information is supplied ACD by the Department of Health's Bureau of Day Care, 212-334-7803, the group charged with licensing pre-school facilities. Their Directory of Day Care Services in New York City is available by mail free of charge.

- **Child Care Inc./The Pre-School Association**, 275 Seventh Avenue, NYC 10001, 212-929-4999, a knowledgeable, non-profit group, has a corporate program. Member firms receive counseling on child care in New York City as well as detailed publications on the subject for distribution to employees. The organization, funded also to assist individual parents, offers telephone counseling to all callers. They also provide three packets ($5 each) \ one each on in-home care, family day care and early childhood programs— which contain an informative booklet, checklist, licensing information sheet and, most helpful of all, names of day care providers appropriate to your needs in your specific neighborhood.

- **The Independent Schools Admissions Association of Greater New York (ISAAGNY)** publishes the *New York Independent Schools Directory* containing page-long descriptions of more than 120 private member schools enrolling pre-schoolers through high schoolers. Nursery schools and toddlers groups, as well as numerous elementary and secondary schools with pre-school groups, are listed, and a useful geographical index is included in the appendix. This directory provides an excellent overview of New York's varied private schools. Copies cost $10 and can be picked up at the office of the Parents League of New York or ordered from them by mail ($11.50).

- **The Lower East Side Family Resource Center**, 137 East Second Street, NYC 10009, 212-677-6602, houses among a variety of other services the Community Child Care Exchange, an information, referral and counseling group. Targeted at Lower Manhattan residents, the exchange helps parents to locate child care centers, family day care providers and sitters and to establish informal cooperative play groups.

- **The New York Public Library's Early Childhood Resource Center** at the Hudson Park Branch on Leroy Street off Seventh Avenue in Greenwich Village, 212-929-0815, devotes one whole floor to resource materials for parents and a playroom for kids.

- **Parents League of New York, Inc.**, 115 East 82nd Street, NYC 10028, 212-737-7385, with 106 member schools, mainly in Manhattan, is an excellent source of private school information. One counseling session with a specialist from their School Advisory Service—for example, their expert on toddler's groups and nursery schools—is well worth the League's annual $30 membership fee. A panoply of other child-related services, not the least of which is their reliable Baby Sitter-Young Helper listing, a great boon to any newcomer with kids, also come with League membership, as does their 80-page *Toddler Activities* directory.

Other Leads

So, you say, all these lists are terrific but they don't adequately apply to your very specific needs. If this be the case, check out some of the following resources for referrals in your particular neighborhood:

- **Churches**, large and small; **bulletin boards**, most often, but not exclusively, found in the larger supermarkets; **private schools**, ask the admissions director for the names of feeder schools, day care centers or playgroups; **pediatricians**; **hospitals**, talk with the administrative officer in charge of residents and interns; and, last but perhaps most accessible and knowledgeable of all, **playground and park bench parents**.

Places of Worship

If you came from a small town, you may have gone to the Methodist church, the Catholic church, or the synagogue. No problem. But there are an estimated 2,300 churches (not counting storefront pentecostals) and some 650 synagogues in New York City. You'll find some, but by no means all, of them listed by denomination in the Yellow Pages. Connecting with a church or synagogue may be as simple as that or the suggestion of an acquaintance. Or it may be as intensely personal and complicated as choosing a spouse. The churches and synagogues listed below by denomination were chosen specifically for their possible appeal to newcomers. It's a place to start.

Roman Catholic Churches

Most Catholics attend Mass near their home or office. But there are a few churches which, for one reason or another, attract worshipers from beyond the parish confines. One of these may suit you.

- **Cathedral-Basilica of St. James**, 230 Cathedral Place (at Jay Street near Tillary Street), Brooklyn Heights 11201, 718-855-6390. Restored to a Georgian brick elegance befitting its new prominence, St. James has experienced a renaissance in recent years. It is Brooklyn's cathedral, but it is also a non-territorial parish, especially popular among young professionals in the area and beyond. Mass here is traditional, and the music quite wonderful. Sunday afternoon vespers feature lay activists often, bishops in the spring. There is a singles group and adult religious education.

- **Church of the Epiphany**, Second Avenue and 22nd Street, NYC 10010, 475-1966, is at once striking and modest, an unusually successful modern structure of rounded verticals in brown brick. It's a family church, with a traditional two-choir Mass at 11 and a popular family Mass to guitar accompaniment at 10. But there's a difference. For one thing, altar girls. Nuns are involved in work traditionally done by priests, and women's issues are addressed. The church is popular with young professionals in the community, and there is an active singles group.

- **Church of St. Thomas More**, 65 East 89th Street between Park and Lexington Avenues, NYC 10028, 876-7718, stone Victorian Gothic, was built as an Episcopal Church and still feels a bit like one, with its intimately peaceful, fragrant interior beneath a timbered ceiling. Ever so decorous. You can linger for coffee in the Chelsea Room after 10 o'clock Mass.

- **Holy Trinity Chapel**, 58 Washington Square South, NYC 10012, 674-7236, is the Catholic chapel at New York University, but its congregants are by no means all students. A moderately liberal intellectual approach and active social life attract a committed band of Catholics from the surrounding Village and beyond to this modest but appealing modern brick structure. Communicants run the Monday soup kitchen and provide legal advice to the homeless. A women's group meets regularly, and there are sessions of silent Christian meditation and Omega gatherings for Mass and socializing in neighborhood apartments.

- **Our Lady of Vilna**, 570 Broome Street, NYC 10013, 255-2648, peers quizzically over the entrance to the Holland Tunnel on the northern edge of Tribeca. This might seem an unlikely place to find a Latin Mass, complete with incense and Gregorian chants, but there it is, every Sunday at 5 p.m. The 11 a.m. Mass is said in Lithuanian.

- **St. Francis Xavier**, 30 West 16th Street, NYC 10011, 627-2100. This hulking, grey stone Jesuit presence dominates the block between Fifth and Sixth Avenues. The style here is rather less formal than you might expect, perhaps because the congregation covers such a broad social spectrum: Hispanics, knowledgeable Catholic activists and young professionals. Actively involved in the community, the church shelters the homeless and serves 1,000 meals a week. It's equally busy on the spiritual front, with lay spirituality group retreats, healing Masses and discussion groups for a fiercely devoted following.

- **St. Ignatius Loyola**, Park Avenue at 84th Street, NYC 10028, 288-3588, solidly limestone Italian Baroque, is definitely high church and upscale: incense, ornate vestments, a fine professional choir and children's choir at the traditionally sung morning High Mass. But the rigorous Jesuit approach is apparent in a strongly social and economic outlook from the pulpit. At 11 a.m. you can attend a folk Mass in the undercroft (the Chapel of St. Laurence O'Toole) and linger over coffee. Young adults meet over wine and cheese, and there's a Yorkshire group for those over 35.

- **St. John's**, 210 West 31st Street, NYC 10001, 564-9070, as a distinct sideline to its normal parish activities, is host to the Catholic charismatic movement in Manhattan. There are seminars, prayer meetings and a monthly charismatic Mass. For these and other details contact (Capuchin) Father Peter Chaffee.

- **St. Joseph's**, 371 Avenue of the Americas at Washington Place, NYC 10014, 741-1274, in the heart of Greenwich Village, appeals to a variety of Catholics in the neighborhood and even outside the city. At once a bustling family church and an esthetic experience, with professional musicians performing at formal, traditional Masses and at evening concerts. Distinctly high church. The lovely stone and stucco Greek Revival structure, newly resplendent inside with creamy plaster, crystal chandeliers and wide, carved balconies, is the oldest Catholic church in the city (1833), and the first to open a shelter for homeless men.

- **St. Paul's Chapel at Columbia University**, 116th Street and Broadway, NYC 10027, 864-5110 (Catholic Campus Ministry Office), is an architecturally stunning Episcopal chapel but other denominations hold services here, and the 5 p.m. Sunday Catholic Mass, with its modern liturgy, lay participation and challenging intellectual content, attracts communicants from beyond campus. Ancillary activities include an active Pax Christi movement, Food Pantry, a shelter, and other community outreach efforts.

Protestant Churches

Baptist

- **Calvary**, 123 West 57th Street between Sixth and Seventh Avenues, NYC 10019, 975-0170, across from Carnegie Hall, is probably the largest Baptist Church in Manhattan. You might begin a typical Sunday at the 9:30 Young Professionals' topical Bible study and fellowship, followed by traditional worship service at 11 along with some 1,400 other fellow Baptists, mostly young educated singles, and then coffee in Fellowship Hall downstairs. The Calvary Gospel Singers might perform at the 7 p.m. service. Young Adult Ministries offers occasional weekend retreats and a coffeehouse with singing. There are outreach programs to the prison population, the poor and welfare hotel children.

Episcopal

- **Cathedral of St. John the Divine**, 1047 Amsterdam Avenue at 112th Street, NYC 10027, 316-7540, dwarfs its rather shabby surroundings even as it awaits completion of its stone towers. The largest cathedral in the world, at once Byzantine, Romanesque and Gothic, it is truly awesome, especially inside, where spectacular stained glass windows light the vast dark vaults and music echoes ethereally. It is also a bustling and exciting community church, a leader in the movement to feed and house the poor. And the performing arts flourish here almost around the clock.

- **Church of the Ascension**, 36 Fifth Avenue at 10th Street, NYC 10011, 254-8620. Its communicants find this church especially challenging intellectually and pleasing esthetically. A LaFarge altar fresco and a St. Gaudens altar relief enliven the quietly tasteful interior, and liturgical music of the highest quality is performed by an exceptional choir Sundays and at special evening concerts.

- **Church of the Heavenly Rest**, 2 East 90th Street at Fifth Avenue, NYC 10128, 289-3400, sits confidently but unostentatiously, stripped contemporary Gothic in pale grey stone, facing Central Park. It's an upscale, neighborhood family church, where the congregants linger casually for coffee after the morning service while the children play decorously about the door.

- **Grace Church**, 802 Broadway at East 10th Street, NYC 10003, 254-2000, despite its rather patrician, lacy English Gothic elegance, is relatively low church. Worship is traditional, however, with wonderful music, especially on holy days. The congregation runs to young families and a variety of artists. Pastoral counseling is available as well as adult classes on a variety of topics, and there are outreach groups to seniors, youth and AIDS victims.

- **St. Bartholomew's**, Park Avenue at 51st Street, NYC 10022, 751-1616. This prestigious, landmarked Romanesque-Byzantine church with some 2,000 members is, nevertheless, warm and friendly. Lay participation in liturgical music, dance and drama is encouraged, and there is Bible study throughout the week, as well as a stimulating Adult Forum Sunday morning. The Community Club next door attracts some 1,500 not-necessarily-church members to its stunning facilities (pool, squash, basketball, gym, 24-foot yacht) for activities ranging from parties, dances and wine tastings to ski trips, St. Bart's Theater auditions, youth work and more. Club membership runs between $200 and $500, ages 18 to 45. Athletic fees are extra. The City Club takes older members.

- **St. James'**, 865 Madison Avenue at 71st Street, NYC 10021, 288-4100. Distinctly Upper East Side, this trim brownstone is a warm, neighborhood family church which is also decidedly activist in the community and beyond: feeding, sheltering, mentoring, supporting, and sometimes even demonstrating. Despite its rather liberal bent, St. James' is moderately high church and boasts a bishop in residence. Its education programs for adults and children are worthy of note.

Lutheran

- **Holy Trinity**, Central Park West at 66th Street, NYC 10023, 877-6815, offers challenging preaching at traditional, rigorously Lutheran services. But it is music, at the regular services and at the Sunday vespers featuring Bach cantatas with professional musicians, for which Holy Trinity is widely known. The sturdy Gothic revival church is the setting for frequent evening concerts as well.

- **St. Peter's**, Lexington Avenue at 54th Street, NYC 10022, 935-2200, nestles, sleek and angular like a modern stone tent, beneath the towering Citicorp Center. A large Louise Nevelson sculpture punctuates the stark, light interior, scene of a sung Mass with traditional liturgy in the morning and Jazz Vespers with jazz as the sermon Sunday afternoons. Classical and jazz concerts, often free, theater and provocative adult Forum lectures attract an ecumenical following, to say the least.

Methodist

- **Christ Church**, 520 Park Avenue at 60th Street, NYC 10021, 838-3036, is sedately Byzantine outside, dazzlingly so inside, every inch covered with mosaics in blazing blues, greens and gold. It's a wonderful setting for the religious music-dramas occasionally performed here. The congregation, though relatively small, supports a twice-weekly soup kitchen and excellent pastoral counseling.

- **John Street**, 44 John Street between Broadway and William Street, NYC 10038, 269-0014. To step into this landmarked little Italianate brownstone church (1841) among the towering monoliths of the financial district is to step out of place and time into a peaceful haven of creamy modest proportions and brass sconces. It's the oldest Methodist society in the US, and few know about it. Inquire about the occasional Wednesday noon hymn-sings.

- **Park Avenue**, 106 East 86th Street, NYC 10028, 289-6997. A mixed and growing congregation, mostly young families and singles, is attracted by the moderately liberal approach and active social scene at this smallish, restfully intimate, Moorish-looking church. A coffee hour follows the traditional Sunday service with volunteer choir. Hounds of Heaven meet regularly for Bible study and dinner in the neighborhood.

Presbyterian

- **Brick Church**, Park Avenue at 91st Street, NYC 10128, 289-4400, staid neo-Georgian with a rather ornate interior, is distinctly Park Avenue. But the welcome is friendly, including a popular Coffee Hour after the Sunday service. Adult Bible study here is meaty, and the church's day school prestigious.

- **Fifth Avenue**, Fifth Avenue at 55th Street, NYC 10019, 247-0490. The city's largest Presbyterian church has a warm, woody interior behind its otherwise undistinguished brownstone facade. A popular volunteer chorus and two mainly social adult fellowship groups (FOCUS and Midtowners) attract large numbers of youngish adults to the traditional services. Activities of these groups include Sunday night church suppers, after-church brunch, movies and ski retreats.

- **Madison Avenue**, 921 Madison Avenue at 73rd Street, NYC 10021, 288-8920, has a cozy, Scottish feel, with its Gothic-timbered white walls, carved pews and galleries. And when the legendary Rev. David Read is in the pulpit, it sounds Scottish. The music program is strong, including a volunteer choir and frequent Sunday afternoon concerts. An Adult Fellowship group meets regularly for Bible study, discussion and socializing.

- **Redeemer**, 111 East 87th Street between Park and Lexington Avenues, church office at 271 Madison Avenue, Suite 1208, NYC 10016, 212-808-4460. This recently organized and rapidly growing congregation of the PCA holds three Sunday services in a Seventh Day Adventist meetinghouse. The scripturally-based emphasis is on preaching which is intellectually engaging and an array of spiritual, social and outreach activities.

Unitarian

- **All Souls**, 1157 Lexington Avenue at 80th Street, NYC 10021,

535-5530. New England simple and elegant, this Federal-style brick church looks Unitarian. As might be expected here, the busy church calendar tends to activism on a variety of fronts and a fairly intellectual approach to adult education, which features book groups, films and lectures. Music is stressed. Social activities are many and varied, including a Career Networking Group.

Interdenominational

- **Judson Memorial** (Baptist-United Church of Christ), 55 Washington Square South, NYC 10012, 477-0351. Fairly worldly young adults and seminarians are attracted to this ornate Romanesque church and its fairly traditional Protestant liturgy with progressive elements, including a monthly Agape Meal. There is an active Central American Committee and refugee ministry as well as a ministry to prostitutes, consumer health library, and support for AIDS victims.

- **Riverside**, 490 Riverside Drive at 122nd Street, NYC 10027, 222-5900. This towering Gothic gift of John D. Rockefeller, Jr. dominates the heights overlooking the Hudson River. Inspired by Chartres, it boasts spectacular stained glass and beautifully carved stone in the large but simple nave and chancel and about the entrance. Activist concerns under the leadership of the Rev. Dr. James Forbes, Jr. are dizzying, as are the opportunities for involvement in activities musical, theatrical, intellectual and social, not to mention spiritual.

Synagogues

Reform

- **Central**, 123 East 55th Street, NYC 10022, 838-5122, is the oldest Jewish house of worship (1872) in continuous use in New York. The Moorish brownstone structure has an interior richly stenciled in red, blue and gold. Traditional in orientation and ritual, the temple tends to the manifold interests, worldly as well as spiritual, of its 1,400-member congregation in groups and classes ranging from Hebrew and Yiddish to Bible to bridge, teens' and singles' groups, and 8 a.m. Women's Focus speakers for working women.

- **Temple Emanu-El**, 1 East 65th Street, corner of Fifth Avenue, NYC 10021, 744-1400, is perhaps a little less traditional, nevertheless classical Reform in approach, and it is the largest Reform temple in the US, with over 3,000 members. The landmarked limestone Moorish-Romanesque temple facing Central Park seats 2,500 beneath a high, colorfully painted wood ceiling and stunning stained glass windows. The temple has a large staff to run its many facilities, classes and community outreach programs, as well as a large religious school. Services are broadcast every Friday evening at 5:30 over WQXR (1560 AM, 96.3 FM).

Conservative

- **Ansche Chesed Temple**, 251 West 100th Street at West End Avenue, NYC 10025, 865-0600, houses *four* separate congregations, each with a different approach to Conservative Judaism, in one medium-sized, squat, brick building. Alternatives within a framework of Jewish tradition are stressed at this much-talked-about West Side synagogue, which offers an adult beginners' service, courses on a wide range of Jewish topics, and social action projects aiding elderly Jews.

- **Brotherhood**, 28 Gramercy Park South, NYC 10003, 674-5750, occupies a landmarked (1859) Friends' Meeting House, starkly beautiful in Italianate brownstone and overlooking lovely Gramercy Park. About its courtyards are housed a shelter for the homeless, a religious school, adult education, an educational program for the developmentally disabled, and facilities to aid Jewish immigrants.

- **Congregation Baith Israel Anschei Emes/Kane Street**, 236 Kane Street at Tompkins Place in Cobble Hill, Brooklyn 11231, 718-875-1550, has grown considerably in recent years, partly, perhaps, because of the emphasis on egalitarianism in its observances. Vibrant and involved, with challenging study groups, it is regularly packed with congregants, mainly young, from Cobble Hill and nearby Brooklyn Heights.

- **Park Avenue**, 50 East 87th Street at Madison Avenue, NYC 10128, 369-2600, is the city's largest Conservative temple and an East

Side Moorish landmark in carved golden stone. The rich interior boasts fine stained glass, sculpture and paintings, and the traditional services are distinctly formal, with organ and choir. There are many programs for children, singles, young marrieds and seniors, and a Food Pantry for the neighborhood's hungry.

- **Tifereth Israel/Town and Village**, 334 East 14th Street between First and Second Avenues, NYC 10003, 677-8090, stresses sexual egalitarianism in its informally innovative, traditional services and attracts an involved family congregation, largely from the adjacent community, including Stuyvesant Town and Peter Cooper Village. Adult education and a young marrieds group are popular. Emanu-El Midtown YMHA next door, with whom it shares a Hebrew school, offers members the advantages of a social center with pool, gym, classes and interesting theatrical offerings on Jewish themes.

- **United Synagogue of Hoboken**, 830 Hudson Street at Ninth, Hoboken 07030, 201-659-2614, is one congregation with two temples, the other being at 115 Park Avenue, a tan brick structure with copper onion domes. Sabbath services are in the converted Victorian brownstone Hudson Street temple, the last of many serving the predominantly German Jewish community here at the turn of the century. The small but growing congregation is youngish and welcoming. There is a "Learners' Minyan", courses in Hebrew reading and Jewish history, a monthly breakfast series with speakers, and dance/movement classes.

Orthodox

- **Civic Center**, 49 White Street west of Broadway, NYC 10013, 966-7141, occupies a small, award-winning, modern structure scrunched among the cast iron manufacturing lofts and loading docks. Its frame-shaped interior houses a membership of some 650 with about 1,300 supporters, including elderly members of long standing as well as artists and young professionals from surrounding Tribeca, Independence Plaza and Battery Park. There are both Hebrew and Sunday schools, and parenting sessions conducted by Educational Alliance West.

- **Congregation Kehilath Jeshurun**, 125 East 85th Street between Lexington and Park Avenues, NYC 10028, 427-1000. Though old and rich and housed in classical Romanesque grey stone, this is probably the most progressive of the Orthodox congregations. Its size makes possible a host of activities for singles, couples and children, recreational facilities, and an educational program including the Ramaz School and "Lunch and Learn" classes.

- **Congregation Shearith Israel**, 8 West 70th Street at Central Park West, NYC 10023, 873-0300, known as the Spanish and Portuguese synagogue, is the oldest Jewish congregation in the US, dating from 1655, when a group of Sephardic Jews arrived from Brazil. In the formal sanctuary scholarly rabbis conduct very formal services, which offer the best opportunity to observe Sephardic tradition and music. Excellent adult education focuses on the differences between Sephardic and Ashkenazic culture and tradition.

- **Lincoln Square**, 200 Amsterdam Avenue at 69th Street, NYC 10023, 874-6100, sometimes referred to as "the hip synagogue", might be described physically as synagogue-modern. Its nickname and popularity among the young professionals who pack five Saturday services is due in large part to the charm and zealous outreach efforts of Rabbi Ephraim Buchwald, who hosts the 9:15 "Learners' Minyan", which is followed by wine and cookies and, if you like, lunch with an experienced family. There are courses at all levels on Jewish law and thought as well as singles and youth groups.

Other

- **Society for the Advancement of Judaism**, 15 West 86th Street off Central Park West, NYC 10024, 724-7000. Known as the SAJ, this is the original Reconstructionist synagogue. Reconstructionism, which attempts to reconcile traditional Conservatism with modern life, views Judaism as evolving rather than divinely inspired. The Torah is observed, and services are largely traditional but egalitarian. The approach here is distinctly intellectual, not social.

- **West End**, 270 West 89th Street at West End Avenue, NYC 10024, 769-3100, is a popular new Reconstructionist congregation meeting in the Lindenbaum Center and flourishing with a slightly more emotional, interpersonal emphasis and monthly Shabbat dinners as well as concerts, debates and social action programs.

- **Young Israel of Fifth Avenue**, 3 West 16th Street at Fifth Avenue, NYC 10011, 929-1525, is one of three such temples in Manhattan. Young Israel can be defined as modern Orthodoxy, observing all the Orthodox forms, including separate seating of the sexes, but emphasizing programs serving the entire family. This includes communal singing and participation, youth and singles programs, outreach, adult education, and attention to community needs.

Mosques

- **Islamic Center of New York**, 1711 Third Avenue, NYC 10029, 722-5234. This imposing structure, the recent gift of a group of Islamic countries, houses a large mosque. The design is modern, with numerous references to traditional elements of Muslim architecture. The effect is at once peaceful and spiritual.

Belonging

The diversity and incredible depth of the city's cultural, intellectual and artistic life is a magnet for many. Nowhere else can such an enormous range of interests and avocations be accommodated on so many levels. While it is impossible to cover all the opportunities New York offers, we *can* help the newcomer assimilate culturally by providing a compilation of ticket, subscription and membership information for leading opera companies, symphony orchestras, dance companies, theatrical repertory groups and museums.

First, a list of publications which cover what is showing where and when.

- **"Weekend," *New York Times* Friday Edition**, features reviews, articles and tips on the endless entertainment possibilities for Friday, Saturday and Sunday. This special section also contains an up-to-the-minute Movie Clock, useful in a town where movie schedules are notoriously unreliable.

- **"Arts and Leisure," *New York Times* Sunday Edition**, besides reviews and critical articles on current trends and upcoming events in the arts, includes listings for the arts with thumbnail reviews.

- *The New Yorker*, on the stands Wednesday, includes not just plays, opera and museums in its comprehensive "Goings on About Town," but also poetry readings, sporting events and night life. Most listings include abbreviated reviews.

- *New York* magazine, on the stands Monday, incorporates *Cue*, "A

Complete Guide to Entertainment, the Arts, and Dining for the Week." Included are brief movie and theater reviews. Comprehensive.

- **The Village Voice**, on the stands Wednesday, is filled with entertainment ads and carries a "Listings" column of weekly free events. Particularly good for alternative events.

- **New York Press** is distributed free in restaurants, stores and in street boxes below 28th Street, sparsely uptown. A favorite with downtowners as a reference for what's going on in arts and music, the weekly also includes restaurant reviews and feature stories.

The latest wrinkle in performance information is **New York City/On Stage**. Dial 212-768-1818 for up-to-the-minute information and ticket availability. Once connected with this 24-hour recorded service, you are asked to choose a category: Press 1 for Theater and Performance, 2 for Dance and Music, 3 for *New York Newsday* listings of borough events, 8 for information on TKTS booths, and so on. Recorded information is also available in Spanish.

Tickets

How can you buy tickets to New York's plays, concerts, ballets, operas and special mega-events? Let us describe the ways.

Box Office

To get the best seats for the day you want, go to the appropriate box office in person well in advance of the performance desired, cash or charge card in hand. Not only can you check the theater's seating diagram (usually posted near the ticket window) but you won't pay a fee for using a credit card. When ordering by telephone or mail, you have no control over the exact row or seat issued because orders are filled automatically on a "best available" basis. Box offices are usually open from 10 or 11 a.m. until the evening performance. Note: Sometimes producers, directors or actors release their personal tickets and these go back to the box office for sale at the last minute, making it possible for the persistent to see a hot show which has officially sold out. Line up.

Telephone Orders

Most theaters list a special number to call for reservations. Billed to credit cards, tickets are mailed if time allows; otherwise pick them up at the theater the day of the performance. Tele-charge, 212-239-6200, represents some 20 Schubert Theaters in New York City and adds $4 per ticket to your bill. Ticketmaster, 212-307-7171, originally an outlet for children's and sports events and rock concerts, now handles theater productions as well, collecting $3 to $5 per ticket plus a one-shot handling fee of $2.

Ticketmaster

Promoters determine how tickets to their events will be sold: at Ticketmaster outlets, by calling Ticketmaster, or both. First call 212-307-7171 to find out what performances they are offering and whether tickets can be ordered by phone and charged to a credit card (fees range from $2.50 to $3.75 per seat) or whether they must be picked up in person and paid for in cash ($2.50 extra for Broadway shows; $1.25 for all other events) at one of Ticketmaster's 2200 outlets in the US and Canada. There are 160 outlets in the tri-state area; prime locations in Manhattan include Tower Records, 692 Broadway corner of East 4th Street and Broadway at 66th Street; Tower Video, 215 East 86th Street, and 42nd Street east of Avenue of the Americas. Call 212-307-7171 for the location nearest you.

Brokers

Unless you have a friend with a personal broker or an "in" with a hotel concierge or unless your corporation runs a ticket service, don't expect to walk into a ticket agency and get front row center for the town's hottest musical the day of performance. These seats are held for valued clients. However, for most events brokers such as Mackey's, 212-944-8910 (see "Ticket Sales—Entertainment and Sports" in the Yellow Pages for some 75 other names), add $18 to $21 to the total price for their service. Brokers, who usually handle only orchestra, mezzanine and box seats, are still probably the easiest way to get into a show or sporting event in a hurry.

Discounts

TKTS is one of the city's great bargains. The Theater Development Fund, operates three outlets for half-price, day-of-performance tickets to Broadway and off-Broadway shows as well as to music programs and dance events. Availability information is posted on large boards near ticket sales booths, and a small fee—currently $2.50—is charged for each ticket. Cash or travelers' check only.

- **TKTS Times Square**, West 47th Street and Broadway, sells Broadway and off-Broadway tickets for evening performances from 3 to 8 p.m. daily. Matinee tickets go on sale on Wednesdays, Saturdays 10 to 2, Sundays noon to 7.

- **TKTS Lower Manhattan**, 2 World Trade Center, mezzanine, open Monday through Friday from 11 to 5, Saturday 11 to 3:30. Seats for Broadway evening performances go on sale here earlier—at 11 a.m.—than those at Times Square, and the lines are a lot shorter at the World Trade Center TKTS, where half-price off-Broadway evening tickets are also sold from 11 a.m. to 1 p.m. on the day of performance. Matinee tickets are sold from 11 to 5 on the day prior to performance.

- **TKTS Bryant Park**, 42nd Street east of Avenue of the Americas, 212-382-2323 and 212-382-2483, open noon to 2 p.m and again 3 p.m to 7 p.m., Tuesday - Sunday and noon to 6 Saturday, sells half-price, day-of-performance tickets for dance and music concerts throughout town. You can call for a recording listing tickets available that day. Tickets for Monday may be purchased on Sunday. Sharing this booth is a Ticketmaster outlet for full-price tickets to all events.

Twofers resemble theater tickets but are, in fact, passes. When exchanged at Broadway (and some off-Broadway) box offices, twofers entitle the bearer to two tickets for little more than the price of one. A convenient way to keep a show open after bad reviews or at the end of a long run, twofers can be found all over town, for example at restaurant cash registers, the New York Convention and Visitors Bureau at 2 Columbus Circle, in college dorms and on hotel desks.

The Theater Development Fund, 1501 Broadway, Attention: Applications, NYC 10036, 212-221-0013, offers tickets to a variety of plays, musicals, dance and jazz performances at about $10 each to its members. If you are retired, a student or teacher, a clergyman, performing professional, union member or in the armed forces, you can get a membership application by mailing a self-addressed, stamped envelope with your request. Upon acceptance and payment of $5 or more, you'll be on the mailing list to receive their offerings. You will also be eligible to purchase their TDF Vouchers for off-off-Broadway shows, music and dance events. For $15 you get vouchers good for five performances over a six-month period, plus a calendar of events to which they apply.

Audience Extras, 109 West 26th Street, NYC 10001, 212-989-9550, provides free tickets to plays in preview and post opening (whose producers wish to "paper" the house, i.e., fill it with freebies to stimulate word-of-mouth) to its members in the theater industry. For $85 you get a one-year membership card and access to their 24-hour hotline, which lists available shows. There is no limit on free shows, and you can bring up to three guests. A service charge of $2-3 per show is levied.

Quicktix, a small allotment of seats for each of the various performances at the New York Shakespeare Festival's Public Theatre on Lafayette Street (see Theater section) go on sale at 5:30 p.m. the day of performance for about half the price of regular tickets. Call 212-598-7150 for information on general availability.

Student tickets at half price or less are often available to those holding bona fide student IDs as follows:

- **New York Philharmonic** at Avery Fisher Hall, Lincoln Center, has two arrangements. They sell $5 tickets for the Thursday morning rehearsals about a month before the actual date. In the Student Rush Program you should line up with ID and $5 at Window 6 about an hour and a half in advance of a Tuesday or Thursday concert. At 7:30 p.m. available tickets go on sale. Call 212-875-5656 to check ticket availability first.

- **New York City Opera**, also at Lincoln Center, sometimes has student tickets for those who line up at the theater by 10 a.m. on the morning of a performance, 11:30 on Sunday. Tickets, if available, are $5. Call 212-870-5570 for more information.

- **Carnegie Hall** sells $5 tickets, when available, on a first-come, first-served basis. You can call 212-247-7800 between noon and 1 p.m. on the day of performance to see if tickets will be available.

- **Grace Rainey Rogers Auditorium** at the Metropolitan Museum of Art sells standing room tickets for half price on the day of a concert. Call the box office at 212-570-3949 to check on availability.

An indispensable aid for the dedicated theater goer, sports fan or classical music enthusiast is **STUBS**, a paperback which publishes the seating plan of every concert hall, opera house, stadium, arena and theater in town. STUBS in hand, you can immediately locate the seats being offered by TKTS booths, brokers, Ticketmaster outlets and others who have no seating diagrams available for ticket purchasers.

Subscriptions

Common practice dictates that new subscriptions to any series...symphonic, operatic, dance, theatrical...must wait to be filled until the previous season's subscribers are given an opportunity to renew. Once the renewal deadline is past, new subscriptions are processed on a first-come, first-served basis. The initial announcement of each new season's schedule is sent to everyone on the mailing list anywhere from six weeks to six months before performances are scheduled to begin. To assure a position near the beginning of the line, call whatever institution interests you well in advance of its season and ask to be put on the mailing list. Upon receipt of the announcement schedule, choose your series and return the coupon and a check quickly. Full-page ads in *The New York Times* Sunday Arts and Leisure section herald symphonic, operatic and dance seasons five to six months before performances begin, but usually a week or two after the first public subscription mailers have been sent out.

Incidentally, certain nights are traditionally more popular than others. If good seats are more important than sitting next to the right people, find out which night or series has the best tickets available.

Grand Opera

Metropolitan Opera, Metropolitan Opera House, Lincoln Center, NYC 10023; Subscriptions, 212-362-2080; Met Ticket Service for current sales, 212-362-6000. Subscriptions range from $160 for an eight-opera series high up in the Family Circle to $1,080 for an eight-opera series in the Center Orchestra. The Met charges $20 per subscription for handling. Renewal notices are mailed to current subscribers, and once these orders are processed in the spring, new subscriptions are filled.

The Met's season is broken into three periods for the sale of individual seats: fall, winter and spring. Subscribers are given first crack, then seats for single performances are offered to the public, first through a mailing, then via newspaper ads about a month and a half before each of the three seasons begins. Standing room goes on sale the Sunday before performance.

New York City Opera, New York State Theater, Lincoln Center, NYC 10023, Subscriptions, 212-496-0600; Box Office, 212-870-5570. The New York City Opera offers around 48 two-to four-opera series for performances between mid-July and mid-November. The cheapest seats for a two-performance series cost $18; the most expensive for four performances, $212. With a top ticket price of $68, City Opera performances are a grand bargain.

Classical Music

New York Philharmonic, Avery Fisher Hall, Lincoln Center, NYC 10023, Subscriptions, 212-875-5656; Center Charge for current sales, 212-874-6770. Fifteen different series are available for a September through June season. Easiest to obtain are subscriptions to the three-concert mini-series. Prices run from $36 in the Third Tier Box with partial sight for the three-concert series to a top of $500 for concerts down front in the Center Orchestra. Fall schedules are announced in late February/early March.

Carnegie Hall, 57th Street and Seventh Avenue, NYC 10019, Subscriptions, 212-903-9700; current sales, 212-247-7800. One hundred years old and still counting, Carnegie is still the concert hall preferred by many performers and it continues to host programs by a variety of virtuosos and orchestras (to say nothing of popular superstars) with age-given grace. The Philadelphia, Cleveland and Boston Symphony Orchestras all hold their New York concert series here.

Call Carnegie Hall for subscriber information. A series can cost anywhere between $37 and $430.

Chamber Music

Several halls traditionally host the extraordinarily popular chamber music groups that perform here regularly. The Guarneri Quartet, the Juilliard Quartet and the Beaux Arts Trio might give two or three New York series during any given year, each at a different location. Only the Lincoln Center Chamber Music Society has a hall—Alice Tully Hall in Lincoln Center—which it can call home. Good seats go fast once the *Times* advertisements appear, so it's important to get on each group's mailing list. The following spaces are most likely to host chamber music performances. Call them or keep your eyes on the Arts and Leisure section of the Sunday *New York Times* in late spring and summer.

- **Abraham Goodman House**, Merkin Concert Hall, 129 West 67th Street between Broadway and Amsterdam Avenue, NYC 10023, 212-362-8719.

- **Alice Tully Hall**, Lincoln Center, NYC 10023, Subscriptions, 212-875-5050; Center Charge for current sales, 212-721-6500. Concerts by the Lincoln Center Chamber Music Society as well as other groups.

- **Carnegie Hall**, 57th Street and Seventh Avenue, NYC 10019, Subscriptions, 212-903-9700; current sales, 212-247-7800.

- **Metropolitan Museum of Art**, Grace Rainey Rogers Auditorium, 83rd Street and Fifth Avenue, NYC 10028, 212-570-3949.

- **92nd Street Y** (YM-YWHA), **Kaufmann Concert Hall**, 1395 Lexington Avenue, NYC 10028, 212-427-6000.

Dance

American Ballet Theater, Metropolitan Opera House, Lincoln Center, NYC 10023, Subscriptions, 212-799-3100; Met Ticket Service for current sales, 212-362-6000. Seventeen series are offered, each with four ballets, for the ABT's nine-week season April through June. The first announcement, mailed to friends in late December, is followed by a new subscriber mailing towards the end of the month and then a week or so later by the traditional January New York Times ad. Subscriptions for seats high up in the Family Circle cost $40 while way down in the Orchestra they command $380.

Individual tickets at the Box Office and by phone from the Met Ticket Service go on sale in March.

New York City Ballet, New York State Theater, Lincoln Center, NYC 10023. Subscriptions and current sale information, 212-870-5580. Two seasons provide balletomanes the opportunity of feasting on dancing by Balanchine's company. Both the Winter Season, November through February, and the Spring Season, April through June, have sixteen four-performance series, and good seats are easiest to come by for weekend matinees. First announcements go out nine weeks before the season begins. A tip for *Nutcracker* ballet fanciers: first mail orders for single, non-subscription performances of the *Nutcracker* are accepted in late October. Call 212-870-5580 for prices and dates, and if certain seats for special performances are important, get your check in the mail several weeks before that time.

The City Center Theater, 131 West 55th Street, NYC 10019, 212-581-7907. Dance companies dominate City Center's performance schedule. The house, open from mid-September through June, is in fact almost totally given over to productions of modern dance and modern ballet. The following are among the major groups performing regularly here:

• **Martha Graham**, 316 East 63rd Street, 212-832-9166.

• **Joffrey Ballet**, 130 West 56th Street, 212-265-7300.

• **Alvin Ailey American Dance Theater**, 211 West 61st Street, 212-767-0590.

• **Paul Taylor Dance Company**, 552 Broadway, 212-431-5562.

• **Dance Theatre of Harlem**, 466 West 152nd Street, 212-690-2800.

As with the chamber music ensembles, it is best to get on each particular company's mailing list. Call the company direct or City Center's Subscription Department. Prices vary for each series. Single tickets average $15 to $45.

The Joyce Theater, 175 Eighth Avenue at 19th Street, NYC 10011, 212-242-0800. Celebrating dance of all kinds—the Joffrey II and Erick Hawkins Company dance here, and the Joyce is practically the Feld Ballet's home—the Joyce is an elegantly revamped former Art Deco movie house in Chelsea. Your reward for buying tickets to performances by four different dance groups during the fall or spring season is a membership that entitles you to 40% off on all tickets purchased subsequently. Your membership card also entitles you to priority seating and various discounts at fifteen Chelsea restaurants located between 14th and 23rd Streets and Sixth and Tenth Avenues.

Theater

A high percentage of the most critically acclaimed plays produced in any given year originate off-Broadway, more often than not in theaters that offer subscriptions as a means of financing productions. Season tickets not only ensure exposure to new artists, playwrights and directors, but in most cases save money as well. A few of the most established groups are mentioned here, but please don't be limited by this list. Many more experimental but no less rewarding companies exist and should be explored.

Circle Repertory Company, 99 Seventh Avenue South at Sheridan Square, NYC 10014, 212-924-7100; Subscriptions, 212-807-1326. Subscriptions for this resident ensemble company's five-play September to June season featuring new works, revivals and classics go on sale in mid-May at prices which ranged to a top of $137 in 1991. The company continually wins awards and citations for its presentations and contributions to the American theater.

CSC Repertory Theater, 136 East 13th Street, NYC 10003, 212-677-4210. Founded in 1967, CSC has been performing Ibsen, Strindberg, Brecht and other mostly-contemporary classics in this comfortably intimate theater since then. It's not a resident company, but three or four plays are performed in repertory throughout the season, with an occasional lecture bonus. The season is announced in August, but you can subscribe anytime for $60 to $95.

Joseph Papp Public Theater, 425 Lafayette Street south of East 8th Street, NYC 10003, 212-598-7100. Joseph Papp was perhaps the single most important figure in the post-WWII American theater. With his death in 1992, and after 40 years of his leadership, it was not surprising that the Public experienced some turmoil as it sought its way through a difficult transition. With the appointment of George Wolfe (acclaimed director of *Angels in America*) as its new artistic director, the newly renamed New York Shakespeare Festival's Public Theater appears once again to be on firm ground, offering events that are hailed for their diversity as well as their excellence.

A bargain subscription plan allows the public inexpensive access to productions. Cheapest is $90. The most expensive subscription, $120, guarantees admission to shows and includes admission on Friday and Saturday nights. Seats are not pre-assigned at The Public. Subscribers write or stop by the box office for tickets once they receive the passes automatically sent to members as each new show is announced. A small allotment of the seats for any performance at The Public are held for same-day sale at a discount. The tickets, called Quicktix (see Discounts section), go on sale at 6 p.m. for about half the price of regular tickets.

Lincoln Center Theater, 150 West 65th Street, Attention: Members Department, NYC 10023, 212-239-6277. Members in this innovative theater program have access, at $10 a ticket, to a potpourri of presentations from Shakespeare to Mamet, with an occasional first-rate musical thrown in, be it at Lincoln Center, on Broadway or off-off-Broadway at the experimental LaMama. The $25 membership fee buys one year's access to Lincoln Center Theater plays already in progress around town and first crack at six new productions a year as they come up. Popular productions with outstanding casts have included *Our Town*, *Sarafina*, *Waiting for Godot* and *Anything Goes*.

Manhattan Theater Club, 321 East 73rd Street, NYC 10021, 212-645-5848. Upper East Siders don't have to go downtown for good theater. The Manhattan Theater Club's critically acclaimed plays have been produced here since 1972. However, productions have proven so popular that the traditional five-play September-through-May series now takes place at The Space, a 299-seat theater at City Center, 131 West 55th Street, while the four-play "Special Events" season occupies the Downstage Theater at the Manhattan Theater Club proper.

National Actors Theatre, Lyceum Theatre, 45th Street (East of Broadway), NYC 719-5783. Despite the ignominy of less than support-ive critics, Tony Randall has persisted in his dream of a theater of American actors performing the classics of the world stage. The former Felix Ungar now presents plays by Chekov, Ibsen, Gogol, Shakespeare and Shaw with actors who have made their careers in America's reper-tory theaters as well as those best known for their work on television. The ingredients seem unlikely but the intent is sincere and the results have begun to pay off. Subscriptions for the four-play series begin at around $120.

Roundabout Theater Company, 1530 Broadway (at 45th Street), 212-869-9400. With a subscription base second only to the Metropolitan Opera, the Roundabout is obviously doing something right. What that involves is presenting plays such as Pinter's *Old Times* and O'Neill's *Anna Christie* and musicals like *She Loves Me* with such stars as Natasha Richardson, Jason Robards, Christopher Plummer and Kelly McGillis. A five-play series starts at around $150, a bargain considering the Roundabout is a Broadway house. The Roundabout has also pio-neered special subscriptions for singles (straight and gay) that are a good way for fellow theater lovers to meet.

All of the Above

Brooklyn Academy of Music, 30 Lafayette Avenue, Brooklyn 12217, 718-636-4100, is a center for all the performing arts. Best known for its Next Wave Festival which takes place September - December, BAM (as it is popularly known) is the premier New York showcase for cutting-edge dance, theater, music and opera. From the intimate LeClerq Space to the magnificent Opera House and the newly renovated Majestic Theater, BAM presents everything from small chamber performances like Eiko and Komo to Peter Brook and Arianne Mnouchkine epics. With several series taking place year-round, it is best to call and get on the mailing list in order to have a shot at getting tickets.

Film

New York is a movie buff's paradise. **The Museum of Modern Art**, 11 West 53rd Street, 212-708-9490, is famous for its carefully planned retrospectives. Screening of new filmmakers' works are a constant at the **Whitney Museum of American Art**, 945 Madison Avenue, 212-570-3617, as well as at most of those all-encompassing, art-encouraging alternative spaces sprinkled throughout New York. **The New School for Social Research**, 66 West 12th Street, 212-229-5600, and the Cinema Department of **New York University**, 721 Broadway, 6th floor, 212-998-1600, explore movies in depth through numerous seminars and courses and, almost every semester, sponsor a film series or two as well.

Some of Manhattan's premier revival and art film showcases include: **Theater 80**, 80 St. Mark's Place, NYC 10003, 212-254-7400; **Cinema Village**, 12th Street east of Fifth Avenue, NYC 10003, 212-505-7320; **8th Street Playhouse**, 52 West 8th Street, NYC 10011, 212-674-6515; **Film Forum**, 209 West Houston, NYC, 212-727-8110; and the **Public Theater**, 425 Lafayette Street, NYC 10003, 212-598-7171. Weekly schedules for these theaters, as well as first and rerun houses, are found in the "Arts and Leisure" section of the Sunday *Times* and *The New Yorker.*

The Film Society of Lincoln Center, 140 West 65th Street, NYC 10023, 212-875-5000, presents the New York Film Festival each fall (late September through October) as well as the New Directors/New Films series in conjunction with the Museum of Modern Art each spring. Established in 1963, the Film Festival presents some 20 films during its annual run. A $50 membership in the Film Society provides the following perks: right to buy two twelve-film subscriptions to the New York Film Festival and first crack at certain other Festival tickets, discounts on tickets for New Directors/New Films at the Museum of Modern Art, and a free subscription to the society's bi-monthly magazine *Film Comment.*

If you're not interested in membership, it's a good idea to get on the society's mailing list before the Film Festival's program is announced the last week in August, in order to obtain the schedule before it appears in the papers. The Box Office for performances at Alice Tully Hall is at 1941 Broadway at 65th Street, NYC 10023, 212-875-5050. It opens the Sunday after Labor Day for single ticket sales to the public.

Broadcasting

The Museum of Television and Radio, 23 West 52nd Street, 212-621-6800, shouldn't be missed as a chance to have a lot of fun experiencing American culture in video and audio tape form. Call for schedule listings of special screening events. Annual memberships begin at $35 and allow you free admission to the museum's theaters and screening and listening rooms. The museum offers 96 video monitors for individual viewing of any television program in their collection. Membership also gives you a discount on museum seminars and magazines as well as all gift shop items. For more membership information, call 212-621-6600.

Memberships

The benefits that can be reaped by joining any of the city's myriad non-profit institutions are really quite amazing. There seem to be museums and societies for every possible interest, and if you're an avid afficionado of a certain discipline, seek out the institution which best reflects your avocation and join. You'll be inundated with free literature, offered perquisites of many kinds and probably be invited to teas, cocktail parties and even banquets if your contribution is big enough. For the generalist, membership in one or two of the city's established cultural citadels is a wonderful way of obtaining well-researched information on any number of subjects. For those who want to keep up with the latest in museum happenings, there's a new, bimonthly magazine *Museums of New York* that will inform you of all the museum news and events in town. Call 800-825-0061 for a subscription. As an indication of the kind of benefits memberships provide, we've noted below details for a few of New York's major institutions.

Metropolitan Museum of Art, Fifth Avenue at 82nd Street, NYC 10028, 212-879-5500. The sumptuous Bulletin published quarterly by the Met, filled with high-quality color photographs and illuminating texts of catalog caliber, comes free with the museum's $70 Individual Membership. Other bonuses include the bi-monthly *Calendar News*, free admission to the museum and the Cloisters, invitations to previews and private viewings of two exhibitions a year, and copies of the Met's Christmas and Spring Catalogues illustrating the museum's publications and glamorous reproductions of everything from Chinese scarves to early American pewter pitchers, which, as a member, you can buy for a 10% discount. But probably the biggest bonus you'll receive is the program and exhibition information, which will impel you to get over to the Met more often than you might otherwise.

American Museum of Natural History, Central Park West at 79th Street, NYC 10024, 212-769-5100. A $25 Associate Membership here entitles you to as many visits to the dinosaurs as you wish, to say nothing of the Hall of Meteorites, a subscription to *Natural History* magazine and a 10% discount in the store; a $45 family membership provides as well a monthly newsletter and calendar, 25% discount on Planetarium tickets and invitations to previews of the exhibitions. You also receive a 10% discount on most educational programs at the museum and a 40% discount at the Naturemax Theater, a thoroughly modern revamping of the old auditorium with an oversized retractable screen and a dizzying IMAX projector.

The Museum of Modern Art, 11 West 53rd Street, NYC 10019, 212-708-9400. With the ambitious expansion program complete, gallery space for the museum's unparalleled collection of 20th century art has been doubled and MoMA now has two theaters for films and a new glass-enclosed garden hall overlooking the sculpture garden. Those who pay $60 for an entry level membership can lunch in the new members' restaurant, receive 25% discounts at the enlarged museum store and on catalog merchandise (10% on non-museum merchandise), free admission to the galleries and daily film programs, discounted admission for guests, reduced subscription rates on major art magazines, invitations to exhibition previews and special events as well as free subscriptions to the monthly Members' Calendar and to MoMA, the quarterly newsletter.

Whitney Museum of American Art, 945 Madison Avenue, NYC 10021, 212-570-3641. An Individual Membership costs $50 and benefits its holder with free museum admission for two, 20% discount on museum publications, two invitations to exhibition opening receptions and a free museum publication, as well as calendars of events. If American art or experimental film interests you particularly, it is worth belonging to the Whitney to have ready access to its excellent series of large and small exhibitions and also to the works presented by the museum's New American Filmmakers series in some 25 or 30 different programs every year.

South Street Seaport Museum, 207 Front Street, NYC 10038, 212-669-9400. Despite the commercial redevelopment of the Seaport's facilities by the Rouse Corporation—in main part the construction of a glimmering glass Pier Pavilion over the East River—Phase I, encompassing the new Fulton Market with its intriguing stores and jolly restaurants, the restoration of Schermerhorn Row's handsome brick houses, and the Museum Block with old shops and new walkways, continues to attract crowds.

For $35, the cost of an Individual Seaport Membership ($25 for students), you become involved with conserving an historically valuable part of downtown and preserving New York's maritime traditions while receiving discounts and free admissions in the city's newest and most vibrant entertainment area. Museum members tend to be a youngish crowd, drawn as much by the ambiance and the idea of the museum as by the perks, which include free admission to the ships and the Seaport Gallery on Water Street, quarterly copies of Seaport magazine and the museum's bulletin, as well as reduced admission to the South Street Venture multimedia show and other special events. Furthermore, you get first shot at seats for the free Summerpier jazz concerts and special member rates on the Pioneer's two-and three-hour sails of New York Harbor.

The Bronx Zoo (new official name: **New York Zoological Society's International Wildlife Conservancy**), Fordham Road and Bronx River Parkway, Bronx, 718-367-1010, is the largest zoo in the five boroughs and, stretching over 265 acres, the largest urban zoo in the world. An annual memberhship costs $38 and gives you free admission to this zoo as well as to the **Central Park Zoo**, Central Park, East 64th Street and

Fifth Avenue, 212-861-6030; the **New York Aquarium**, Surf Avenue and West 8th Street, Coney Island, Brooklyn; and the **Queens Zoo** and **Children's Farm**, 111th Street at 54th Avenue, Corona Park, Flushing, Queens. Bronx Zoo membership also includes three free parking passes and tickets to seven seasonal attractions. Call 718-220-5111 for membership information.

For the record, the comprehensive **New York City Culture Catalog**, compiled and published by the Alliance for the Arts, 330 West 42nd Street, NYC 10036, 212-947-6340, briefly describes and gives directions to scores of local institutions and attractions—from historic houses and botanical gardens to alternative spaces and zoos. Call for further details.

Volunteering

Despite the city's rapid pace and anonymity, or perhaps because of it, New Yorkers by the thousands volunteer their services to hundreds of worthy causes. Motivations are as varied as the tasks. So are the rewards. The pragmatist can benefit the community while making new friends; humanitarians can meet kindred souls as well as help mankind; idealists will find no dearth of worthy causes.

A mind-boggling array of public, private and non-profit organizations will gladly put to use whatever talents or interests you have. Experience is not necessarily required; most institutions provide training. What kinds of jobs are available where? Read on. We've also listed the names of agencies which refer volunteers to other organizations and included a few alternative suggestions as well.

How You Can Help

The Hungry and the Homeless

Scores of volunteers concern themselves with shelter for the city's homeless. Jobs include: monitoring and organizing the shelters, providing legal help, ministering to psychiatric, medical and social needs, raising money, manning phones, and caring for children in the shelters. Many people solicit, organize, cook and serve food to the destitute at sites throughout the city. Still others deliver meals to the homeless from portable kitchens.

Children

If involvement with children is especially appealing you can: tutor in and out of schools, cuddle a foundling, be a big brother or sister, teach music and sports in shelters, parks and hospitals, and accompany kids on weekend outings.

Hospitals

The need for volunteers in both city-run and private hospitals is manifold: chaplain's aides, interpreters, laboratory personnel, admitting and nursing aides are required; assistants in crisis medical areas—emergency rooms, intensive care units and the like— are wanted; so are ambulance drivers, and volunteers to work with victims of sexual abuse.

The Handicapped and the Elderly

You can read to the blind, help teach the deaf, work to prevent birth defects, help the retarded and developmentally disabled, among others. You can also make regular visits to the homebound elderly, deliver them hot meals, and teach everything from nutrition to arts and crafts in senior centers and nursing homes.

Extreme Care Situations

Helping with cancer, Alzheimer's and AIDS patients, rape victims and abused children is a special category demanding a high level of commitment—not to mention emotional reserves.

The Culture Scene

Unpaid stamp-lickers and benefit chairmen keep the city's cultural institutions afloat. Consider guiding tours, raising funds or assisting the staff at your favorite museum, library or ballet company.

The Community

Work in your neighborhood. Block associations and community gardens are run strictly by volunteers. You can help out at the local school, nursing home, settlement house or animal shelter.

Where You Can Help

Specific-Need Organizations

The organizations in New York City that address a major disease, disability or social problem are legion. For example, there's the Memorial Sloan-Kettering Cancer Center, The Coalition for the Homeless, Volunteer Services for Children, New York Association for the Blind (The Lighthouse), Literacy Volunteers of New York, Women in Need, and City Harvest, which collects and distributes food to the hungry.

Institutions

New York's health, education and, some would say, its very civilization rest upon the city's institutions. Hospitals, museums, libraries, schools, opera and ballet companies are mostly underfunded and rely on a veritable army of volunteers to prosper.

The Religious Connection

Individual churches and synagogues (in particular, those serving the homeless and the needy) and church federations such as the Federation of Protestant Welfare Agencies, the Catholic Charities and the UJA-Federation of Jewish Philanthropies use volunteers for a variety of activities.

The Community

More than 5,000 block associations and neighborhood-wide organizations, like Greenwich House in the Village and Yorkville's Civic Council (see below), can use your talents. Citywide there is a need for volunteers in the schools, parks, shelters and in consumer affairs.

Multi-Service Organizations

Don't forget such well-known groups as the Salvation Army, American Red Cross and the Visiting Nurse Service (it's not just nurses).

The Corporate Connection

Corporations encourage employee voluntarism through company-supported projects such as literacy programs, pro bono work and management aid to non-profit groups. Check with the company personnel or public relations department to see if your firm is involved in any specific project. Many corporations have set up programs with the help of Corporation Volunteers of New York, 17 John Street, NYC 10007, 212-696-2442.

Referral Services

If you don't know which way to turn, try one of several umbrella organizations which find volunteers for affiliated agencies. At these referral services, staff members will help you determine the tasks you would be interested in doing, where and when. Your interviewer will make specific suggestions and appointments at the places that sound appealing. Interview at several sites if you wish, and return to the referral agency until you find something you want to undertake.

- **Catholic Charities of New York**, 1011 First Avenue, 212-371-1000, are affiliated with more than 100 different agencies dealing with shelters, food kitchens and the homeless. An interview may be requested.

- **The Federation of Protestant Welfare Agencies**, 1 Whitehall Street, 212-425-7060, open 8:30 to 6 Monday through Friday. This ecumenical group, with connections to some 800 agencies in the metropolitan area, finds jobs for volunteers of any religious persuasion.

- **The Mayor's Voluntary Action Center**, 61 Chambers Street, 212-566-5950, open 10 to 3 Tuesday and Thursday, to 7 Wednesday. The city's largest referral agency has 10,000 job openings in nearly 5,000 public and private non-profit organizations. This enormous clearing house can place just about anyone in a useful job, especially in the human services and cultural areas.

- **New York Cares**, 140 East 58th Street, NYC 10022, 212-753-6670, is a favorite volunteer organization among young professionals. It was founded in 1986 by people anxious to volunteer but discouraged by other organizations' long waiting lists and required time commitments. New York Cares lets its 8,000 volunteers choose from a monthly calendar of events set up with the more than fifty not-for-profit organizations they serve. These projects include reading with homeless children, serving brunch at soup kitchens, cleaning public parks and visiting elderly homebound. "Joining a volunteer team within a month after my move to New York gave me an immediate sense of belonging to the city. It's also been a great place to meet people," says a two-year New York Cares volunteer. He adds, "The funny thing is, most of the volunteers I meet here are somewhat new to New York themselves." Call to attend one of two weekly orientation meetings.

- **The United Jewish Appeal-Federation of Jewish Philanthropies**, 130 East 59th Street, 212-753-2288, open 9 to 5 Monday-Friday. The Jewish Information Referral Service sends callers a catalog describing nearly 200 agencies and projects. Programs include revitalizing old neighborhoods and synagogues as well as working with children, immigrants, the elderly and the homeless.

- **The Volunteer Referral Center**, 161 Madison Avenue, 212-889-4805, 212-745-8249, interviews by appointment, 11 to 3 Tuesday through Thursday, and 5:30 to 7 Tuesday and Wednesday. The Center can place adult and student volunteers at some 350 not-for-profit agencies throughout Manhattan.

Other Connections

Check bulletin boards at your office, church, neighborhood grocery store, laundromat and school.

- **WBAI-FM** (99.5 FM) discusses, and occasionally stimulates, volunteer projects, especially those involving the homeless and the hungry.

- The **Yellow Pages**, under "Social and Human Services," contains more than five pages of organizations and institutions—in categories from Abortion Alternatives Counseling to Youth Services—many of which welcome volunteers. It's a great source of ideas, as well as a tool for follow-through.

Sports

In New York you can root, root, root for the home team, canter along Central Park's cinder track, join a pickup basketball game, work up a water ballet, or sit spellbound at the US Open Tennis Championships. The city hosts events for every season and activities for every appetite. As an aid to sorting out the teams you wish to follow and the activities you wish to pursue, ticket information and other details about the area's major teams are listed below followed by a section devoted to **Participant Sports**. For specifics about ticket sales see also **Tickets** in the chapter on **Belonging**.

Professional Sports

For weekly specifics on leading amateur and professional sporting events check "This Week in Sports," a box in the Sports section of the Sunday *New York Times*, and *The New Yorker* magazine's Sports section.

Baseball

The season begins in late March and lasts until early October. General admission costs $5.50 at Yankee Stadium in The Bronx. Single tickets for Yankee games are $13.50 and $14.50 for box seats, $9.50 and $12.50 for reserved seats; Mets tickets cost $15, $12 and $6.50; there is no general admission to Shea Stadium in Queens, the Mets' home base. Reserve seats for Yankee games through Ticketmaster, 212-307-7171; you can charge tickets to a credit card and have them sent or pick them up at one of 20 locations in Manhattan. The Mets use Ticketmaster, 212-307-7171, for phone orders and for direct sales.

New York Mets (National League), Shea Stadium, 126th Street and Roosevelt Avenue, Flushing, NY 11368, 718-507-8499. The Mets have innumerable subscription plans ranging in cost in 1992 from $336 for 28 weekend games to $1230 for the full plan of box seats. Call Shea for everything in between. Availability is generally good, and applications for new subscriptions are filled around January.

New York Yankees (American League), Yankee Stadium, 161st Street and River Avenue, Bronx, NY 10451, 718-293-6000. Season tickets at Yankee Stadium run from $80 for a reserved seat for a mini-series to $984 for a full season's box seat. For a chance at the most desirable location, get on the mailing list by November.

Basketball

Basketball begins when baseball leaves off, around late October, and continues through mid-April. Home games are played in Madison Square Garden and at the Meadowlands, the huge sports complex in New Jersey that each year seems to have attracted yet another New York City team across the Hudson and into the marshlands. Single seats for the Nets and the Knicks range between $10 and $75 each and go on sale late October. Call Ticketmaster, 212-307-7171, for mail orders; visit an outlet to pick up your tickets.

New Jersey Nets (NBA) play in the multimillion-dollar Byrne Meadowlands Arena, East Rutherford, NJ 07073, six miles west of the Lincoln Tunnel; call 201-935-8888 for ticket information. Season tickets for the 41-games start at $410 and reach a top of $3,075 for first row (which you'll never get!). They go on sale at the end of the previous season.

New York Knickerbockers (NBA), Madison Square Garden, 33rd Street between Seventh and Eighth Avenues, NYC 10001, 212-563-8300. Prices for tickets will remain near last year's $576 to $1075 level. Individual tickets for all games go on sale in early September and can be purchased through Ticketmaster outlets, 212-307-7171, as well as at the Garden Box Office.

Football

The popularity of Jets and Giants games during the pro football season, September through December, is clearly demonstrated by ticket scarcity. Business contacts or generous friends are about the only ticket sources for Giants games; chances of buying Jets tickets are slightly better.

Giants (NFL), Giants Stadium, Meadowlands, East Rutherford, NJ 07073, 201-935-8111. Regular season tickets, $184 to $208 for eight home games, are sold out about thirty years in advance at this point. Individual tickets, $23 and $26 each, are also sold out for next season.

New York Jets (AFL) play at the Giants Stadium in the Meadowlands too. Call 516-538-6600 for ticket information. Renewals for season tickets to the eight home-game season are filled by May 15. New subscriptions ($180 a seat) are then issued from the fairly long waiting list on a first-come, first-served basis in early June.

Hockey

The New York Rangers play their home games at Madison Square Garden between late September and early April. An alternative to the Rangers are the Islanders, considered a local team by many New Yorkers. Call the Nassau Coliseum, the Islanders' home rink in Uniondale, Long Island, NY 11553, 516-587-9222, for information and tickets.

New York Rangers (NHL), Madison Square Garden, 33rd Street between Seventh and Eighth Avenues, NYC 10001, 212-563-8300. Rangers management must be overjoyed with the team's present "sold out" state. Waiting list requests are accepted only for seats in the Blue and Green sections near the Garden's ceiling. Individual tickets, again available only in the Blue and Green sections, go on sale in early September.

Racing: Harness and Thoroughbred

All the local tracks are easily reached by public transportation. Call the numbers listed below for directions.

Aqueduct, Jamaica, Queens, 718-641-4700. The track is open from October until May for thoroughbred races starting at 1 p.m. daily.

Belmont Park, Elmont, Long Island, 718-641-4700. Thoroughbred races May through July and again, after the Saratoga meet, August through October begin at 1 p.m. every day (1:05 p.m. Sunday) except Tuesday.

Meadowlands Racetrack, East Rutherford, NJ, 201-935-8500. Harness racing every day but Monday at 6 p.m., January through mid-August. Thoroughbreds run September through December.

Monmouth Park, Oceanport, NJ, 201-222-5100. Thoroughbred races daily except Sunday at 1:30 p.m., June through late August.

Yonkers Raceway, Yonkers, NY, 718-562-9500. The season's dates for the trotting races at Yonkers are determined by the New York State Racing Board. The post time is 8 p.m., and the track is closed Sundays.

Tennis

The two biggest tournaments held in the New York area are listed below. The West Side Tennis Club at Forest Hills, once the site of the US Open, now hosts the Tournament of Champions for men in May.

United States Open Tennis Championships, United States Tennis Center, Flushing Park, Queens, NY 11365, 718-592-8000. The US Open consists of 13 days of afternoon and evening matches held in late August and early September. The finals take place the weekend after Labor Day. Individual tickets for the finals and semifinals are sold as soon as the first mailing goes out in late March or early April and cost $12 to $45. Tickets for matches earlier in the tournament aren't so hard to come by and are sold at Ticketmaster outlets, 212-307-7171, as well as the Tennis Center.

Virginia Slims Tennis Championships, Madison Square Garden, 33rd Street between Seventh and Eighth Avenues, NYC 10001, 212-465-6000. Box seats for the five-day women's tournament, held in the Garden annually in November, sell out fast. Call 212-563-8957 in early December for information. Individual tickets usually go on sale at Ticketmaster and the Garden in mid-December and cost between $10 and $30.

Participant Sports

Swimming pools, tennis, squash and racquetball courts, bowling alleys and billiard parlors as well as roller and ice skating rinks dot the island for your sporting pleasure, and practically any outdoor recreation you want can be found in Central Park. It's not just a super place to ride bikes or listen to classical performances of a summer evening. You can also schedule football and baseball games, play tennis or row a boat around The Lake. Flanked by Central Park West and Fifth Avenue to the east, the park covers some 750 acres between 59th and 110th Streets and is Manhattan's prime outdoor recreation area. So, before listing information about sports citywide, as well as multipurpose facilities such as health clubs and Ys, we've detailed opportunities to be found in the park sport by sport.

Central Park

The park's Visitor's Information Center run by the Department of Parks and Recreation is located at the Dairy, 65th Street between the Zoo and the Carousel. Call 212-360-1333 for taped event information. The Arsenal, 830 Fifth Avenue at East 64th Street in front of the Zoo, is the park's administrative hub. For Parks Information call 212-360-8236 or the switchboard at 212-360-8111 for general information.

- **Baseball, Softball, Football, Rugby and Soccer** Fields are located in the North Meadow, at the Great Lawn and Heckscher Playground. Call 212-408-0209 for permits.

- **Bicycling** Cycling is encouraged when the park drives (but not the sunken crosstown transverses) are closed to motorized traffic on weekends from 7 p.m. Friday to 6 a.m. Monday (all day on holidays), and from 10 a.m. to 3 p.m. and 7 p.m. to 10 p.m. weekdays from April through October as well. For rentals, see Bicycles under Participant Sports for names of bicycle shops near the park.

- **Boating** The Loeb Boathouse, near East 74th Street, 212-517-2233, rents rowboats at $6 per hour for sorties onto The Lake between 9 a.m. and 5 p.m. daily in season. For $20 per half hour you can glide beneath Bow Bridge in a black Venetian gondola, complete with (not necessarily Venetian) gondolier. Armchair sailors can enjoy the comfort and cuisine of the glass-enclosed Boathouse Cafe March 21st through Thanksgiving. Fast food is available year round.

- **Horseback Riding** The Claremont Riding Academy, 175 West 89th Street, 212-724-5101, rents mounts to experienced riders for rides along the six miles of bridle paths that circle the park. You must reserve in advance.

- **Ice Skating** The park boasts two rinks: the beautifully renovated Wollman Memorial on the East Side near 62nd Street, 212-517-4800, and Lasker Memorial Rink, Lenox Avenue at 110th Street, 212-996-1184, open daily. Skate rentals $2.50, $1.50 for children.

- Every Saturday and Sunday morning between 7:30 and 9 a.m., **Ice Hockey** games are played at the Lasker Rink. The fee is $4 and anyone can join in the mayhem. Call the rink for more information.

- **Miniature Golf** A recent addition to the park is Donald Trump's nine-hole Gotham Golf. It covers 10,000 square feet and includes replicas of the Statue of Liberty and of course Trump Tower and the Plaza Hotel.

- **Paddleball and Handball** You can use the ten courts located near the North Meadow at 97th Street and Transverse Road on a first-come, first-served basis. Watch the all-City and Budweiser Championships on the park courts or join the informal round robin tournaments held during the summer. Call the Department of Parks and Recreation, 212-408-0209, for more information.

- **Roller Blading/Roller Skating** In-line skaters and old-fashioned roller skaters can be found strutting their stuff (or falling down) throughout the park, but the road west of the Sheep Meadow near 69th Street is designated specifically for blading and skating. Skates can be rented for use at Wollman Memorial (see above) April through November. Hours and admission are the same as for ice skating.

• **Running** Joggers traditionally work out on the 1.58 mile cinder track girdling the Reservoir between 85th and 96th Streets, but running isn't limited to that patch. The New York Road Runners Club, 9 East 89th Street, 212-860-4455, sponsors races and clinics during the season.

   The 97th Street Field House has boasted men's lockers for some time but, thanks to the efforts of Road Runners, women obtained equal opportunity to shower and change when the park's first locker room for women opened there recently.

• **Sledding** The park has hills for all kinds of sledders, from the beginner to the more advanced. For children or timid sledders, a perfect spot is Pilgrim Hill by the 72nd Street and Fifth Avenue entrance closest to the pilgrim statue. For more of a challenge, try Cedar Hill close to the Belvedere Castle at the 77th Street entrance off Central Park West.

• **Tennis Courts** 26 clay and four all-weather courts, open from 7 a.m. to dusk, are located on the west side of the park near 95th Street. In the summer, play necessitates tennis permits, which in turn require a 1 1/2" x 1 1/2" photo (there's a photograph machine in the Arsenal), a completed application blank and $50 (no personal checks). Permits can be obtained by mail or in person at the Arsenal Building, Fifth Avenue and 64th Street, NYC 10021, 212-360-8204, between 9 and 4 weekdays. Permit holders can reserve a court for $3 by going to the Tennis House adjacent to the 95th Street Courts, 212-397-3194. Single play tennis tickets cost $4 for one hour of court time and are issued at the Arsenal on a first-come, first-served basis.

Basketball

The Department of Parks and Recreation maintains over 1,000 courts throughout the city in gyms (see **Swimming** below) as well as in city parks, large and small. Call 212-408-0209 for the location nearest you.

Baseball

Most of Manhattan's 26 diamonds, seven of which are located in Central Park, are under the aegis of the DPR. Call 212-360-8111 for information.

Bicycling

- **American Youth Hostels**, 891 Amsterdam Avenue, 212-932-2300, the city's largest cycling organization, sponsors the Five Borough Bicycle Race which bumps and winds its way through New York each spring. AYH also promotes a number of day rides as well as weekend trips for enthusiasts.

- **Hungry Pedalers**, 212-222-2243, arranges gourmet bicycling tours in all five boroughs including a "Harlem Sights and Souls" tour in the fall.

If you don't own a bike, you may well want to rent one on a beamish spring day. At least half of Manhattan's bike dealers rent both three-and ten-speed bicycles. Rates average $4 an hour for a three-speed, $6.50 for a ten-speed bike. You'll have to leave money, or a driver's license or major credit card behind as a rental deposit. A handful of the many bike rental outfits include (all telephone numbers are Area Code 212):

- **Bicycles Plus**, 204 East 85th Street, 794-2201.

- **Fourteenth Street Bicycle Discount House**, 332 East 14th Street at First Avenue, 228-4344.

- **Metro Bicycles**, 1311 Lexington Avenue at 88th Street, 427-4450; 360 West 47th Street, 581-4500; 231 West 96th Street, 663-7531; 332 East 14th Street, 228-4344; 417 Canal Street, 334-8000; and 546 Avenue of the Americas at 15th Street, 255-5100.

- **Midtown Bicycles**, 360 West 47th Street at Ninth Avenue, 581-4500.

- **Stuyvesant Bicycle**, 349 West 14th Street, 254-5200.

Billiards

There are 29 pool halls in New York City, at last count, and no doubt Minnesota Fats would still be comfortable at many of them. Others, hardly the smoke-filled hustler hangouts of yore, have attracted women and teenagers to the traditionally male pastimes of pocket pool, billiards and snooker and have brightened the sport's image in the process.

- **The Billiard Club**, 220 West 19th Street between Seventh and Eighth Avenues, 212-206-7665, open 10 a.m. to 3 a.m., Friday and Saturday until 5 a.m. It's $5 an hour to shoot pool here, $10 after 7, on two floors of a converted warehouse with 33 tables beneath brass chandeliers, two private rooms and a snack bar with waitresses. In fact, you can rent the whole place for a party, or rack 'em up with the lunch crowd.

- **Chelsea Billiards**, 54 West 21st Street west of Fifth Avenue, 212-989-0096, open 24 hours, is the biggest in the country at this writing, with 44 Brunswick pool tables, four antique snooker tables and two billiard tables on two floors of a converted printing plant. Yet you might have to wait for a table, Friday nights especially. Best times are mornings and Sunday daytime. The tariff is $6 per hour 9 a.m. to 5 p.m., $8 per hour 5 p.m. to 9 a.m. and $10 on weekends, $2 per hour each additional person. Snooker costs $10 and $12 per hour, $2 for each additional person. There is a private room with two tables for private parties.

Bird Watching

- **The American Museum of Natural History,** 212-873-1300; the **Brooklyn Botanical Garden,** 718-622-4433; and the **New York Botanical Garden** (Bronx Park), 718-220-8747, make the guide-books as good bird-watching areas. Rare Bird Alert, 212-979-3070, provides recorded information on interesting sightings in the New York City area.

- **Linnaean Society of New York**, 15 West 77 Street, NYC 10024, holds its meetings at the American Museum of Natural History and is open to amateurs and professionals interested in ornithology. The organization does not list a phone number; for more information, write to the address above.

Bowling

- **Bowlmor Bowling**, 110 University Place, between 12th and 13th Streets, 212-255-8188, 44 lanes, open 10 a.m. - 1 a.m. Sunday - Thursday, 10 a.m. - 4 a.m. Friday and Saturday, call for lane availability.

- **Gil Hodges Lanes**, 6161 Strickland Avenue, Brooklyn, 718-763-6800, named after the famed Brooklyn Dodgers first baseman. This 68 lane alley is the biggest in the five boroughs, open 9 a.m.- midnight Sunday - Tuesday, 9 a.m. to 2:30 a.m. Friday, 9 a.m. to 2 a.m. Saturday.

- **Leisure Time Bowling**, 625 Eighth Avenue (in the Port Authority Building), 212-268-6909, 30 lanes, open 10 a.m. - 11 p.m. Sunday - Thursday, 10 a.m. - 2 a.m. Friday and Saturday.

Fencing

- **The New York Fencers Club**, 154 West 71st Street, 212-874-9800 (after 4:30 p.m.), offers duelists a place to parry and thrust, as well as a space for lessons to better foil their opponents. Dues for this membership organization cost an average of $650 a year.

- **Blade**, 212 West 15th Street, 212-620-0114, teaches fencing to beginners, intermediate and advanced students, supplying equipment if necessary. Four group lessons cost $65, plus a $10 registration fee. Private sessions are more expensive.

Football

Most playing fields fall under the Department of Parks and Recreation, call 212-408-0220 for information and permits. Eighteen football fields, some of which are suitable also for soccer, are located in Manhattan.

Games

- **The Mayfair Club**, 51 East 25th Street, 212-779-1750, is not a casino or a gambling house, says its owner. "It's a place to play games." Poker is the game mostly played, but there's bridge and backgammon too.

- **Hackers, Hitters and Hoops**, 123 West 18th Street, 212-929-7482, offers 23,000 square feet of miniature golf courses, each hole a replica of a famous course. You'll also find batting cages, ping pong tables, and basketball courts as well as an amusement park space ride called Orbitron.

Golf

Manhattan boasts no 18-hole golf courses, though a 17-acre course is in the planning stages for Randall's Island, but each borough's Department of Parks and Recreation—that of Brooklyn, The Bronx, Queens and Staten Island, too—operates courses open to the public. The fee is $14.50 for daytime play on weekends and holidays, $13.50 during the week. Call 718-390-8000 for details. Marine Park, 718-338-7149, in Brooklyn and Silver Lake, 718-447-5686, on Staten Island are typical of these courses.

Plenty of slightly tonier public clubs surround the metropolitan area. Higher fees, averaging $14 Monday to Friday and $15.50 on weekends, are the norm at suburban courses. Typical of the county-run golf links is Mohansic Golf Club, 914-962-4065, in Yorktown Heights. Rental equipment is available here, just as it is at other clubs found in New Jersey, Long Island and Connecticut, but balls must be purchased.

With a little imagination, Manhattan-locked golf enthusiasts do have an alternative. Miniature golf courses abound, and with the help of video you might even find yourself yelling "Fore" down a causeway at Pebble Beach, in midtown.

- **Midtown Golf Club**, 7 West 45th Street, 212-869-3636. Open 8 to 11 weekdays, 10 to 7 weekends. Admission: $35 an hour, $5 each additional person per group. This fore-runner offers what might be the golf of the future. With video screens and computers to simulate images of sand traps, roughs, and water, frustrated city golfers can drive down the grassy fairways of four different golf courses without leaving the building.

Horseback Riding

Care to canter Central Park bridle trails, or brush up on your dressage in the ring? Manhattan has one stable.

- **Claremont Riding Academy**, 175 West 89th Street corner Amsterdam Avenue, 212-724-5101 for reservations, essential weekends. Open 6:30 a.m. to 10 p.m., 6:30 to 5 on weekends. They stable about 100 horses here, some 70 for rental, English saddle only, at $30 an hour either in Central Park or in the ring. Private lessons cost $32 per half hour, group lessons $32 per hour.

- **Lynne's Riding School**, 88-03 70th Road, Forest Hills, 718-261-7679. Open daily 8 to 4. You can take public transportation—the F train and then the Q23 bus—to Queens where Lynne's offers riders a choice between Eastern or Western tack. Private lessons cost $20 a half hour, $40 an hour, and renting a horse costs $17 an hour English, $20 Western.

- **Van Cortlandt Stables**, West 254th Street and Broadway, inside Van Cortlandt Park, 718-543-4433. Open 9 to 5, Saturday and Sunday 8:30 to 6 or 6:30. Rabbits, raccoons and other wildlife are a bonus on the guided trail rides in this large city park, but be prepared to wait—up to a couple of hours—for your turn on fine spring and summer weekends. Tack is English or Western, and the cost is $15 per hour, $18 on weekends. Lessons in the outdoor ring are $15 per semi-private half hour, $23 per hour; $25 per hour for a private lesson, $20 for a one-hour group lesson. Pony rides for children are $1, and pony parties can be arranged. To get there by public transportation take the # 1 Seventh Avenue IRT to 242nd Street (last stop) and the # 9 bus (262nd Street) from there; ask to get off at the stables.

- **Overpeck Riding Center**, 40 Fort Lee Road, Leonia, NJ 07605, 201-944-7111. Open 9 to 5, Saturday and Sunday to 6 p.m., by appointment. By # 4 Red and Tan Lines or # 166 New Jersey Transit bus from the Port Authority Terminal, have the driver let you off at Overpeck Park. By car, take Route 80 off the George Washington Bridge, off at the first exit ("70—Leonia"). A quarter mile south on the right are the stables, which are run by Claremont, offering private lessons at $28 a half hour, $56 an hour, and group lessons for $28 an hour. There are riding clinics, shows and competitions in the indoor and outdoor rings. Boarding is also available.

Ice Skating

Besides the Wollman and Lasker rinks (and the Sailboat Pond at 73rd Street when it freezes) in Central Park, Manhattan boasts three other fine places to skate. In Queens try the Flushing Meadow rink.

- **Rivergate Ice Rink**, First Avenue and East 34th Street (next to the Rivergate apartment complex), 212-689-0035. This outdoor rink is open daily through March.

- **Rockefeller Center Rink**, 50th Street off Fifth Avenue, 212-757-5730. Open daily and evenings in season; skate rentals.

- **Skyrink**, 450 West 33rd Street between Ninth and Tenth Avenues, 16th Floor, 212-695-6555. A year-round, indoor, Olympic-sized rink, open daily and evenings, but schedules vary so call ahead; skate rentals.

- **Kate Wollman Rink**, sister to Central Park's Wollman Rink, is located on the east side of Prospect Park, off the Parkside and Ocean Avenue entrance, in Brooklyn, 718-965-6561. Open 10 to 5:30 Wednesday, 10 to 9 Thursday and Friday, 10 to 10 Saturday and 10 to 8 Sunday, to 6 on holidays. Closed Monday and Tuesday.

- **World's Fair Skating Rink**, 111th Street, Corona, Queens, in Flushing Meadow Park, 718-271-1996. You can walk to this large, indoor rink from the Shea Stadium—111th Street stop on the #7 (Flushing) Line. Open Monday, Wednesday, Friday, Saturday and Sunday, call for hours and prices; skate rentals.

Lacrosse

- **New York Lacrosse Club**. This dues-paying amateur group fields both an A and B team and competes against members of an Eastern Seaboard league of lacrosse clubs. New York City is their home base but the home field is on Long Island. Write Dr. Bernard Schflnbaum, 21 Ridge Road, Little Falls, NJ 07424 for information.

Racquetball

Devotees of this popular sport can burn off calories at two of the Ys we mention below—the West Side YMCA at 5 West 63rd Street and the 92nd Street YMHA at Lexington Avenue (three practice courts only)—as well as:

- **Club La Raquette**, 119 West 56th Street at Avenue of the Americas (Hotel Meridien), 212-245-1144. Buried beneath the hotel are four racquetball courts and two squash courts which are open to the public by reservation.

- **Manhattan Plaza Racquet Club**, 450 West 43rd Street, 212-594-0554, a tennis club with two regulation courts. Use does not require membership.

Roller Blading/Skating

For exhilarating outdoor fun, try Central Park blade action. Roller disco, though passe, still has followers here also. Other in-line skating (its official moniker) hot-spots: Union Square, the World Financial Center and Brooklyn's Prospect Park. If you plan on renting, bring a credit card for a deposit on the equipment.

- **Blades East and West Skate and Sport**, 160 East 86th Street, 212-996-1644; 105 West 72nd Street, 212-787-3911; open 10 to 8 weekdays and Saturday, 10 to 6 Sunday. With the help of the friendly staffers at either of these locations, you too can join the fun (and risk your neck) by in-line skating. Rollerblades, the best-known brand, can be rented for two hours ($15, weekends,) or the whole day ($25), wrist guards and knee pads included. And if you want to join the growing army of neon-clad bladers permanently, you can also buy skates, equipment, and gear here ($95-$350).

- **Crunch Fitness**, 140 Charles Street, NYC 10014, 212-639-8863; offers Saturday classes for beginners; blades rent for $12.99 for two hours, $25 per day.

- **Lezly Dance and Skate School**, 622 Broadway between Bleecker and Houston Streets, 212-7773232, holds classes for every level; skate rentals available for classes only.

- **Manhattan Sports**, 2188 Broadway (at 78th Street), 580-4753 and 2901 Broadway (at 113th Street), 749-1454; blades rent for a reasonable $10 per day weekdays, $15 per day weekends. Also sell and repair in-line skates.

Rugby

- **Van Cortlandt Park**, 212-548-7070, in The Bronx is the center of rugby play in New York City.

Running

- **The New York Road Runners Club** with over 25,000 members, "the world's largest running club," maintains an "International Running Center" at 9 East 89th Street, NYC 10128, 212-860-4455. Road Runners sponsors the New York Marathon and more than 150 other races a year. Regular annual membership costs $25.

Sailing

If you want to bound over Long Island Sound, City Island in The Bronx is an accessible starting point. Take the IRT # 2 (Seventh Avenue) or # 6 (Lexington Avenue) train to Pelham Parkway and transfer to the Bronx # 12 City Island bus.

- **The New York Sailing School**, 697 Bridge Street, City Island, The Bronx 10464, 718-885-3103, offers a 28-hour sailing course for $445 on board one of its Solings, Sonars, Merit 25s or J-22s. You can also rent boats here for $70 to $185 a day, depending on the size of the boat, day of the week and whether or not you are a Sailing School graduate. (1994 rates.)

- **Offshore Sailing School**, locations in Port Washington, Long Island, Jersey City, NJ and Greenwich, CT, 800-221-4326, has a fleet of 27' to 43' boats on which they teach beginning three-day courses for $450 weekdays, $475 weekends. Advanced courses available for slightly more. (1994 rates.)

Scuba

While no one's suggesting dives to the murky depths of the Hudson, you can take certification courses in local pools preparatory to plunging into the Caribbean's turquoise waters.

- **PanAqua Diving**, 166 West 75th Street, 212-496-2267, is the only dive shop with a compressor on site. In addition to selling and repairing equipment, they organize group and individual diving travel and run certification courses of six evening sessions each, over a two-week period at the West Side Y and the Vanderbilt Y, over three weeks at Manhattan Plaza, and Sunday evenings over five weeks at the 92nd Street Y. The cost for each is $200 to $225.

Skiing

You won't schuss downhill in New York City, but cross country skiers take to the gentle slopes of Central Park and, in the boroughs, Van Courtland Park, Split Rock Golf Course in Pelham Bay Park, The Bronx, Prospect Park in Brooklyn and Flushing Meadow Park in Queens.

The New York-New Jersey Trail Conference, 232 Madison Avenue, 212-685-9699, can provide ski touring information by phone.

Soccer

The Cosmopolitan Soccer League, 201-861-6606, represents amateur and semi-pro clubs from New York, New Jersey and Connecticut. The League has one semi-pro and two amateur divisions consisting of about 20 clubs each. You don't have to join a club to play on a team, but club facilities are limited to members. Coaches are available for training; all age groups are welcome.

Squash

When you consider that a tennis court takes up about ten times as much space as a squash court, it is easy to understand the great attraction squash holds for sports club operators as well as for a population determined to exercise, but at the lowest cost possible. Numerous commercial clubs have opened recently, but still the pressure grows for more.

- **New York Sports Club**, 404 Fifth Avenue at 37th Street, 212-594-3120, four courts; 61 West 62nd Street, 212-265-0995, four courts; and 151 East 86th Street, 212-860-8630, eight courts, two international.

- **Park Avenue Athletic Complex**, 3 Park Avenue at 34th Street, 212-686-1085; one squash court.

- **Park Place Squash Club**, 25 Park Place at Church Street, 212-964-2677; five courts.

Swimming—Beaches

City strands traditionally open on Memorial Day and close the day after Labor Day. Managed by national, state and city park departments, all the beaches mentioned below are staffed with life guards. For information on beaches open to the general public, as opposed to residents with permits, in Nassau and Suffolk Counties, call the Long Island Tourism and Convention Commission, 516-794-4222.

- **Jones Beach State Park**, 516-669-1000. No car? Take a bus from
  the Port Authority Terminal, 42nd Street and Eighth Avenue, or the
  Long Island Railroad from Penn Station as far as Freeport, and
  change to a bus for the ride direct to the beach.

- **Riis Park**, managed by the Gateway National Recreation Area,
  718-338-3687, can be reached by taking the IRT # 2 (Seventh
  Avenue) or # 5 (Lexington Avenue) train to Flatbush Avenue and
  changing to the Q35 Queens Green Line bus.

Call the Transit Authority, 718-330-1234, for directions on how to reach
the following beaches managed by the city Parks Department:

Brighton Beach and contiguous **Coney Island Beach**, two of
Brooklyn's Atlantic Ocean beaches; **Orchard Beach** on Long Island
Sound in The Bronx; **Rockaway Beach** (near Riis Park) on the Atlantic
in Queens; and **Great Kills Beach**, **South Beach** and **Wolf's Pond
Park** on Staten Island.

Swimming—Pools

The Department of Parks and Recreation maintains a number of indoor
and outdoor pools with inexpensive admission. In the heat of summer,
the outdoor pools are more for play and cooling off than serious lap
swimming. The swimming's easier during off hours in winter. Note that
gyms are attached to the three city pools listed. Winter indoor pool hours
are generally 3 p.m. to 10 p.m. weekdays, 10 a.m. to 5 p.m. Saturday,
closed Sunday. Summer hours for the outdoor pools are 11 a.m. to 7
p.m. daily. The indoor pools are closed in summer.

- **Asser Levy Pool**, 23rd Street between First Avenue and FDR
  Drive, 212-447-2020. Built in 1906 as a public bath modeled on the
  Roman baths, this granite gem with a marble lobby and 20-foot ceilings reopened in 1990 after extensive renovations. A $25 member-
  ship donation ($10 for seniors) gives you a year's entree to the 21
  by 65 foot indoor pool and the very popular workout room, which is
  used from 7:15 a.m. until 10 p.m., including some 60 classes from
  aerobics to yoga. The 50 by 125 foot outdoor pool is free.

- **Carmine Street Gymnasium and Pool**, Clarkson Street and Seventh Avenue South (Greenwich Village), 212-397-3107. 20' by 70' indoor pool; 50' by 100' outdoor pool. Two upstairs gyms and a running track.

- **East 54th Street Gymnasium and Pool**, 348 East 54th Street between First and Second Avenues, 212-397-3154. 50 by 54 foot indoor pool (open year round). Upstairs gym and running track. $25 annual membership donation.

- **West 59th Street Gymnasium and Pool**, West 59th Street and West End Avenue, 212-397-3159. 34 by 60 foot indoor pool; 75 by 100 foot outdoor pool. Gym has basketball and paddleball courts. $25 annual registration fee.

Health clubs and Ys with pools are described at the end of this chapter. Dedicated swimmers might wish also to check out other swimming situations such as:

- **Manhattan Plaza Swim and Health Club**, 482 West 43rd Street at Tenth Avenue, 212-563-7001. The handsome, verdant, glass-enclosed 40 by 75 foot pool with four lap lanes is the main lure here, but there is also a gym and sauna. Annual membership costs $832, renewal is $675.

- **Trinity School Swim Club**, 91st Street between Columbus and Amsterdam Avenues, 212-873-1650. The Olympic-sized 45 by 75 foot pool is available to members for swimming six nights a week. Membership is for a summer session and for a winter session that corresponds to the academic year (and therefore includes fall and spring). Currently, there's a long waiting list.

If a dip for a day is all you require, try one of these two West Side hotel pools:

- **Ramada Inn**, Eighth Avenue at 48th Street, 212-581-7000. 20' by 30' outdoor rooftop pool, call for seasonally changing hours, $20 a day weekends, $15 weekdays.

- **Sheraton City Squire**, 790 Seventh Avenue at 52nd Street, 212-581-3300. Covered 20' by 40' pool with outdoor sunning area, open 7:30 a.m. to 8 p.m., $12 a day weekends, $10 weekdays.

Tennis

The Department of Parks Permit Office in each borough issues tennis permits for city courts. Manhattan permit particulars are detailed under Central Park—Tennis. Of the city's 535 public courts, more than 100 are located in Manhattan at nine sites. The largest single concentration, 30 courts, is in Central Park off 96th Street. Seven of the other locations are north of 96th Street, and the eighth is at East River Park at Broome Street on the Lower East Side.

In Brooklyn, permits are sold at the Brooklyn Borough Parks Department office in Litchfield Mansion, 95 Prospect Park West off Fifth Street, 718-965-8900, Monday through Friday 9 to 4. The ten city courts located at the Parade Grounds, Coney Island and Parkside Avenues, open from April through November, are probably those most popular with tennis permit holders. The same courts are covered with a bubble and run as a concession in the winter. Call 718-236-7045 for hours and rates.

Seven private clubs with four or more courts in Manhattan and across the East River in Queens are listed below. Check the Yellow Pages for other facilities near you.

- **Armory Tennis**, 643 Park Avenue at 66th Street, 212-772-6015. Five indoor courts; hourly and seasonal rates.

- **Crosstown Tennis**, 14 West 31st Street, 212-947-5780. Four indoor courts; hourly and seasonal rates.

- **East River Tennis Club**, 44-02 Vernon Boulevard, Long Island City (located on the East River; courtesy minibus service leaves hourly on the half-hour from 57th Street and Third Avenue), 718-937-2381. 20 courts, under bubble in winter; membership.

- **Manhattan Plaza Racquet Club**, 450 West 43rd Street, 212-594-0554. Five courts, two racquetball courts and swimming pool privileges; membership, hourly and seasonal rates.

- **Midtown Tennis Club**, 341 Eighth Avenue at 27th Street, 212-989-8572. Eight courts; hourly and seasonal rates.

- **Tennisport**, Borden Avenue and Second Street, Long Island City (opposite Manhattan on the East River near Midtown Tunnel exit), 718-392-1880. 16 indoor, 13 outdoor courts; membership.

- **Trinity School**, 91st Street between Columbus and Amsterdam Avenues, 212-873-1650, has two outdoor courts open April 1 through December 1 and one indoor court open September thru May; seasonal memberships.

Windsurfing

- **Island Windsurfing**, 1623 York Avenue, 212-744-2000. This full-service shop provides everything from boards to wetsuits. They can arrange lessons at and transportation to either of their two Long Island locations for $65 for three hours. In summer they run day trips to both; call for current rates. The Manhattan store is open year round and has ski gear and snowboards as well.

- **Olympic Windsurfing**, 475 Port Washington Boulevard, Port Washington, Long Island, 516-883-8207. Call during the season for information.

Health Clubs, YMCAs, YWCAs and YMHAs

Most of the city's seemingly hundreds of local health clubs fall into one of two categories. Newest are clubs applying a scientific approach to physical health, clubs featuring cardiovascular and "health enhancement" facilities where fitness regimes are custom-designed after a thorough physical and where a trainer is assigned to supervise progress. More traditional are those ubiquitous all-purpose spas where you set your own pace using the most appealing facilities. These usually include a pool (varying from postage stamp to Olympic in size), exercise equipment, steam rooms, whirlpools and saunas, as well as exercise, yoga and calisthenics classes. To indicate the amenities available a few of the many health facilities located here are described.

- **Bally's Jack LaLanne Fitness Center**, five locations in Manhattan: Broadway at 75th Street, 212-877-1111; Lexington Avenue at 86th Street, 212-722-7371; Fifth Avenue at 53rd Street (women only); Madison Avenue and 55th Street, 212-688-6630; 233 Broadway near Wall Street, 212-227-5977; three locations in Brooklyn; three locations in Queens; one Bronx location. This is one of the few New York City clubs that does not require a full year's payment upfront but allows you to pay on a monthly basis. Includes Universal and Lifecycle exercise machines, free weights and daily aerobics classes. Some membership packages provide for use of other Bally centers throughout the country.

- **Cardio-Fitness Centers** at 79 Maiden Lane, 943-1510; 345 Park Avenue at 53rd Street, 838-4570; 1221 Sixth Avenue at 48th Street, 840-8240; 200 Park Avenue at 45th Street, 632-4440; and 9 West 57th Street, 753-3980. (All Area Code 212.) Some corporations pay part or all of their employees' fees for the individualized, instructor-designed exercise programs at the Cardio-Fitness Centers (members can use the clubs interchangeably). Saunas are in place, as are exercise machines, bikes and treadmills. A medical history is required and a stress test as well for those over 35.

- **Downtown Athletic Club**, 19 West Street, 212-425-7000, occupies a 35-story building housing numerous dining rooms, hotel rooms on 15 Floors, and sports and fitness facilities on 13 floors. These include a 30' by 75' pool, two handball and/or racquetball courts, ten squash courts, a basketball court, Nautilus and Universal exercise machines, saunas, steambaths and a whirlpool. You must be proposed by a current member.

- **New York Health and Racquet Club**, 212-797-1500, has six locations. Rates go down considerably in the summer (watch for ads offering discounts, and ask about corporate discounts). Membership includes use (for a fee) of the club's tennis court in the Village and admission to any of its locations: 20 East 50th Street, 18' by 50' pool; 1433 York Avenue at 76th Street, 30' by 35' pool; 24 East 13th Street, 20' by 35' pool; 132 East 45th Street, 18' by 50' pool; 110 West 56th Street, 20' by 60' pool; and 39 Whitehall Street, Olympic-sized pool. Other facilities include tennis courts downtown, a yacht and the midtown Kimberly Hotel.

• **New York Sports Club**, ten locations: 30 Cliff Street (Seaport), 212-349-7700; 541 Lexington Avenue at 50th, 212-838-2102; 404 Fifth Avenue at 37th, 212-549-3120; Madison Avenue at 46th, 212-983-0303; 61 West 62nd Street, 212-265-0995; 100 Old Slip (downtown), 212-785-3000; 151 East 86th Street, 212-860-8630; 614 Second Avenue, 212-213-5999; 110 Boerum Place, Brooklyn, 718-643-4400; 151 Reade Street (Tribeca), 212-571-1000. Eagle and Nautilus circuits, Lifecycles, Stairmasters, Gravitron and other equipment are available in all clubs. Most have one-on-one training, pools, squash courts, whirlpools and saunas. Membership includes entrance to all clubs and access to tennis courts (additional court fee) in Brooklyn. This is one of the few clubs that does not require payment for a full year upfront but will bill you monthly.

• **The Printing House Fitness and Racquetball Center**, 421 Hudson Street at Leroy, 212-243-7600. On the first Floor are five racquetball and four squash courts; on the ninth floor four kinds of gym machines, treadmills, locker rooms and a sauna, a steam room and whirlpool as well as a cardiovascular fitness center, two dance studios and a full-service salon. On the roof above is a seasonal 20' by 30' foot heated outdoor pool. There are three different membership rates here, depending on whether you want to use just the racquetball and squash courts, just the gym, or everything. Call for specifics.

• **The Sports Training Institute**, 239 East 49th Street, 212-752-7111, specializes in one-on-one, personalized training on Nautilus, Universal, Orthotron and Cybex machines. Besides their strengthening regime, one that has kept numerous sports personalities in the very best of health, the institute offers aerobic equipment, including Nordic skis, Sitron bicycles and rowing machines, a mat-covered area and a stretch class every 15 minutes.

- **The Vertical Club**, 330 East 61st Street, 212-355-5100, is that glamorous seven-story building you see when entering Manhattan on the 59th Street Bridge from Queens: lots of tinted glass, gleaming chrome and lithe-looking figures back-lit and working out. The big club accommodates a 20' by 40' pool, exercise machines, squash and racquetball courts, an indoor track, sundeck, restaurant and juice bar, among other amenities, and is slick and classy.

- **Brooklyn YWCA**, 30 Third Avenue between State Street and Atlantic Avenue, Brooklyn, 718-875-1190. For a reasonably priced $395 Athletic Membership plus a $35 Y membership, both men and women can work out on the Universal machines, punching bags, the large basketball court, jogging track and in the 20' by 60' swimming pool, as well as relax in the sauna.

- **McBurney YMCA**, 215 West 23rd Street, 212-741-9216. This Y has a carefully developed children's after-school program as well as adult gymnastics, adult lap and recreational swimming, full-court basketball, indoor jogging track, fencing, handball, volleyball and weight lifting room. Annual adult membership costs $624 for those over eighteen, with a $125 joiner's fee for the first year.

- **92nd Street YMHA**, 1395 Lexington Avenue, 212-427-6000. The cost of Athletic Memberships are determined by the member's sex (men are charged more because their locker facilities are better): $695 or $960 for men; $695 or $860 for women. If you know a member, the Y takes $150 off the price; your friend receives one month free. The program provides indoor jogging, weight training, volleyball and handball as well as fitness programs and use of the 50 by 75 foot pool.

- **Vanderbilt YMCA**, 224 East 47th Street, 212-755-2410, offers yoga, handball and paddleball, along with swimming, basketball, volleyball, indoor jogging, Nautilus and aerobics. Regular memberships cost $624 and include use of the gym, 25' by 60' swimming pool, a 40' by 75' lap pool and other sports facilities. Annual dues for the Businessman's Club and the men's Athletic Club are higher.

- **The West Side YMCA**, 5 West 63rd Street, 212-787-4400, is justifiably proud of its Sports Fitness Department, which keeps both men and women members in the very best of shape. The seven-story building houses two pools, a wrestling room, indoor running track, handball, squash and racquetball courts, Universal exercise machines and numerous other facilities. Annual adult membership is $749, plus $125 initiation fee.

Transportation

Subways

The subway is still the quickest way to get around New York City. All city subway lines are administered by the New York City Transit Authority, and recently they've been considerably improved, particularly the IRT lines. Call 718-330-1234 for train information or stop by one of the authority's Information Booths, open from 7 a.m. to 11 p.m. at Pennsylvania or Grand Central Station. Subway and bus maps for all five boroughs are readily available there. In theory, token sellers at the subway stops also distribute maps, but in practice they are often out of stock.

Subway trains operate 24 hours a day, but service slows appreciably after 11 p.m., when it is generally best to take a cab or bus anyway. Subway tokens currently cost $1.25 each. Subway entrances with red lights have no token booths; avoid them.

PATH

The PATH (for Port Authority Trans-Hudson) tubes provide clean and efficient service connecting Manhattan with Hoboken, Jersey City and Newark for $1 round the clock. Trains leaving 33rd Street at Avenue of the Americas (Sixth Avenue) go to Hoboken or Jersey City, with stops along the way at 23rd, 14th, 9th and Christopher Streets. From the World Trade Center in Lower Manhattan trains leave for Hoboken and for Newark by way of Jersey City. Schedules are available in most stations, or call 800-234-7284.

Buses

Independent bus lines found mainly in boroughs other than Manhattan co-exist with those run by the New York City Transit Authority. Call 718-330-1234 for Transit Authority information as well as telephone numbers for the independents. Maps are sometimes available from drivers but are always stocked at the Information Booths mentioned under Subways above.

Buses cost $1.25. Transfers in Manhattan are free at the moment (but not always free in other boroughs). Exact change is required for buses and tokens are also accepted.

Ferries

Time was, before the advent of the auto, when some 125 passenger boats plied 50 different routes across the Hudson and East Rivers. With the closing of the Hoboken Ferry in 1967, only the Staten Island Ferry remained, both a commuter necessity for Staten Islanders and an excursion delight for Manhattanites and tourists alike.

The water commute is once again a reality on a dozen privately operated routes connecting Manhattan with New Jersey, Brooklyn and Queens. In increasing numbers commuters are choosing this alternative to gridlock, exorbitant parking fees and expressway dementia, especially during the oppressive heat of summer. As more passengers take to the water, increased service comes on line. Most recently re-opened is the link between Hoboken and a floating terminal at Battery Park City (call 201-902-8850 for information).

- **Staten Island Ferry**, at 50¢ still New York's best transportation (and entertainment) buy, leaves the South Ferry Terminal at Whitehall in Battery Park for St. George, Staten Island, every half hour between 6:30 a.m. and 11:30 p.m. and every hour between 11:30 p.m. and 6:30 a.m. Car service was suspended in 1991 after fire in Whitehall and, according to ferry personnel, resumption of car service is "under consideration." Call 212-806-6940 for information.

- **New Jersey passenger ferries**, TNT Hydro Lines, are operated from Highlands and Keyport to Pier 11 at the foot of Wall Street on the East River Monday through Friday during commuter hours (call 800-B-O-A-T-R-I-D for times). The fare is $26 round trip for the 55-minute ride.

From Weehawken, Port Imperial Clipper Service, 201-902-8735, operates between 6:45 a.m. and midnight Monday through Friday, with runs to Pier 78 at 38th Street and Twelfth Avenue and to Slip 5, Whitehall, next to the Staten Island Ferry. The fare, $4 each way to midtown and $5 each way to downtown, includes connecting buses in Manhattan.

- **LaGuardia Airport service** is described below under Airport Transportation.

Taxis and Car Services

All car services in New York City, unlicensed as well as licensed, come under the jurisdiction of the Taxi and Limousine Commission (TLC: 212-221-8294 for questions or complaints; 212-869-4513 for lost and found).

Licensed cabs in New York City tend to be reliable and safe although in 1994, for the first time, the TLC is requiring licensed cabs to install plexiglass shields between driver and passenger. This is intended more for the driver's safety, however. The TLC licenses chauffeur-driven stretch limos as well as three types of cabs:

- **Yellow cabs**, or "medallion"—for the emblem affixed to the hood—cabs, are the only taxis authorized to pick up passengers on the street. There are 11,787 of these charging $1.50 for the first 1/5th of a mile, 25¢ for each additional 1/5th of a mile, and 20¢ for each 60 seconds waiting time. A 50¢ surcharge is collected between 8 p.m. and 6 a.m. No legal surcharge for luggage. Tips in the 15% to 20% range are expected. If you're going crosstown, especially mid-day in the crush of midtown traffic, it pays to take a crosstown bus. Better yet, walk; it's faster.

- **Black cars**, the trade term for those high-quality (somewhat limousine-like), radio-dispatched fleet cars you see around, aren't licensed to stop for street hails. Corporations, and private charges, account for most of the "black car" business. That's why shiny

Oldsmobiles and Buicks with quivering radio antennas, discretely lettered fleet plates and the official blue decal of the Taxi and Limousine Commission affixed to the passenger side of the windshield blanket Wall Street. In theory, these meterless "voucher cabs" (which charge by zone or by mileage registered on the odometer) will respond to telephone requests from charge-accountless individuals; in practice few do.

• **Car services** are licensed to work only from a telephone base and can't legally pick up passengers on the street. The vehicles, of which there are some 36,000 licensed, range from the less-than-lovely to the pristine-upscale, but they are never yellow. Each vehicle, as proof of licensing, must display the blue decal of the Taxi and Limousine Commission on the passenger side of the front windshield. Especially useful to residents of the outer boroughs, where cabs rarely cruise, and to baggage-laden wayfarers, these for-hire vehicles charge fat rates per trip, sometimes less than the cost of a metered cab. In fact, with two or three sharing a car, it may be cheaper and more pleasant to go out of town, to Washington or Philadelphia, say, by car service than to fly.

It pays to shop around by phone. Some rides can be reserved 20 minutes before departure, others require a day's notice. Rates and features vary: you may wish to pay a few dollars extra for a station wagon or for a Lincoln Town Car, and you may wish to arrange to have the car wait for you for the return trip from out of town, for which some services charge only half fare. In any case, be sure the service is licensed, and don't hesitate to ask how much liability insurance they carry for passenger injury; they should carry a minimum of $1 million.

The car lurching to your side looks a wreck, and there's no decal? Then it's probably an unlicensed **gypsy cab**, in which you'll ride at your own risk without recourse in case of bad service.

Limousines

For those occasions when you wish to ride in style or have a car and driver at your beck and call, consider hiring a limousine. Many car services also operate limousines; rates are usually on a per hour basis although some firms set flat rates for trips to airports or for dinner-and-theater evenings. White, 40-foot-long strrrretches such as those operated by Amex Limousine Service, 212-696-4088, are the current ultimate. These block-long beauties carry 14 people including two in the rumble seat; the garden-variety stretch limos offer stereos, color TV and a stocked bar with ice for five or six. One day's notice is usually required, though cars (but not necessarily your first choice) are sometimes available on short notice. Most firms accept major credit cards but check when you call. Below are some representative rates. Add 15% gratuity for the driver.

- **All-State Car and Limousine Service, Inc.**, 446 Hudson Street, 212-741-7440. This service requires a two-hour minimum plus gratuity when you rent a sedan at $18 an hour or stretch limo at $40 an hour plus 20% gratuity. All-State also offers good rates to LaGuardia ($16 plus toll and gratuity), JFK ($25 plus toll and gratuity) and Newark ($26 plus toll and gratuity). A stretch to any airport is $70 plus tolls and a 20% gratuity.

- **Carey Limousine**, 62-07 Woodside Avenue, Woodside, Queens, 212-599-1122. Cadillac sedans cost $44 per hour, limousines $52 per hour, starting from the time the car leaves the garage on 34th Street, Manhattan, until it returns. You pay tolls or parking fees plus 7% service charge.

- **Communicar Ltd.**, 129-02 Northern Boulevard, Corona, Queens 11368, 718-457-7777. Call 15 minutes ahead of time to have an unmetered maroon Oldsmobile at your door. Flat rates depend on pickup point and destination (fees are listed in a book). East Side to LaGuardia Airport is $25, to JFK $39. Cars are available hourly at $30 per and can be reserved one day in advance at an additional $4.

- **Dav-El Livery**, Pier 62, North River at 23rd Street, 212-645-4242. Sedans cost $42 per hour or $1.45 per mile and stretch limos cost $50 per hour or $1.60 per mile, beginning when the car leaves the garage. A trip to or from all airports is charged at the two-hour rate. There is a one-and-a-half-hour minimum before 6 p.m., two-hour minimum after 6.

• **Fugazy International Corp.**, 212-661-0100. Sedan town cars for $35 per hour, beginning at the scheduled pickup time. Stretch limos at $46 per hour, with a two-hour minimum, from the time of pre-arranged pickup.

Airlines

The Port Authority of New York and New Jersey manages John F. Kennedy, LaGuardia and Newark Airports and strives mightily to upgrade airport transportation and services and to disseminate information to the public about the facilities. To this end, they distribute particularly helpful materials and staff several telephone information numbers.

Since deregulation, the 90-plus airlines serving the three airports seem to be perpetually changing flight schedules, destinations and names, to say nothing of fares. To order this chaos, the Port Authority publishes the *International and Domestic Consolidated Airline Schedule*, a pocket-sized quarterly useful for finding the flight to fit one's needs.

The Port Authority also publishes the *Airport Map/Guides*—one each for JFK, LaGuardia and Newark—illustrating the locations of parking lots, airlines, access routes and other services. Call the 800 number listed below or write or phone the Aviation Public Service Division, Room 65N, One World Trade Center, NYC 10048, 212-466-7510, for copies of either series.

Call **800-A-I-R-R-I-D-E** 9 to 5 weekdays and a particularly helpful staff will try to answer your questions about any of the airports; if the question is too detailed, they'll suggest the right number to phone.

Airport Transportation

The easiest, fastest, and most expensive way to reach JFK is by **helicopter**. New York Helicopter, 800-645-3494, has ten-minute flights between JFK and the 34th Street Heliport every half hour between 1:30 and 7:30 p.m. for $71.50 one way, reservations required.

At $2.50, the cheapest and one of the slowest methods is to take a subway to Queens, changing there to public bus for either LaGuardia or Kennedy. Between these two extremes are other possibilities.

First, a word about airport parking. You can, of course, drive to the airport and park there for up to 30 days at Kennedy International or Newark (tab: $150). LaGuardia has no long-term parking. Short-term parking at all airports is closer to the terminal and more expensive, $48 per day after the first day, for example, at Newark. Only LaGuardia accepts credit cards for parking. Remember that Fridays and holiday periods most lots are full. Business travelers fill short-term lots on Wednesdays. Arrive at the lot before 3 p.m. most days to be sure of a parking spot, and don't expect to find a space at LaGuardia Sunday night.

John F. Kennedy International Airport

Call 718-656-4520 for information; 718-656-4120 for lost and found; 718-495-5400 for parking.

- **Taxis** to and from midtown cost about $35 to $40 each way not including tolls and tip. There is no formal Share and Ride system at Kennedy, but if you can find a "friend" with whom to split the fare, so be it.

- **Carey Transportation**, call 718-632-0500 for exact schedules, leave approximately every half hour from four different locations: East Side, 125 Park Avenue, across from Grand Central between 40th and 41st Streets; West Side, Air Trans Center located in the Eighth Avenue and 42nd Street wing of the Port Authority Bus Terminal, and the New York Hilton and Marriott Hotels. Fares are $11 one way, $22 round trip.

- **Shared minibus service**, call 212-757-6840 for information. Gray Line Air Shuttle provides minibus service every 15 minutes to major Manhattan hotels from 7 a.m. to 11 p.m. for $15 per person.

- **Public Subway and Bus** Call the Transit Authority, 718-330-1234, and Green Bus Line, 718-995-4700, for information. Handling lots of luggage along this route is difficult, but the bargain $2.50 cost one way (two tokens) is attractive if you're going to pick someone up or are on your way home from saying goodbye. Take the E or F train to Kew Gardens, the BMT J train to 121st Street or the A Lefferts

Boulevard (not Far Rockaway) train to the last stop, which is Lefferts Boulevard. In each case you change to the Q10 bus to Kennedy Airport. The Q10 circles the airport, stopping at each airline terminal where you can also pick it up for the return trip home.

LaGuardia Airport

Call 718-476-5000 for information; 718-476-5515 for lost and found; 718-476-5507 for parking.

- **Taxis** to and from midtown cost about $18 to $20 without tip. If you can find a friendly fellow Manhattan (or wherever you are going) bound traveler you can split the fare.

- **Carey Transportation,** call 718-632-0513 for exact schedules, leave approximately every 15 minutes from four different locations: East Side, 125 Park Avenue, across from Grand Central between 40th and 41st Streets; West Side, New York Hilton at 53rd Street, Sheraton City Squire at 50th Street, and Marriott Hotel at 48th Street. Fares are $10 one way, $20 round trip.

- **Shared minibus service,** call 212-757-6840 for information. Gray Line Air Shuttle provides minibus service to major Manhattan hotels every 15 minutes from 7 a.m. to 11 p.m. for $12 per person.

- **Public Subway and Bus Call the Transit Authority,** 718-330-1234, and Triborough Coast Line, 718-335-1000, for information. Take the E or F train to the Roosevelt station in Queens and change to the Q33 bus which runs to LaGuardia every 15 minutes 24 hours a day. Total cost $2.50 one way.

    The LaGuardia "Q.T." (Quick Trip) leaves from all LaGuardia terminals and the Marine Air Terminal every 20 minutes from 6:35 a.m. to 11 p.m. The express bus leaves you at 21st Street and 41st Avenue in Long Island City, where you can catch the B or Q into Manhattan. Total cost is $5 in exact change or tokens.

- **Delta Water Shuttle,** 800-54-F-E-R-R-Y, operates a regularly scheduled launch shuttle between LaGuardia and East 34th Street and Pier 11 at the foot of Wall Street Monday through Friday. The trip takes 25 minutes from East 34th Street, 40 minutes from Pier 11 and costs $20 one way, $38 round trip.

Newark International Airport

Call 201-961-2000 for information; 201-961-6230 for lost and found; 201-961-4755 for parking.

The Port Authority, which runs all three NYC area airports, supervises efficient, inexpensive transportation to and from Newark.

- **Taxis** can legally add $10 to the meter rate, and the trip from midtown to Newark Airport costs about $40 without tolls and tips. Returning to Manhattan, New Jersey cabs are limited to fixed fares determined by location, for example $25 to the West Side between the Battery and 59th Street; $32 to anywhere on the East Side above 86th Street. Share and Save rates for groups of up to four passengers cut costs by almost half and are available between 8 a.m. and midnight. Check with the dispatcher at the terminal's hackstand.

- **Bus Service** by New Jersey Transit to and from the Port Authority Bus Terminal, 212-564-8484, uses a special air-conditioned airport departure lounge, the Air Trans Center, in the North Wing of the terminal at 42nd Street and Eighth Avenue. Buses leave every 15 minutes from 6:45 a.m. to midnight and cost $7 one way, $12 round trip.

- **Olympia Trails Bus Company**, call 212-964-6233 for information, runs a bus about every 30 minutes during rush hours that stops first at 125 Park Avenue, between 40th and 41st Streets across from Grand Central, then at One World Trade Center on West Street next to the Vista Hotel before arriving at Newark Airport some 25 minutes later. The cost is $7 one way.

- **Shared minibus service**, call 212-757-6840 for information. Gray Line Air Shuttle provides minibus service every 15 minutes to major Manhattan hotels from 7 a.m. to 11 p.m. for $17 per person.

Inter-Airport Service

Every half hour between 6:30 a.m. and 11:30 p.m. **Carey**, at

718-632-0513, runs a shuttle bus that loops between the passenger terminals at **Kennedy and LaGuardia Airports**. The fare is $11 one way. If you are traveling with a companion, or can find someone to share with, it is probably worth taking a taxi. The fare is about $12 to $15 without tip.

As described above, Carey also provides transportation from these airports to the Air Trans Center at the Port Authority Bus Terminal. Because New Jersey Transit, 212-564-8484, also uses the Air Trans Center as a depot for Newark Airport service, a direct bus link has been forged between **Newark, LaGuardia and Kennedy Airports**. Just change at the Air Trans Center from Carey to New Jersey Transit or vice versa. The fares remain the same: $11 from Newark to New York, $11 from New York to LaGuardia, $11 to Kennedy.

Satellite Airports

Two airports outside the city offer an attractive alternative to the JFK-LaGuardia-Newark axis: uncrowded access roads, easy parking and fewer delays all around for domestic flights.

- **Long Island MacArthur** in Islip, Long Island, is served by American Airlines and USAir, plus the commuter lines of Continental, Delta, Northwest and United, with direct flights to ten cities in the East. Call 516-467-6161 for information.

- **Stewart Airport**, a former Air Force base 60 miles north of the city in Newburgh, NY, at the juncture of I-87 and I-84, opened for commercial service in 1990 and offers service by American and USAir and the commuter lines American Eagle and United Express to five cities and Kennedy Airport. Call 914-564-2100 for information.

Commuter and National Rail Service

Pennsylvania Station, between 31st and 33rd Streets and Seventh and Eighth Avenues, with the Long Island Railroad Station adjacent between 33rd and 34th Streets, and Grand Central Station at 42nd Street between Vanderbilt and Lexington Avenues at Park are the railroad hubs in New York City. The waiting room at Grand Central has recently been renovated in celebration of the grand old station's 75th birthday and is once again habitable. The Oyster Bar downstairs, unbelievably, is one of New York's best restaurants.

- **Amtrak** trains, call 212-582-6875 for information and reservations, leave Pennsylvania Station for the Northeast Corridor between Washington and Boston and for destinations throughout most of the country and to Canada. For **Metroliner** service between New York and Washington call 800-523-8720 for information and reservations.

- **Metro-North trains**, 212-532-4900, leave from Grand Central Station and include the Hudson Line to Poughkeepsie, New York; the Harlem Line to Brewster, New York; and the New Haven Line to New Haven, Connecticut.

- The **New Jersey Transit** Information Center, 201-762-5100, is the place to call for Pennsylvania Station-New Jersey train schedules.

- **Long Island Railroad** trains, 718-217-5477, leave from their own station next to Penn Station.

Commuter and National Bus Service

The Port Authority Bus Terminal, between 40th and 42nd Streets and Eighth and Ninth Avenues, 212-564-8484, strikingly modernized and enlarged, is the center for almost all intercity bus traffic. The exceptions are interborough expresses, which have designated pickup points at certain Manhattan intersections, and buses, mostly from New Jersey, that arrive and leave from the Port Authority Bus Station at the George Washington Bridge, 212-564-1114.

- **Greyhound/Trailways Bus Lines**, 212-971-6363, has its principal ticket offices in the Port Authority Terminal, and their buses arrive and depart from the Lower Level of the North Wing with entrances on both 41st and 42nd Streets.

Car Rentals

If you let your fingers do the walking through the 19 Yellow Pages of car rental firms in the Manhattan Telephone Directory, you will undoubtedly come up with the best rate for your particular needs. National and local companies rent everything from the latest model cars in all sizes to sub-compacts, station wagons, vans and "oldies." Prices vary widely from firm to firm, and special rates (for a weekend, say, or midweek) are common; call around for cost comparisons. Keep in mind that companies located just outside the city may have low enough rates to more than compensate for the lack of convenience.

Be sure to ask if there is a charge for leaving the car at another location, if that is your plan. Some other helpful hints: Manhattan car rental companies run out of availability quickly, especially before summer and holiday weekends. *Do not wait until the last minute!* Calling early may also get you a better discount. You may be able to get discount packages through your employer's company policy. Finally, becoming a member of New York City's AAA, 212-757-2000, even if you do not own a car, is a good idea. Aside from access to good discount rental rates, you're guaranteed the protection you might not otherwise get from a small rental company.

Here are most of the largest companies. All of them accept major credit cards.

- **Avis** In New York City call 212-308-2727 for information and reservations; elsewhere call 800-331-1212. Eleven locations in Manhattan; cars available at John F. Kennedy International Airport, LaGuardia Airport and Newark International Airport.

- **Budget** 800-527-0700. Nine locations in Manhattan and at all three airports.

- **Dollar** 800-800-4000. Three locations in Manhattan and at all three airports.

- **Hertz** 800-654-3131 anytime. Eleven locations in Manhattan and at the three airports.

- **National** 800-328-4567. Nine locations in Manhattan and at all three airports.

- **Thrifty** 800-331-4200. One location in Manhattan and at all three airports.

Lodgings

Summer accommodations in university dorms, Ys, church-run women's residences, hotels and even B & Bs provide temporary shelter enroute to a permanent living situation. Descriptions of these varied lodgings are furnished, together with a selection of hotels categorized by price and location.

The rates quoted are from 1993-94. Increases during the year are a good bet, particularly in the case of hotels which traditionally hike prices in April or September.

Summer Only

Dorm accommodations and other special situations include (all Area Code 212):

- **Barnard College**, contact Ms. Jean McCurry, Director, Summer Program, 2009 Broadway, NYC 10027, 854-8021. During the summer, Barnard opens the doors of its dorm and student apartment rooms to men and women students both, as long as they have jobs, an internship or are attending an accredited school. 1992 rates: an air-conditioned room is $96 to $124 per person per week, two-week minimum. Meal plans are extra.

- **Columbia University's Intern Housing**, c/o Conference Housing Office, 116 Wallach Hall, Columbia University, NYC 10027, 854-2946. Columbia's traditional summer hostel is open to anyone, including June graduates, with a current student ID and a paying or non-paying internship. There is a one-month minimum stay payable in advance. Rates run about $100 a week.

- **International House** (near Columbia University), 500 Riverside Drive at 123rd Street, NYC 10027, 316-8400. You don't have to matriculate at Columbia to be eligible for one of the approximately 700 dorm rooms and suites available to students, interns and other visitors from late May to mid-August on a first-come, first-served basis. Rates are $400 and up a month; for short stays, $25 a night. Write or call for information or to reserve. These bargain accommodations are sometimes available during the school year as well.

- **New York University Dormitories**, c/o New York University Housing Office, 14 Washington Place, NYC 10003, 998-4620. There is a three-week minimum stay requirement at the NYU dorms, which are open to other students and June graduates from early June through early September. Room rates range from $95 a week for a double or triple room without air conditioning to $210 per week for an air-conditioned single with kitchen, but occupants are obliged to sign up for a meal plan which costs extra.

See also **Sublets** and **Sharing** in the chapter on **Apartment Hunting**.

Transient YMCAs
Two of the three Ys in Manhattan offering accommodations house both men and women; all rent rooms on a daily basis only and all subscribe to the "Y's Way" central booking office. Anyone (member or no) can write or call the "Y's Way" booking office located in William Sloane House, 356 West 34th Street, NYC 10001, 212-760-5856, to obtain confirmed reservations at the three YMCAs listed below. "Y's Way" rates are a Flat $36 single, $46 double. Rates vary if you book direct at a specific Y. In all cases the room rate includes use of all athletic facilities on the premises (see YMCAs under Participant Sports). These accommodations have not been inspected.

- **McBurney YMCA**, 206 West 24th Street, NYC 10011, 212-741-9226. Co-ed. 279 single rooms, $32 to $48 per day ($1 less if Y member).

- **Vanderbilt YMCA**, 224 East 47th Street, NYC 10017, 212-755-2410. Men only. 439 rooms, $45 single, $65 double.

- **West Side YMCA**, 5 West 63rd Street, NYC 10023, 212-787-4400. Coed, with men and women on separate Floors. 550 single rooms, $45 single, $55 double.

Residences

Daily transients are not accepted by any of the residences noted below which, with the exception of the 92nd Street Y, are for women only. Weekly rates are the norm and many include two meals a day in the price. Full occupancy is the rule at most of these places, as is the requirement for a personal interview, and you should therefore make arrangements for a room well in advance of arrival. Selections were made from *A Temporary Place to Live* published by the Open Housing Center, 150 Fifth Avenue, NYC 10011, 212-941-6101.

- **92nd Street YM-YWHA**, 1395 Lexington Avenue, NYC 10128, 212-427-6000. Co-ed, for men and women ages 18 to 26. 400 rooms, $350 to $600 a month.

- **Katherine House** (Ladies Christian Union), 118 West 13th Street, NYC 10014, 212-242-6566. 82 rooms, $115 a week includes two meals a day; three-month minimum stay.

- **Markle Residence** (Salvation Army), 123 West 13th Street, NYC 10014, 212-242-2400. $195 a week for private room and bath includes two meals a day.

- **Parkside Evangeline Residence** (Salvation Army), 18 Gramercy Park, NYC 10003, 212-677-6200. About 200 rooms, $163 a week including two meals a day. Require $500 refundable security deposit and a $15 non-refundable registration fee.

- **Roberts House** (Ladies Christian Union), 151 East 36th Street, NYC 10016, 212-683-6865. $105 a week including two meals a day; three-month minimum.

- **St. Mary's Residence** (Daughters of the Divine Charity), 225 East 72nd Street, NYC 10021, 212-249-6850. $120 a week, with a three month minimum, no meals.

Bed and Breakfast

In Manhattan? Yes! Many a resourceful New Yorker has let out that extra room and thrown a Continental breakfast into the bargain. It's even possible to have the whole apartment, in a charming brownstone or a high tech high rise, to yourself, which is to say unhosted. In any case, it will be cheaper than comparable digs in a hotel, but the visitor may give up something in privacy, service or convenience. However, don't look for handlettered shingles advertising availability because owners require anonymity and an agency acts as intermediary.

This cottage industry is unregulated, though reputable agencies inspect the properties they represent and attempt to monitor the quality of service and accommodations on an ongoing basis through visitor critique cards. Shop around by phone; be as specific as you can be about preferred location, likes and dislikes, allergies and other restrictions. There is usually a two-night minimum stay, but there may be exceptions off-season. For the best choice, book well in advance if possible, and expect to pay a 25% deposit or more. The commission is included in the fee. Some accept credit cards. Unless stated otherwise, all telephone numbers are Area Code 212.

- **Abode Bed and Breakfast,** P.O. Box 20022, NYC 10028, 472-2000, represents about 200 hosted and unhosted apartments, mostly in Manhattan, a few in Brooklyn, and some long-term locations. They request business references from guests. Two-night minimum. Rates range from $75 to $85 for a hosted single, $85 to $100 double, and $90 to $300 for unhosted apartments. AE.

- **Bed, Breakfast and Books,** 35 West 92nd Street, NYC 10025, 865-8740, so named because the owners also operate a book business, attracts a fairly bookish clientele, not surprisingly. One of the more established agencies, they handle about 35 apartments, mostly hosted, all over Manhattan and a couple in Brooklyn. In telephone interviews they attempt to match the visitors' background, age and preferences to the location. Prices range from $65 and $70 for a hosted single, and $75 and $80 double, to $90 to $125 for an unhosted one-bedroom apartment. Two-night minimum, with a surcharge for a one-night exception; some long-term stays. AE.

- **Bed and Breakfast Network**, 134 West 32nd Street, Suite 602, NYC 10001, 745-8134, lists 145 places, hosted and unhosted, and suggests a few weeks' advance notice. Rates range from $50 to $60 single, $70 to $80 double, and $80 to $200 for an unhosted apartment. There is a two-night minimum in most cases.

- **Bed & Breakfast on the Park,** 113 Prospect Park West, Brooklyn 11215, 718-499-6115. An exquisitely appointed Victorian townhouse off Brooklyn's Prospect Park. Prices start at $75 per weekday night for a single with private bath and rise to $150 per night for a weekend double. Breakfasts are hearty and delicious.

- **New World Bed and Breakfast**, 150 Fifth Avenue, Suite 711, NYC 10011, 675-5600, or 800-443-3800 from out of town, represents about 120 apartments, all in Manhattan. Perhaps because the owner is a woman, the agency tends to attract working women. Rates for hosted rooms range from $55 to $65 single, $75 to $85 double; unhosted apartments from studios to two-bedroom, two-bath spreads in the theater district go for $70 to $200 a night, with a two-night minimum. AE, MC, V.

- **Urban Ventures, Inc.**, P.O. Box 426, NYC 10024, 594-5650, the first to enter the field, offers over 500 rooms with local residents, mainly in Manhattan. Daily rates vary with location and degree of comfort: presently $65 to $80 for hosted singles, $80 to $120 double, and $85 to $350 for unhosted apartments. There is a two-night minimum, three nights for apartments. AE, MC. V.

Residential Hotels

A number of hotels, particularly smaller neighborhood properties equipped with kitchenettes, quote weekly and monthly, as well as daily, rates. You'll find several listed under Inexpensive Hotels below. There is also a group that offers monthly rates in eight apartment hotels located in some of New York's nicest neighborhoods:

- **Manhattan East Hotels**, call 800-637-8483, represents the Shelburne (Murray Hill), Eastgate Tower (fringes of Murray Hill),

Beekman Tower (near Sutton Place), Plaza 50 and Lyden/53 (Midtown East), The Surrey and Lyden/64 (Upper East Side) and Southgate Tower (Penn Station area). The least expensive rental, a studio in Southgate Tower, costs $2,950 a month, a one-bedroom apartment in the more prestigious Beekman Tower goes for $4,500 and up.

Inexpensive Hotels

Doubles for $75 to $180 not including tax may not seem cheap but that's the price separating New York's hotel bargain category from the rest of the flock this year. All telephone numbers are Area Code 212.

- **Allerton Hotel for Women**, 130 East 57th Street, NYC 10022, 753-8841. The commendable location of this more-residential-than-transient hotel (it offers weekly as well as daily rates) keeps the place full to overflowing in spite of the fact the rooms are small, spartan and occasionally unkempt. $76 double with private bath ($60 single without bath), taxes included.

- **Best Western Seaport Inn**, 33 Peck Slip, NYC 10038, 766-6600. A pleasingly restored 19th century building one block from the waterfront at the very lower tip of Manhattan. Doubles start at $135 per night, a bargain if you get one of the upper floor rooms with great views of the Brooklyn Bridge.

- **Chelsea Inn**, 46 West 17th Street, NYC 10011, 645-8989, is reminiscent of many a small European hotel, guests included. Of the 27 rooms on the first two floors of two converted brownstones, eight share a bath with one other room. All rooms, which are clean and simple, have kitchenettes, and guests have their own front door key for the evening hours, when the desk is untended. Rates: single with a shared bath, $85; studio, $110; suite for two, $135; two-room suite for up to four, $165.

- **Empire**, 44 West 63rd Street, NYC 10023, 265-7400. The major selling point for the basic but cheerfully furnished 507-room Empire is its location next to Lincoln Center and near Columbus Circle. $120 to $230 double.

- **Excelsior**, 45 West 81st Street, NYC 10024, 362-9200. A great location facing the Museum of Natural History and Central Park compensates for occasionally grungy rooms. $65 single, $75 double, $99 for a one-bedroom suite.

- **Gramercy Park**, 2 Lexington Avenue at 21st Street, NYC 10010, 475-4320, or 800-221-4083 from out of town. Idiosyncratic and a little threadbare, perhaps, the Gramercy is not as cheap as some hotels, nor as fancy as others, but the location on and access to private, graceful Gramercy Park is appealing, especially if you can arrange for a room with a view. Doubles are $140.

- **Gorham**, 135 West 55th Street, NYC 10019, 245-1800. All 116 rooms in the narrow, 17-story Gorham just off Sixth Avenue have kitchenettes and dining tables; many have black/gold/beige decor too but are clean and a good buy. $145 to $185 for a double.

- **Esplanade Hotel**, 305 West End Avenue at 74th Street, NYC 10023, 874-5000. About a third of the 170 two-room units in this sturdy, brick housekeeping hotel on the Upper West Side are available to transients. The spacious brown and beige suites, not elegant, mind you, but each with a kitchenette, count writers, musicians and UN personnel among their full time occupants. In fact, the hotel was recently refurbished. $95 to $200 for a double.

- **Paramount**, 235 West 46th Street, NYC 10036, 764-5500. The designer of the avant-garde Royalton, Philippe Starck, turned his charms on a lower-priced venue. This whimsical effort aimed at the young, hip and financially strapped offers amenities including a $1 screening room with penny candy, a 24-hour day-care center designed by the Pee Wee Playhouse people, and a Dean & Deluca store. Rates are between $130 and $400 with special weekend rates from $130 to $165.

- **Pickwick Arms**, 230 East 51st Street, NYC 10022, 355-0300. Bits of peeling paint, randomly-sized rooms, some without baths, don't deter fans from this slightly flaky place with its East 50s location and doubles for $85 with shower.

- **The Hotel Wales**, 1295 Madison Avenue corner of 92nd Street, NYC 10028, 876-6000. Long an annex for guests of Upper East Siders with too-small apartments, the recently renovated Wales is clean, cheerful and a good value for $145 double a night.

- **Westpark Hotel,** 308 West 58th Street, NYC 10019, 246-6440. With a grand location facing Columbus Circle and Central Park and coordinated, tidily-renovated rooms—those 16 (out of 99) with park views are especially nice. At $65 to $70, the Westpark is an especially good buy for a single, doubles $80 to $180.

Hotels

Prices and occupancy rates fluctuate seasonally depending on location. The friendly, and sometimes frenetic, first-class commercial establishments along Central Park West and Lexington and Park Avenues in the East 40s and 50s are impossibly full weekdays in the fall, winter and spring, but both occupancy and prices languish during the summer dog days. This is the season, however, when the comparatively feisty West Side tourist class hotels sprinkled around the Broadway theaters in the West 40s cost the most and are the fullest. Low rates are never in season at the town's justifiably famous deluxe hotels, be they large and extravagant, quietly posh or smoothly contemporary—but many do have weekend plans.

Anyone who wants to lessen the blow of oppressive hotel prices should know where to find the lower rates at various times of the year (or week), and some generalizations are included here. *The rates quoted are for two people in a room, week nights.* All Manhattan hotels are Area Code 212.

Weekend Rates are almost always lower than prices charged during the week. However, flossy "weekend packages" with champagne, flowers and free brunches for two don't represent the best values. Ask about the no-frills prices available Friday, Saturday and sometimes Sunday nights. Weekend rates are, in effect, contingency plans to fill the house. If full occupancy looms, off they go.

Unadvertised Discounts As a result of the unprecedented (at least since the late 1920s) hotel building boom in the late 1980s, the occupancy rate of some hotels is erratic, with the result that accommodating, unadvertised prices are occasionally available. After you've been quoted the standard rates, ask for information about any special deals.

West Side Tourist Hotels

The cheapest rates for reliable, if far from classy, rooms are found in the tourist hotels along Eighth Avenue and in the West 40s surrounding the theater district. Better deals are offered here in the winter than in the summer.

- **Hotel Edison**, 228 West 47th Street, NYC 10036, 840-5000. A thousand rooms convenient to the theater and reasonable: $90 single, $100 double, $120 quadruple.

- **Howard Johnson's Motor Lodge**, Eighth Avenue and 51st Street, NYC 10019, 581-4100. A HoJo's is a HoJo's even in New York: clean, decent and about $118 to $154 for two, with parking at a rate of $7.50 for every 24 hours.

- **Milford Plaza**, Eighth Avenue and 45th Street, NYC 10036, 869-3600. Big, basic and sometimes exceedingly reasonable. Normally $110 to $150 double.

- **Ramada Inn**, Eighth Avenue and 48th Street, NYC 10019, 581-7000. Recently refurbished, and as a result, the nicest motel in town. Pool and free parking make this a good buy for $120 to $150 double, high season.

First-class Commercial or Deluxe Hotels

As said, discounts and good weekend values in these hotels are generally available only in the summertime. Suggestions for this location are given on the basis of glamour and singularity as well as fair prices when they can be found.

- **Berkshire Place**, 21 East 52nd Street at Madison Avenue, NYC 10022, 753-5800. Carefully created bouquets frame the elegant marble lobby and provide a backdrop for the toney (in a low key) tea and cocktail area on the far side of the flowers. An accommodating concierge caters to clients with dispatch in this bijou hotel, where the only major drawbacks are the smallish rooms and higher than average prices: $198 to $300.

- **Doral Court**, 130 East 39th Street between Park and Lexington Avenues, NYC 10011, 685-1100, or 800-624-0607 from out of town. The rooms are large and sunny, the youthful staff delightful and the dining al fresco in the Courtyard Cafe and Bar of this quietly elegant hotel. A double here is runs from $199 to $250.

- **Doral Inn**, Lexington Avenue between 49th and 50th Streets, NYC 10022, 755-1200. Flight crews compete for space with Latinos laden with shopping bags in the relatively spacious lobby of this popular, mildly chaotic commercial hotel where the small yet tidy rooms are a good value for this location at $145 to $160 double. Special rates are available for government and non-profit employees.

- **The Drake**, 440 Park Avenue at 56th Street, NYC 10022, 421-0900. Glowingly updated in the Continental manner complete with attractive lobby bar, the Drake is now owned by Swissair's hotel division. Doubles cost $240 to $290 weekdays but weekends here are a bargain: $150 to $175.

- **Grand Hyatt New York**, 42nd Street and Lexington Avenue at Grand Central Station, NYC 10017, 883-1234. Fast paced and glitzy with a terrific lobby, especially when the fountains are splashing, and a dramatic bar cantilevered over 42nd Street. Rooms carefully but unobtrusively furnished. $195 to $205 for two. Weekends are cheaper: $145 per night.

- **Journey's End**, 3 East 40th Street between Fifth and Madison Avenues, NYC 10016, 447-1500. Reasonably priced and centrally located, this midtown newcomer offers spacious, no-frills comfort. You can walk to Grand Central Station and the newly expanded Morgan Library. But don't walk to Times Square at night, when this area is a bit eerie. Single: $141.99, Double: $151.99.

- **The Mark**, 25 East 77th Street at Madison Avenue, NYC 10021, 744-4300, or 800-T-H-E-M-A-R-K from out of town. Your Frette linens are tended to twice daily in this handsome, sophisticated recent arrival in Carlyle country. Dining is on a par with its "glorious" rooms, which run $275 to $295 double, $235 weekends.

- **Mayfair Regent**, 610 Park Avenue at 65th Street, NYC 10024, 288-0800, or 800-545-4000 from out of town. Personalized attention and pretty rooms decorated in the English style make this small, dignified hotel on the city's Gold Coast feel like an exclusive Old World mansion. It also has one of the city's most appealing drawing rooms for tea, not to mention Le Cirque, dining preserve of the rich and famous. Doubles are $225 to $325.

- **Middletowne Harley**, 148 East 48th Street near Third Avenue, NYC 10017, 755-3000. One-, two-and three-room suites all with kitchenettes and cheerful flowered decor. A favorite of UN personnel when the General Assembly's in session. Weekdays, a double is $155, weekends it drops to a very reasonable $119.

- **The Millenium**, 55 Church Street, NYC 10007, 693-2001. Easily the classiest and most elegant of the downtown hotels. Modern and convenient (if you're visiting Wall Street), the Millenium offers stunning views as well as first-class amenities such as computers and a health club with an attractive pool. Service too is top-notch at the Millenium. Doubles start at $190 per night.

- **Morgan's**, 237 Madison Avenue between 37th and 38th Streets, NYC 10016, 686-0300. Morgan's, which is sleek and swings with pals of Manager Ian Schrager, he of Studio 54 fame, doesn't much resemble its staid neighbor and namesake, the Morgan Library next door. An upstart on New York's rather traditional hotel scene, this narrow, vertical little place has stereo cassette players in every (small) room and VCRs for rent ($6.50 a night). Rates have come down at this once-trendy spot to $195 and up for a weekday double, $150 weekends.

- **Park 51**, at the Equitable Center, 152 West 51st Street at Seventh Avenue, NYC 10019, 765-1900. The old Taft Hotel resurrected in Eurostyle elegance with well-designed rooms and great baths attracts a glitzy crowd. Bring the kids, but avoid the slow, overpriced room service. Doubles run $225 to $450.

- **The Peninsula**, 700 Fifth Avenue at 55th Street, NYC 10019, 247-2200, or 800-262-9467 from out of town. The Hong Kong Peninsula Group took over the old Gotham and restored it to its former art nouveau elegance, updated with a contemporary spa and the like. The entrance up a flight of stairs is somewhat eccentric. Doubles from $295 to $395.

- **Plaza Athenee**, 37 East 64th Street, NYC 10021, 734-9100. Very international, this British-run import from Paris. Rumor has it that Le Regence restaurant, a favorite of Jackie O and the Upper East Side ladies-that-lunch, is more enchanting than the rooms, which cost between $280 and $390 double.

- **Royalton**, 44 West 44th Street off Fifth Avenue, NYC 10036, 869-4400. With mahogany beds, Danish faucets, French and Italian furniture, Ian Schrager (see Morgan's) has fashioned a swinging silk purse out of a sow's ear. You can have a gym, a computer and a fireplace too in your room, which will run about $275 for a basic double, loft suites more.

- **San Carlos**, 150 East 50th Street, between Lexington and Third Avenues, NYC 10022, 755-1800. Quiet, small hotel with pleasantly spacious rooms and kitchenettes. $139 to $149 for two.

- **St. Regis**, 2 East 55th Street at Fifth Avenue, NYC 10022, 753-4500. This grande dame of Fifth Avenue reopened in all her Beaux Arts glory, and then some, after an endless, multi-million dollar restoration in 1991. A continental hotel in the old style with no modern convenience overlooked. And, yes, you *can* still dance on the St. Regis Roof. Doubles $350 to $450.

- **The Stanhope**, 995 Fifth Avenue at 81st Street, NYC 10028, 288-5800, or 800-828-1123 from out of town. Quiet, discrete, Old

World luxury is what the Stanhope has achieved with its recent $30-million facelift. It's all French antiques, crystal ashtrays, Egyptian cotton sheets, fresh flowers, that sort of thing, not to mention unrivaled views of Central Park and the Metropolitan Museum. Superb food and impeccable service gild the lily at $225 to $300 for a double.

• **United Nations Plaza**, 44th Street and First Avenue, NYC 10017, 355-3400. Superior service and sensational views from every room because they begin on the 28th Floor. A good-sized pool, health club, tennis court and free limousine rides to Wall Street make this classically modern hotel unique. Doubles $225 to $230, $155 to $175 weekends.

• **Waldorf-Astoria**, Park Avenue at 50th Street, NYC 10022, 355-3000. Doubles in this marvelously grand place can be had for $290 to $330 if you reserve far enough ahead. The public rooms and large, high-ceilinged lobby are amazingly svelte and polished, considering the Waldorf's size, popularity, and the fact that the hotel celebrated its sixtieth birthday in 1991.

Central Park and Vicinity

Rooms without park views cost less than those overlooking the park, but few bargains are to be had in this neighborhood. Some of the more remarkable establishments include:

• **Pierre**, Fifth Avenue at 61st Street, NYC 10021, 838-8000. A gracious and rather grand landmark, with punctilious but friendly service, and a particularly fashionable cafe-restaurant. Not cheap. $310 to $490 double.

• **Parker Meridien**, 119 West 56th Street, NYC 10019, 245-5000. Air France manages the Meridien, but you don't have to stay here to marvel at one New York real estate baron's gift to the city: the hotel's 57th Street entrance, a narrow, arched galleria complete with columns diminishing in size as they reach upwards toward a colorfully frescoed ceiling. $255 to $300 double, weekend special: $155 per night.

- **Plaza**, Fifth Avenue at 59th Street, NYC 10019, 759-3000. The marvelous mix of movers and shakers who stay here or use the Plaza's renowned public facilities creates an especially vibrant and exhilarating atmosphere. Trader Vic's is out now, and the new, Trumped-up luxe is in. $255 to $415 double.

- **Ritz Carlton**, 112 Central Park South, NYC 10019, 757-1900. A proper haven for 21 Club types, the decorous and very secure Ritz Carlton contains 240 rooms decorated by Parish-Hadley with hunting prints, flowered chintzes, fourposter mahogany beds and antique reproductions. $195 to $330 double, weekends $245 to $305.

- **Windsor Harley**, 100 West 58th Street, NYC 10019, 265-2100. Adequate, nicely located accommodations with weekend rates almost half the weekday price. $145 to $155 double, $119 weekends.

Six Favorites

Small, charming, personal hotels are not the city's forte, but there are six fairly priced, medium-sized hotels *in other Manhattan* areas that deserve special mention.

- **Algonquin**, 59 West 44th Street, NYC 10036, 840-6800. Little has changed under the new Japanese ownership. All muted rose, green and burnished wood, the famous lobby bar combines with anachronistic elevators and smallish, genteel rooms to make you feel welcome, secure and part of a pleasantly elite and talented group. $215 to $300 double.

- **Embassy Suites**, 1568 Broadway, NYC 719-1600. Overlooking Times Square, this newly renovated hotel rents suites (sitting room and bedroom) rather than single rooms, at the reasonable rate of $189 to $209 for a double.

- **Lowell**, 28 East 63rd Street, NYC 10021, 838-1400. Once the haunt of independent parents come to visit their well-established Upper

East Side children, the Lowell has recently been totally refurbished and now lets only a quarter of its 60 rooms to transients. But the more-attractive-than-ever Art Deco hotel remains intimate and friendly. Studios for $340 to $540.

- **Salisbury**, 123 West 57th Street, NYC 10019, 246-1300, or 800-223-0680 from out of town. Pleasant, pastel rooms in a relatively intimate setting attract a high percentage of women travelers. $135 for a double.

- **Sheraton Russell**, 45 Park Avenue at 37th Street, NYC 10016, 685-7676. The wood-paneled, book-lined lobby (perfect for tea after 3), the agreeable welcome, and carefully decorated rooms are testimony to the taste and capability of Janice Clatoff, one of the few women general managers in town. $215 to $230 double.

- **Wyndham**, 42 West 58th Street, NYC 10019, 753-3500. Small, attentively managed and nicely furnished, the Wyndham is home to numerous theatrical luminaries whenever they're in town and is one of the very best buys around at $130 to $140 double.

The hotels mentioned here reflect a purely personal taste and are not meant to be an all-city catalog of lodgings. For a free comprehensive compilation, get *Hotels in New York City* published by the New York Convention and Visitors Bureau, 2 Columbus Circle, NYC 10019, 212-397-8200. The Bureau's **New York City Tour Package Directory** lists bargain weekend rates.

Useful Telephone Numbers

Call 911 for Police, Fire and Ambulance Emergencies

All numbers are Area Code 212 unless otherwise indicated. All numbers listed below are answered 9 to 5 weekdays unless otherwise indicated.

An asterisk (*) indicates a recorded message.

Animals

ASPCA
American Society For The Prevention of Cruelty to Animals 876-7700

Animal Bites
Bureau of Animal Affairs, NYC Dept. of Health 566-2068

Animal Emergency Care
Animal Medical Center 838-7053
Open 24 hours; phone calls 9 a.m. to 11 p.m.

Nuisance Complaints
Bureau of Animal Affairs, NYC Dept. of Health 442-1999

Consumer Complaints and Services

Better Business Bureau *533-6200

Cable Television Complaints
NYC Office of Telecommunications 800-342-3330

Consumer Complaints
NYC Dept. of Consumer Affairs 487-4398

Moving and Storage Complaints
Interstate Commerce Commission 264-1072
New York State Dept. of Transportation 718-482-4816

Crime

Crime Victim Hotline
Non-profit Metropolitan Assistance Corp. 417-5160
24 hours a day

Police Emergency Number 911

Police Headquarters
24 hour number for precinct referrals 374-5000

Sex Crime Hotline
Sex Crimes Unit, Police Dept. 267-7273
24 hour service staffed by female NYPD detectives

Discrimination

Complaints
NYC Commission on Human Rights 417-5041

Dow Jones Report *976-4141
24 hour number

Education, Board of 718-935-2000

Elections, Board of...886-3800

Entertainment

Cultural Affairs Department Hotline 765-2787

Parks and Recreation Department
Current events *360-1333

Sports Phone
Schedules, scores...*976-1313
Supplemental information *976-2525

Fire
Emergency Number...911

Health and Medical Care

Ambulance Emergency Number 911

Animal Bites
Bureau of Animal Affairs, NYC Dept. of Health
24 hour service: 9 to 5 weekdays..788-4204
Evenings, weekends and holidays 340-4494

Dental Emergencies
First District Dental Society
Names of members on call 9 a.m. to 8 p.m. *679-3966
Names of members on call 8 p.m. to 9 a.m. *679-4172

Department of Health Central Complaint Bureau *442-1999

Doctor Referrals
New York County Medical Society, AMA 684-4670
Doctors on Call 212-737-2333, 718-238-2100

Drug Store
Kaufman Drugstore, 557 Lexington Avenue corner 50th 755-2266
Open 24 hours a day

Medical Help
Doctors-on-Call, private group 718-745-5900
24 hour house-call service

New York Doctor Line
Referrals to St. Luke's-Roosevelt Hospital physicians 876-5432

Poison Control Center
NYC Dept. of Health..764-7667
24 hour service...340-4494

Suicide Prevention...718-389-9608
24 hours a day...532-2400

24 hours a day..673-3000
After 6 p.m..718-389-9608

Housing

Electrical and Steam Emergencies
Consolidated Edison 683-0862
24 hour service

Gas Leaks
Consolidated Edison 683-8830
24 hour service

Heat Complaints
NYC Housing Preservation and Development 960-4800
24 hour service of the Central Complaint Bureau

Housing Complaints
(In general) 960-4800
See "Heat" above

Rent Stabilization Information
Rent Stabilization Assn. 944-4700

Income Tax

Federal Tax Information
Manhattan and The Bronx..732-0100
Brooklyn, Queens and Staten Island............................718-596-3770

Federal Tax Forms
24 hour number...800-829-3676

New York City and State Information 718-935-6000
New York City and State Tax Forms
24 hour number... 800-462-8100

Library

New York Public Library Information 340-0849
Bronx Reference Service 718-220-6576
Brooklyn Reference Service....................................... 718-780-7700

Manhattan Reference Service...340-0849
Queens Reference Service 718-990-0714
Staten Island 340-0849

Marriage Licenses

NYC Marriage License Bureau *669-2400

Motor Vehicles

Alternate Side of the Street Parking Regulations
NYC Bureau of Traffic Operations *566-4121

Highway Emergencies
NYC Dept. of Highways..566-3406
24 hour service; calls tow trucks for highway (not street) breakdowns

Motor Vehicle Department, New York State
Licenses and Registration Information 645-5550
7:30 a.m. to 4 p.m.

Parking Violations Help Hotline
NYC Dept. of Transportation 477-4430

Property damage claim forms
NYC Controller 718-830-7500

Towed Away Cars
NYC Bureau of Traffic Operations..924-6036
7 a.m. to 10 p.m. daily

Ombudsman

Complaints, City Agencies
Office of City Council President..669-7638

Complaints, State Agencies
New York Dept. of State...417-5760

Consumer Frauds
NY State 416-8345

Post Office

General Information 967-8585
8 a.m. to 8 p.m., Saturday 8 to 4, closed Sunday

Sanitation and Garbage

Complaints
NYC Department of Sanitation 219-8090
Environmental Action Coalition
Recycling..677-1601

Street Maintenance

Potholes
NYC Bureau of Highways...768-4653
After 4:30 p.m. and weekends...964-2110
Streetlights
NYC Bureau of Electrical Control 669-8353
Water Mains, Sewers
NYC Dept. of Environmental Protection............................718-699-9811
24 hour service

Telephone

Credit Card, Special Services
AT&T 800-C-A-L-L-A-T-T
Equipment Sales and Leasing
AT&T 800-555-8111
Equipment Service and Complaints
AT&T 800-526-2000
24 hour information

Federal Communications Commission 620-3436
Advice on any interference in television, radio, and telephone reception
Information
Nynex/New York Telephone..411
24 hour service

Repairs
Nynex/New York Telephone 611
24 hour service

Residential Installation and Information
Nynex/New York Telephone
Bronx...718-890-2450
Brooklyn 718-890-1200
Manhattan, Downtown...890-2100
Manhattan, Uptown 890-2100
Queens...718-779-9950
Staten Island 718-779-9950

Wiring Service and Complaints
AT&T 800-247-7000
24 hour information

Time /Temperature...*976-1616

Tourism and Travel

New York City Information
New York Convention and Visitors Bureau 397-8222

New York State Information
New York State Dept. of Commerce 827-6100
Vacation Information 800-225-5697
Recording after 5 p.m.

Passports
US Passport Agency 399-5290

Traveler's Aid Services
Metropolitan Assistance Bureau....................................944-0013

Transportation

Airports
Port Authority of NY & NJ 800-A-I-R-R-I-D-E

John F. Kennedy International
Information 718-656-4520
Lost and Found 718-656-4520
Parking Information and Conditions 718-656-5699

LaGuardia
Information 718-476-5000
Lost and Found 718-476-5115
Parking Information...*718-476-5105

Newark
Information 201-961-2000
Lost and Found 201-961-6230
Parking Information and Conditions..................................*201-961-2013

Buses
Lost and Found (NYC Transit Authority) 718-625-6200
Bus Schedules (NYC Transit Authority) 718-330-1234
Port Authority Bus Terminal Information 564-8484
George Washington Bridge Bus Terminal Information..............564-8484
Greyhound/Trailways Bus Lines 800-231-2222

Ferry
Staten Island Ferry 806-6940

PATH
(Hudson Tubes)
Travel Information 800-234-7284

Railroads
Staten Island Rapid Transit...718-447-8601
Amtrak (Penn Station and Grand Central) 582-6875
Metroliner Reservations (Penn Station) 800-523-8720
Metro-North (Grand Central) 532-4900
Long Island Railroad (Penn Station) 718-217-5477
New Jersey Transit (Penn Station) 201-762-5100

Subways
Lost & Found (NYC Transit Authority)...............................718-625-6200
Subway Schedules (NYC Transit Authority) 718-330-1234

Taxis
Complaints (NYC Taxi and Limousine Commission) 221-8294
Lost & Found (NYC Taxi and Limousine Commission) 302-8294

Transit Authority Customer Service Office
Complaints about service..718-330-3322

Weather *976-1212

Index

Need More NEWCOMER'S?

	#/COPIES		TOTAL
NEWCOMER'S Chicago	_____	× $12.00	$_____
NEWCOMER'S Los Angeles	_____	× $12.95	$_____
NEWCOMER'S New York City	_____	× $15.95	$_____
NEWCOMER'S Washington, DC	_____	× $13.95	$_____
		SUBTOTAL	$_____
	TAX (IL residents add 8.75% sales tax)		$_____
POSTAGE & HANDLING ($6.00 first book, $.75 each add'l)			$_____
		TOTAL	$_____

How did you hear about NEWCOMER'S? _____

SHIP TO:

_____
Name

_____
Title

_____
Company

_____
Address

_____
City   State   Zip

_____
Phone Number

Send this order form and a check or money order
payable to First Books, Inc.

First Books, Inc. Mail Order Department
P.O. Box 578147, Chicago, IL 60657
(312) 276-5911

Allow 2-4 weeks for delivery.

Smart Business Travel
How to Stay Safe When You're on the Road

Most of us take precautions every day to make our lives more safe. Business travel, however, presents a new and constantly changing set of circumstances that we don't deal with on a daily basis. This book is not intended to scare people, but instead offers some simple tips that can make your business travel more secure. *Smart Business Travel* contains common sense as well as lesser-known but useful ideas that help the busness traveler travel safely.

	#/COPIES		TOTAL
Smart Business Travel	_____	× $12.95	$_____
TAX (IL residents add 8.75% sales tax)			$_____
POSTAGE & HANDLING ($6.00 first book, $.75 each add'l)			$_____
		TOTAL	$_____

SHIP TO:

_____
Name

_____
Title

_____
Company

_____
Address

_____
City   State   Zip

_____
Phone Number

Send this order form and a check or money order
payable to First Books, Inc.

First Books, Inc. Mail Order Department
P.O. Box 578147, Chicago, IL 60657
(312) 276-5911

Allow 2-4 weeks for delivery.

Fit to Travel:
How to Stay in Shape When You're on the Road

	#/COPIES	TOTAL	
Fit to Travel	_____	× $12.95	$_____
TAX (IL residents add 8.75% sales tax)			$_____
POSTAGE & HANDLING ($6.00 first book, $.75 each add'l)			$_____
		TOTAL	$_____

SHIP TO:

_____
Name

_____
Title

_____
Company

_____
Address

_____
City   State   Zip

_____
Phone Number

Send this order form and a check or money order
payable to First Books, Inc.

First Books, Inc. Mail Order Department
P.O. Box 578147, Chicago, IL 60657
(312) 276-5911

Allow 2-4 weeks for delivery.

Reader Response Form

We welcome comments regarding the *Newcomer's Handbook for New York City*. If you have suggestions or if you have found any mistakes/omissions or if you would just like to express your opinion about the guide, please let us know! We will consider any comments for our next edition. Also, for any suggestions we use, respondents will receive a 50% discount off the next edition. Please send this response form to:

First Books, Inc.
P.O. Box 578147
Chicago, IL 60657

Comments:

_____

_____

_____

_____

_____

_____

_____

_____

_____

_____

_____

_____

_____

_____

_____
Name

_____
Address

_____ _____ _____
City   State   Zip